The War for Talent

Michael Williams read psychology with moral philosophy and then took his MSc (in management performance and potential) at the University of Aston. Following eight years of full-time and reserve service with the Royal Navy and then the Royal Marines he began a career in business management, which has taken him from shop-floor production trainee to senior management in a range of industries. He set up his own consultancy – Michael Williams & Partners – in 1979, and now works with clients from the UK, USA, Canada, Ireland and much of Western Europe in the pharmaceutical, aeronautical, info-tech, electronics, mail-order, food, beverage, banking and insurance businesses. He also works in the fields of management and organisational behaviour with major consultancy organisations such as Management Centre Europe, Hawksmere, MbO (Denmark) and Leading Ventures (Amsterdam), and with leading business schools, principally IMD, Lausanne, and the Theseus Institute at Sophia Antipolis, France. He is a member of the British Psychological Society, the Institute of Directors and the Association of Management Education and Development. He is also the author or co-author of eight books on management and organisational behaviour.

The Chartered Institute of Personnel and Development is the leading publisher of books and reports for personnel and training professionals, students, and all those concerned with the effective management and development of people at work. For details of all our titles, please contact the Publishing Department:

tel. 020-8263 3387

fax 020-8263 3850

e-mail publish@cipd.co.uk

The catalogue of all CIPD titles can be viewed on the CIPD website:

www.cipd.co.uk/publications

The War for Talent

Getting the best from the best

Michael Williams

CHARTERED INSTITUTE OF PERSONNEL AND DEVELOPMENT

Design by Action Publishing Technology Ltd, Gloucester

Typeset by
Action Publishing Technology Ltd, Gloucester

Set in 11/13pt Berkeley OldStyle Book

Printed in Great Britain by
the Cromwell Press

British Library Cataloguing in Publication Data
A catalogue record for this book is available from the
British Library

ISBN 0-85292-872-6

The views expressed in this book are the author's own and
may not necessarily reflect those of the CIPD

CIPD House, Camp Road, London SW19 4UX
Tel: 020-8971 9000   Fax: 020-8263 3333
E-mail: cipd@cipd.uk Website: www.cipd.co.uk
Incorporated by Royal Charter. Registered Charity No. 1079797.

Contents

Acknowledgements   vii

Introduction   1

1 The War for Talent   5
2 The First Imperative at Work   21
3 What is 'Talent'?   34
4 The Second, Third and Fourth Imperatives   53
5 Managing Knowledge – More Than a Fad   81
6 'Enabling' Leadership – The Basis of Talent Management   101
7 Talent Management – The Coaching Leader   119
8 Mentoring and Sponsoring Talent   138
9 Empowering Talent   166
10 Managing Talent – New Mindsets, New Actions   191

Appendix
    Talent Management Profile   209
    Emotional Intelligence Profile   213
    Talent Coaching Profile   231
    Developing Coaching Skills – A 'Coaching Challenge' Workshop   234
    Talent Mentoring Profile   235
    Talent Sponsoring Profile   239
    Power and Empowerment Profile   242

For Brenda, Susie and Jonathan, whose love and talents I constantly and gratefully draw upon

Acknowledgements

A great many people have contributed, knowingly or otherwise, to the thinking that lies behind this book. Especially helpful and always so positive in their ideas – as well as a challenge and fun to work with – were the following clients, several of whom I have collaborated with for a good many years. Their experience has been invaluable in my own development. They include:

Howard Mann, OBE, President and CEO of McCain Foods, Toronto
Dr Patrick Dixon, CEO of Global Change Ltd, London
John Bridgeman, Director of the Office of Fair Trading
Nick Kendal, CEO of Ekco Packaging
Dr Patrick Haren, CEO of Viridian, Northern Ireland
Harry McCracken, CEO of Northern Ireland Electricity
Dr Ole Staib-Jensen, Chairman of MbO International, Copenhagen
John Coles, Managing Director of Huck International
Philip Loring, Operations Manager of First Quench
James Pratt, Sales and Marketing Director of Lucent Technology
Ian Butler, Director, Human Resources, ADtranz, Berlin
Brian Cocksedge, General Manager of Wellstream Northsea
Chuck Ytterberg, Deputy General Manager of Wellstream Inc., Panama City, Florida
Dr Peter Richardson, External Affairs Director of Astra-Zeneca
Tim Evitt, CEO of British Ceramic Tiles and one of the most talented and exciting CEOs I have ever worked with

People within my own field of organisational behaviour who have contributed enormously to my learning and to the flow of pure adrenaline on consultancy assignments, and with whom it is always a pleasure to work, are:

Professor Alden G Lank, formerly of IMD Business School, Lausanne

Tex Smiley, formerly Professor at IMI, Geneva, and IMD, Lausanne

Professors Jim Dowd and Jack Wood, of IMD Business School, Lausanne

Professors Ahmet Aykac, Francis Bidault and Linda Stoddart, at the Theseus Institute, Sophia Antipolis, France

Judith Lorick, OB Consultant, the Theseus Institute

Mary Rose Greville, Visiting Academic at Trinity Institute, Dublin

Martin Van Manen, ING Group Business School, Amsterdam

Dr Chiara Bolognesi, Group School, Generali, Mogliano Veneto

Professor Dave Buchanan, of the Simon de Montfort University, Leicester

Karen McCormick, Director of Organisation Development, GUS Home Shopping

Bob Thomas, VP Human Resources, McCain Foods, Chicago

Jan Versteeg, VP Corporate Management Development, ABN AMRO, Amsterdam

Tom Cummings, Managing Director, Leading Ventures Consultancy, Amsterdam

Jerome Trancart and Philippe Haberer, SLT, Aix-en-Provence

Linda Zaccharia, Management Centre Europe, Brussels

Ann Milne, Training Manager, First Quench

Carita Wahlberg, Training Manager, Stora Enso, Stockholm and Helsinki

Hermann Fischer, Organisation Psychologist, Geneva

Neill Jackson and Nigel Erwin, HR, Viridian, Northern Ireland

Hilary and Barrie Smith, Insight, Geneva

Ian McMonagle, McMonagle Partnership

Karen Phillips, Suzette Castle and Angela Spall of Hawksmere

Steph Wholey and Karen Good, HR, British Ceramic Tiles

Professor John Adair, for his endless wisdom and good company

Dr Andre Vandermerwe, formerly Professor IMD – scholar, bon viveur and true gentleman.

I appreciate enormously the instant warmth, genuine interest and real help that I have always received from Richard Goff and Matthew Reisz at CIPD Books. Working with Richard and Matthew has been one of the real bonuses in writing this book.

For Marie Westbury, I have unbounded thanks for uncomplainingly typing the manuscripts for four books – all within the space of 20 months, and this on top of our daily office administration and typing.

To Professor Jonathan Williams, my son, I owe an inestimable debt for his good-natured and instant rejection of humbug, as well as his ability to put life into such manageable and humorous perspectives.

To Susie, Countess Goess-Saurau, my daughter, who has never failed to amaze me, I will be eternally grateful for her devastating ability to cut through waffle and put me straight whenever I lose focus or logic.

Now, for the eighth time in our married life, I express my gratitude and thanks to Brenda, my wife, for her readiness to suspend her own writing in order to help me in the preparation of one of my books. Without her love, quiet common sense and professional perspective, such writing would be impossible.

Introduction

More and more of my consultancy work involves helping clients to source appropriate talent – much of which is often under their noses – and to find the most effective ways to develop, *use* and retain people capable of consistent high performance. The idea of a 'war' for talent was one that I came across many times when working with Baxter International. It crystallises the critical challenges of creating and mobilising the productive synergy so essential to competitive advantage – and survival – in today's markets. And it suggests that there will always be winners and losers, competing to obtain the best people, to hold on to them and not to lose them to the 'enemy'.

Identifying potential and developing people with talent are issues that I have pursued with passion and conviction since my first attempts, some 40 years ago, to recruit into the Royal Marine Reserve the right candidates for both Commando and the Special Boat Service. They have remained an essential driving force in my subsequent professional careers in business management and consultancy. My company has also carried out in-depth research into talent management practices in over 20 organisations in the UK, Europe, the USA and Canada between 1993 and 2000.

The war for talent is not *simply* a matter of offering better material packages. Rather, it is about developing mindsets and focused strategies that will provide talented people with the certainty of an environment where they can continually learn, contribute and excel – to their own advantage and that of the business.

To identify differences between recognised 'best' practice and *current* practice in talent management, I have drawn upon other research sources, including PDI, operating principally in Europe; Global Change Limited, based in London; and my associates in both Geneva and Copenhagen, who, like me, operate globally as HR consultants.

Clearly, there are many issues involved in talent management, not least the 'chemistry' of the relationships that exist between an executive and his or her talented individuals. (Individuals' success and growth are strongly dependent upon *quality dialogues* with appropriate authority figures, which serve to reinforce the certainty that capable, high-performing people's talents will be regularly recognised, developed and put to the most productive use.) Yet over and above interpersonal alchemy is the need for intelligent, sensitive and, at times, *courageous* thinking and action, which take full account of the four imperatives of talent management covered in Chapters 1 to 4. These are to:

❐ build a 'winning' environment that will make people want to join and stay with you

❐ make talent management a critical priority of the business

❐ create the means to select outstanding talent

❐ engage talent, develop it and *use* it.

Outstanding performers who are allowed to use their talents and knowledge are the strongest guarantee of competitive advantage that a company has. They are the people who ensure that a business has the best chance of getting to tomorrow before the competition does. Indeed, people of high potential are an organisation's best insurance policy for a successful tomorrow.

Making the most of outstanding ability is an organisational, strategic and cultural issue that depends upon *corporate* as well as individual know-how and commitment. This book sets out to explore and interweave the personal and organisational aspects of such leadership accountability and skill. Its messages and ideas are offered to anyone who leads and manages others, but especially to those who are in a position to influence talent management practices on a wider front within their organisation.

The concentration upon the management and leadership of high-performing, talented individuals and people of high potential is not intended to be merely elitist. However, where budgets for the development of people are not inexhaustible, it seems sound common sense to 'invest in the best', so that you neither squander talent nor allow it easily to be taken away from you by the competition. More than anything else, business results and standing in the market place reinforce the message that high-calibre talent *is* worth fighting for.

The book's subtitle 'Getting the best from the best', suggested by one of the editor's colleagues, really says it all. Identifying, developing and building upon talent is one of the most exciting and rewarding aspects of business, which itself remains one of the best games in town. Experimenting, taking risks and being prepared to break with wasteful past practices are, at times, essential to intelligent, effective talent management. The key theme throughout the book is: change the mindset and the know-how – and you change the business . . .

CHAPTER

The War for Talent

There is something much more scarce, something rarer than ability. It is the ability to recognise ability.

Robert Half

There is a war for the best managerial and professional talent. What is more, the competition for high-calibre people, with the right mindsets and skills, is intensifying. One of the major challenges facing management currently is to be able to change fast enough, to cope with new technology and new, environmental, social and professional values. The consequent need for high-calibre, outstanding performers is perhaps greater now than it has ever been.

> **❝ There continues to be an unacceptably wide gulf between state of the art and state of the practice in the management of talented people ❞**

Several recent surveys conducted by recruitment organisations and major global consultancies such as McKinsey and PDI, as well as in-company experiences of placement and deployment of high-potential managers and specialists, indicate that there are obvious winners and losers in the battles for talent. Dedicated strategies of talent management are a major determinant of companies becoming – and remaining – talent-rich. There continues to be an unacceptably wide gulf between state of the art and *state of the practice* in the management of talented people in far too many organisations.

Our own research, in a great number of countries and across a wide spectrum of industries, businesses and professions, confirms that managerial and specialist talent consistently remains the most under-developed and undermanaged corporate resource. In too few companies is talent management, *per se*, expressly identified – and rewarded – as a crucial area of executive accountability for requisite results. Neither the necessary mindsets, nor the specific executive competencies, which emerge from – and, in turn, reinforce – focused talent management, are actively developed and fostered in enough organisations.

This is *not* a plea for more formalised performance and potential appraisal 'systems' – heaven forbid! Rather, it reflects a concern that not enough of the *right* conversations – and necessary actions – are taking place between executives and their people of talent, about the 'what', 'why', 'who', 'how' and 'when' of developing and retaining the capabilities of the most talented.

At the other end of the scale, research shows that there *are* organisations where what could justifiably be described as talent management 'best practice' does regularly and consistently occur. What is more, such organisations generally – and almost inevitably – emerge as the 'winners' in the war for talent.

However, as recruitment increasingly shifts to poaching and selective headhunting, so the competition for talent is likely to become more a matter of guerrilla warfare, rather than 'set-piece battles', conducted to formal codes of behaviour and practice. Where identified people of talent are repeatedly under pressure to turn coat and defect to the opposition, then even the most enlightened organisations will need to look to their laurels and constantly review, develop and renew their strategies and practices of talent management.

Highly talented and gifted people may sometimes be a pain but, well managed, theirs are so often the contributory perspectives and competencies that are crucial to competitive advantage and success in today's world. Just as the 'solid citizens' have a role in bringing stability and common sense into a business, so the high-performing 'stars' have their crucial part to play in creating wealth, adding value and initiating necessary change.

A Changing, Confusing, but Exciting World

A fundamental leadership issue in the information age is that of leading people – and organisations – in what White, Hodgson and Crainer[1] term 'complex, rapidly changing social systems'. 'The new era of uncertainty, the one we label white water,' they explain, 'will not come to an end. It is not a blip. It is here to stay.'

> **66** *It is no longer sufficient to meet the financial and commercial dictates of economic survival* **99**

A new revolutionary order of things has already replaced what many people in leadership roles could not have envisaged disappearing, even less than a decade ago. As a consequence, we need people of outstanding ability – with commensurate resolve – who can function effectively in conditions where, as Patrick Dixon[2] puts it, there will be:

❏ more 'wild cards' and a greater need to prepare for the unexpected

❏ faster reaction times and a need to gear up for more rapid response

❏ more adaptable and flexible organisation structures, dictated by changing market needs

❏ greater investment in IT and a greater need for people who can use it *creatively* and intelligently

❏ teams and partnerships where there are necessarily diverse competencies and productive synergy

❏ greater cultural sensitivity as globalisation makes cultural differences more immediate

❏ a rapidly increasing significance for the 'global village', as technology shrinks geography (as Dixon says, 'We ain't seen nothing yet!')

❏ a greater need to create a sense of 'family', especially in 'virtual' organisations, to give people a feeling of identity, personal value and belonging

❏ a stronger focus on purpose and meaning, because people need to feel they are adding value and learning legacies

❏ strong emphasis upon leadership, particularly leadership by vision, trust, motivation and example.

It is no longer sufficient to meet the financial and commercial dictates of economic survival; we also need to take into account environmental imperatives and a bottom line of what amount to 'planetary' issues. There is also the social bottom line and our responsibility – moral, legal and professional – to people, which is where the management of talent largely, though not exclusively, lies.

The emergence of virtual organisations, deriving from successive, changing and therefore adaptive networks of people, makes redundant many of our traditional and conventional approaches to managing and leading relatively stable structures or hierarchies. The growing shift from 'corporation' to *enterprise* marks a major transition in the life cycle of many businesses and institutions, with increased autonomy within interdependent 'frameworks'.

Recent surveys conducted in the USA and Europe, largely by academic David Hall and by Ernst and Young,[3] suggest that not only do 'corporate' executives and their 'New Age', more entrepreneurial colleagues behave differently from one another, they even speak differently, using different vocabulary and terminology (see Table 1).

Dr Robert McHenry,[4] Chairman of the Oxford Psychology Press (leading providers of psychometric instruments), makes the point:

> These people [entrepreneurs] are selling the future in words, they are energetic and of the moment. They want things to sound easy and accessible, to get people to buy into it.

David Wilkinson,[5] Head of Entrepreneurial Services for Ernst and Young, comments:

> Entrepreneurs are closer to the customer and more likely to reflect the language of the customer ... businesses need to become more entrepreneurial and introduce change into their culture. Perhaps they would be well advised to examine the specific, which is the way they speak, to make them think, act and talk in a different way, to bring about the change and success we are all after.

TABLE 1 Corporate v Entrepreneur Speak

'Corporate speak' tends to be:	'Entrepreneur speak' is more:
• cautious, guarded and considered	• colourful, descriptive and flamboyant
• precise and formal, eg 'business plan'	• casual, 'vox pop' and easy, eg 'recipe for success'
• systematic, but removed	• inspirational and energising
• matter-of-fact	• evocative
• organisational clichés	• attuned to the real world
• 'establishment' and 'official'	• more contemporary and 'with it'
• stylised jargon	• user-friendly

An Intensifying War

Attracting – and retaining – the best available people is likely to become even more challenging as the competition for high-performer and high-potential executives intensifies. As the business world changes, so newer, different, more sophisticated, yet radical, skills and understanding will be needed. The inevitable trend towards globalisation, higher technology and more diffuse organisation structures and information networks is likely to mean a far greater demand for:

❏ much more informed and complex entrepreneurial capability

❏ expertise in managing multinational and multicultural transactions and relationships

❏ skills in transforming and renewing businesses, in order to win in tomorrow's world

❏ the skills – and mindsets – necessary to manage and add value to information and knowledge in so-called 'virtual organisations' where networks, rather than formal hierarchies, are the primary vehicles for decisions and action

❏ the wide-ranging capability and integrative thinking increasingly needed to manage and *lead* companies through the challenging interplay of higher uncertainty, more complex paradox and greater opportunity than hitherto

❏ the rare capacity to generate the 'alchemy' of contributive synergy and willing commitment fundamental to team, group and cross-functional enterprise

❏ finally, consistent capability in delivering to the increasingly imperative *'triple bottom line'* of:

● commercial viability

● ecological soundness

● social responsibility.

" There is growing awareness and acknowledgement that lack of the right talent can be a major competitive disadvantage. "

All of these reflect the high premium being placed, more and more, upon *credible* leadership, professional acuity and political acumen, which, increasingly, are talents where demand outstrips availability – and, often, accessibility. In addition to the above seven issues, the competition for high-calibre talent and people of outstanding potential is further heightened by the following factors:

☐ More organisations are simply becoming aware of their need for – and lack of – talent, and are putting increasing energy and money into the recruitment of capable, bright people.

☐ There is growing awareness and acknowledgement that lack of the *right* talent can be a major competitive disadvantage.

☐ More and more poaching aimed at winning hearts, minds – and bodies – is tending to supersede traditional rules of engagement in the recruitment of the best people.

☐ Businesses with a strong achievement ethic, challenging roles and manifest track records of success in the market place – or city – attract the best candidates more readily than the less impressive performers.

☐ Similarly, organisations that possess compelling visions and values that are demonstrably exemplified in a 'living' work ethic have a head start in drawing in and keeping people of high potential. High performers work with authenticity far better than they do with charades or parodies of effectiveness.

☐ More flexible, smaller organisations frequently offer higher, more immediate exposure and so may provide faster opportunities to create wealth, make an impact, add value to the business or 'leave a legacy' – and, hence, offer more fulfilling and exciting career prospects, especially to high performers, in a hurry.

☐ The 'better' organisations, paying more than simply lip service to people as an asset, are more inclined to make talent management a corporate priority, evolve effective human resource strategies and consciously recruit, develop and manage pools of professional talent and executive potential.

☐ On the other side of the coin, high-calibre people are themselves becoming increasingly discriminating, selective and mobile in their search for what, to them, currently represents the 'right' company, right job and right career move. As Professor Manfred Kets de Vries[6] says, 'Today's high-performers are like frogs in a wheelbarrow: they can jump out at any time.'

A successful, highly talented executive team, backed by comparably capable professionals, is without doubt the most critical asset that any organisation can have. Yet, paradoxically, most organisations need to develop radically different mindsets and fundamentally more effective approaches to managing talent – their primary resource.

Franz Landsberger,[7] human resources director (Europe) of Baxter International (the global healthcare organisation), emphasises the point that talent management, taken seriously, is much more than executive exhortation, or an annual company conference, shot-in-the-arm theme:

Talent management is a mindset. It is a process – not an event. We must *consciously* –

❐ bring in new talent

❐ develop talent

❐ engage talent

❐ share talent

❐ above all, *manage* talent.

> **❝ A successful, highly talented executive team, backed by comparably capable professionals, is without doubt the most critical asset that any organisation can have. ❞**

In some organisations, like AT&T, talent management is made an explicit and formal accountability of individual executives' contribution to the business. Their performance as directors and managers, based upon the achievement – or otherwise – against agreed targets, includes goals expressly and specifically focused on talent management. Formal merit reviews for executives build in appropriate levels of reward for demonstrating competence, commitment and, hence, results in the continual, systematic development of people, especially key players.

The Four Imperatives of Talent Management

Consultant surveys and in-company *experience* confirm the major imperatives in talent management as essentially the following:

❏ Build a winning environment, for commitment, achievement and success.

❏ Make talent management a critical corporate priority.

❏ Create the means to identify and select outstanding talent.

❏ Engage talent, use it and develop it.

❝ In the teaching organisation, leaders see 'teaching' and development as conscious processes, synonymous with leading and doing. ❞

As Noel Tichy[8] states in the first chapter of his book *The Leadership Engine*:

> Winning is about leadership. Winning individuals are leaders, people with ideas and values and the energy and guts to do what needs to be done ... Winning companies ... have lots of leaders because they deliberately and systematically produce them. This is what separates the winners from the losers.

Such applied talent management is typical of the winning companies Tichy prefers to call 'teaching organisations' (as opposed to 'learning' organisations). In the teaching organisation, leaders see 'teaching' and development as conscious processes, synonymous with leading and doing. In such environments, personal experience and learning are continually evaluated and translated into teachable concepts, 'models' and precepts. Such learning is also passed on in ways so as to stimulate, encourage and energise others to lead, teach and do.

What Tichy advocates is primarily a *continuous* process of feedback, teaching and coaching that is expressly aimed at generating positive intellectual and emotional energy – and commitment – in others. A core theme of Tichy's thinking and teaching is that one of the leader's priority tasks is to develop other leaders. In essence, this is what much of talent management is about – after recruitment and selection. *The Leadership Engine* eloquently describes the hallmarks of best practice – and of winning organisations.

In the effective business – where leaders can lead from the front when necessary, but will also act as essential 'enablers', 'facilitators' and 'catalysts' – talent management is likely to emerge as a *natural, organic and day-to-day process*, not an annual, ritualised 'exercise in compulsory insincerity'.[9] At times, the leader's role, above all else, will be to 'coach the process', by acting variously as mentor, sponsor, empowerer, enabler – or irritant – to ensure that what needs to happen, by way of talent management, *does* happen – and continues to happen.

In the effective management of talent, so much of the leader's role will be influenced and shaped by the four imperatives, identified above. Figure 1 summarises these imperatives, expanded to include key, specific 'do-how'. In Chapter 2, the first of the four imperatives – and the specific actions and activity it demands – will be explored in more depth and detail.

Build a winning environment

❝ Why would people of outstanding talent want to join our company? ❞

The first imperative – build a winning environment – typically seeks to answer the following questions:

❐ Why would people of outstanding talent want to join our company?

❐ What, specifically, would they be likely to get from working with us?

❐ What, about our business, the way we work, what we do and our culture, vision and values, would be likely to attract – and keep – high performers?

Essentially this imperative is about the key 'pull' factors within an organisation, or business, that people *want* to identify with, become part of and grow with. The imperative has its roots in values, beliefs, aspirations, standards, obligations and achievements – in other words, *what the organisation and its people stand for*. For example, apprentice and trainee gunsmiths still work within the time-honoured ethos, values and traditional practices that were largely developed two centuries ago, in what are known as the makers of 'best guns'. Consistency, extremes of painstaking accuracy and what is virtually a sense of perfection are the standards that dictate the quality of craftsmanship and, therefore, admission to the ranks of a small, select band of highly skilled professionals. Furthermore, membership of such an exclusive craft instils into the young craftsman a sense of personal commitment, pride, self-respect and fulfilment – and, above all, a sense of identity with the business.

As is stated at Holland & Holland, designers and makers of some of the finest English sidelock shotguns and sporting rifles, 'Building best

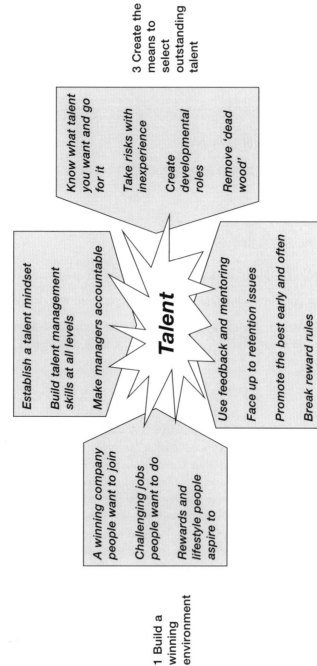

2 Make talent management a critical priority

- Establish a talent mindset
- Build talent management skills at all levels
- Make managers accountable

3 Create the means to select outstanding talent

- Know what talent you want and go for it
- Take risks with inexperience
- Create developmental roles
- Remove 'dead wood'

Talent

1 Build a winning environment

- A winning company people want to join
- Challenging jobs people want to do
- Rewards and lifestyle people aspire to

4 Engage talent and develop it

- Use feedback and mentoring
- Face up to retention issues
- Promote the best early and often
- Break reward rules

FIGURE 1 Talent Management: Four key imperatives

guns is simple. It is merely a matter of refusing to compromise at any stage in their manufacture. This unforgiving ethos is applied to all that we do.' Russell Wilkin, director of gun-making, further emphasises the company's uncompromising but unifying values and vision: 'The standard we set here, in Holland & Holland, is that of – "effectively just unobtainable". It is one we all believe in.' Interestingly, these deep-rooted values and standards have not only survived, but continue to flourish, despite a takeover by the French concern Chanel – which, to say the least, is hardly identified with 'best London' guns!

United Distillers and Vintners (UDV), which has as one of its declared aims 'to be one of the world's very best consumer goods companies', espouses four crucial values that influence its day-to-day working. They are:

❐ to be the best

❐ to be passionate about consumers

❐ to be proud of what we do

❐ *to give our people freedom to succeed.*

Wellstream Northsea, a specialist flexible steel tube company with manufacturing plants in Newcastle-upon-Tyne and Panama City, Florida, has a strong culture of 'doing the right thing' by its customers. Its four 'cornerstone' values are:

Trust	Integrity
Clarity	Tenacity

Managers at Wellstream define success as 'the upward flow of ideas from an involved workforce'. Consultancy experience in the two plants confirms this as a typical day-to-day reality, and labour turnover in both is exceptionally low.

Make talent management a critical priority

Imperative number two – make talent management a critical priority – is, of course, fundamental to the whole process of attracting, developing, using and retaining the best people. It underlines the crucial importance of appropriate mindsets, talent management skills and both personal and corporate accountability and commitment for the continually effective development and deployment of high-performing people to become a reality. Without the collective *conscience professionelle* and sustained corporate drive indicative of commitment from top management, talent management will remain piecemeal, *ad hoc* and fortuitous, which, unfortunately, remains state-of-the-practice in so many organisations.

Create the means to select outstanding talent

The third imperative – create the means to select outstanding talent – involves knowing exactly what talent is needed in order to achieve the predicted – or expected – future goals and necessary transformation of the business. Aggressive sourcing and a willingness to take risks, by promoting people of high potential but little experience, are also fundamental to the third imperative. Just as the talented and those of high potential need to be sponsored and pushed forward into high-profile roles, so 'dead wood' and the consistently unproductive, below-par performers need to be removed, or moved aside, to enable those who will deliver actually to do so.

Engage talent and develop it

❝ High performers almost instinctively expect reward systems based upon differentials that reflect achievement, contribution and results. ❞

The fourth imperative focuses effort, energy and intelligent management on the need to confront the real issues of talent retention – or lack of it – within the organisation. It involves, too, the importance of challenging the sacred cows of the reward policies and systems in order to reward merit and talent *realistically* and appropriately. High performers almost instinctively expect reward systems based upon differentials that reflect achievement, contribution and results. To them, nothing is more unequal – and illogical – than the equal reward of unequal performance. The fourth imperative emphasises the crucial importance of engaging and aligning talent with the goals and direction of the company. It is therefore a means of legitimising and ensuring:

❐ promotion of the best people, early in their careers and as often as possible, as the organisation transforms and develops

❐ development of them, in a systematic, positive and realistic way, constantly giving feedback, and both coaching and mentoring them regularly, to ensure maximum learning, as well as optimal use of their growing talent.

Continuous development is fundamental to the fourth imperative. Diageo, a £12 billion company of 8,000 employees whose businesses include such well-known names as Guinness, Grand Met, Burger King and Pillsbury, consciously seeks to allocate the *best people* as well as the best resources to brand and business development. As John McGrath, group chief executive, says: 'When you have great brands, you've got to have great people to manage and grow them.'

❝ It is the effectively managed interplay of the individual's developing ability – and contribution – with the perceived changing direction and focus of the business that is the real essence of talent management. ❞

The function of the four imperatives is primarily to invest the process of talent management with major significance and urgency, and to raise it to the level of a continually regenerating major corporate priority. *It is the effectively managed interplay of the individual's developing ability – and contribution – with the perceived changing direction and focus of the business that is the real essence of talent management.* Developing a conducive environment that offers not only opportunity to experience and grow, but also operates and 'lives' to values with which capable, gifted people can readily identify and so give of their best, is a core competence in talent management.

SUMMARY

There has always been competition for the best talent, particularly in the world of business, where winning and losing can often mean the difference between succeeding or failing. Because of the trend towards globalisation, and aspirations to become world-class players, the rapid growth in technology and the pace of the information age revolution has enormously increased the demand for what are still relatively scarce mindsets and skills.

The consequences of this are only too obvious. The competition for talent is intensifying and will continue to do so. Not only is there a major problem in trying to attract the best people with the right competencies, there is the matter of how to keep them so that they continue to:

- remain motivated and committed to the organisation and its goals
- add value to the business and its principal activities
- sustain competitive advantage for their organisation over its rivals.

There is comprehensively effective talent management in too few companies. In practice, this means that neither the right sorts of conversations nor decisions are taking place regularly, between executives and those who report to them, about:

- building and developing the competencies of high performers and people of high potential
- making the most of talent, in the most appropriate roles, early enough in people's careers
- realistic career progression – including lateral fast-tracking.

Not only are insufficient feedback, coaching, mentoring and empowerment taking place in many companies, but also little strategic and conceptual thought appears to be given to ways in which environments for growth, based upon clear visions and values, should be developed to make the greatest use of outstanding talent.

Four strong imperatives aimed at giving pace, focus and necessary critical importance to talent management have emerged, empirically, as a result of interventions and surveys by major consultant groups, by direct in-company experience and by fortunes in the market place. They are as follows:

- *Build a winning environment for commitment, achievement and success,* ie develop:
  - ○ 'winning' companies
  - ○ 'winning' roles and jobs
  - ○ vision, mission and values that people of high talent can identify with and want to subscribe to.

- *Make talent management a critical priority.* People remain the most undermanaged and underused asset in too many organisations, because of the lack of importance given to talent management as a strategic, as well as operational, priority.

- *Create the means to identify and select outstanding talent.* Know what talent you need now and in order to win tomorrow, then go out, get it and deploy it in the most intelligent ways. In practice, this third imperative involves being prepared to push talented people forward even though they may be inexperienced. It also involves moving aside 'dead wood' and those who consistently fail to deliver, to make way for those who can and will.

- *Engage talent and develop it.* Face up to the real retention issues in your business and deal with them realistically. This also requires intelligent breaking of the rules of reward, to ensure that those who can and will are rewarded appropriately and realistically. Finally, it means ensuring that feedback, coaching and mentoring are taking place systematically and continually. *Develop, develop and continue to develop* is the key message of the fourth imperative.

Talent management is about constantly engaging the aspirations and developing capabilities of the individual with the transforming needs, vision and goals of the organisation. For that to be done consistently, with optimum pay-off, there needs to be far more than haphazard or *ad hoc* commitment, 'being there at the right time' or the odd twinge of conscience on the part of an organisation's executive body. The organised, committed and *managed* alternative to serendipity, piecemeal intervention – or sheer indifference – is what this book is about.

Before reading Chapter 2, please work through the issues of talent management that follow.

ACTION – THEORY INTO PRACTICE

- Please complete the *Talent Management Profile* on page 209. *Remember to score your answers to represent what actually happens, typically, most of the time, in your organisation.*

- Please answer the three questions that follow the score interpretations.

- What, currently, is your company losing, or missing, as a result of less than fully effective talent management?

- Use the questionnaire and explore the implications at the highest level at which you are able, within your organisation. What, then, are the first actionable steps to be taken to put energy, direction and necessary commitment into revitalised talent management within your organisation?

- In the absence of a dedicated, highly co-ordinated and integrated approach from the top, what can – and should – *you* do to initiate effective talent management within the areas of the business for which you are accountable?

Endnotes

1   WHITE R. P., HODGSON P. *and* CRAINER S. *The Future of Leadership: A white water revolution.* London, Pitman, 1996.
2   DIXON P. *Futurewise: Six faces of global change.* London, HarperCollins, 1998.
3   HALL D. and ERNST & YOUNG, in Smith W., 'Corporate Language – Do you walk the talk?' *Director*, November 1999.
4   MCHENRY R., in Smith W., 'Corporate Language – Do you walk the talk?' *Director*, November 1999.
5   WILKINSON D. *ibid.*
6   KETS DE VRIES M. *Proceedings*, INSEAD Business School.
7   LANDSBERGER F. *Proceedings of the Baxter International Euroboard Meeting on Talent Management.* Brussels, May 1999.
8   TICHY N. *The Leadership Engine.* London, HarperCollins, 1997.
9   *Ibid.*

CHAPTER

The First Imperative at Work

The ultimate insult for a 2005 business colleague: 'You're stuck in a late-twentieth-century time-warp – get into the third millennium.'
Dr Patrick Dixon, Global Change Ltd

Why Would People Want to Work for Us?

What is it that attracts highly talented people to an organisation? What, specifically, are the principal 'pull' factors that make people want to work with a particular company and regularly give upwards of 50 hours a week, commuting and pushing themselves on someone else's behalf? Why are people prepared to give up more time than most actually *need* to – with their loved ones, in enjoying sports and other absorbing leisure activities or in simply relaxing and taking life easy? The answers – as we all know from classic psychological theories[1] and from our own experience – centre around work itself, and the particular personal satisfactions – *self-fulfilment, intellectual stimulation, status, power, social and even physical benefits* – that we derive from engaging in a task where often there are like-minded spirits around us.

But what is it exactly that makes us *want* to work with one particular company, or group of people, or in a specific role? What, precisely, leads people – especially those of talent and high potential – to discriminate between organisations, roles and tasks, choosing one and discarding the others? Are there, for example, any consistent patterns, or most frequently occurring variables, in both the attraction and retention of the most able people that companies can learn from?

McKinsey Management Consultants are leaders in the field in understanding the dynamics of success, or otherwise, in companies' ability to 'pull' and retain the best people. Their research has been conducted with customary rigour, and their survey samples are statistically significant and comprehensive. PDI, also operating globally, has conducted several well-structured surveys into various aspects of corporate culture, including talent management, and especially into the practices of coaching and development, across a wide range of organisations and countries. Global Change Ltd, a UK-based group led by Dr Patrick Dixon, has carried out impressive research under the heading 'Mindsets and Trends Influencing Multi-National Leadership'.

Their cogent conclusions provide powerful arguments for many executives to change, fundamentally, the way they run their businesses and manage people. From their findings come sharply focused definitions of the transforming world. These provide a clear insight into the new, different talents that are now urgently needed to steer companies to success through current – and predicted – change.

The conclusions on which this book is largely based emerge from consultancy and research within 22^2 companies and organisations over a period of seven years from 1993 to 2000, plus the findings of the major global consultancies referred to above.

It is from such research and experience that answers to the questions at the start of this chapter can be developed and translated into necessary strategies and practices of talent management.

The first imperative of talent management – *build a winning environment* – was crystallised as a result of consultancy findings and anecdotal evidence, and focuses attention on the following as major 'pull' and retention factors:

❐ *the outstanding company* and its

- public image and reputation
- culture, vision and demonstrable values
- high-achievement ethic
- role in the market place, as a product or market leader
- brand image of its products or services
- professionalism, values and style of management – especially its leadership

- quality of its people

❑ *the exciting job* and its

- stimulating, testing challenges – and sheer fun
- scope for innovation and experimentation
- opportunities to create wealth and add value
- chance to make a mark or 'leave a legacy'
- manager who commands respect and admiration
- degree of empowerment and autonomy
- level of team synergy and rich mix of talents
- scope to grow and expand its contribution to the business
- exposure to an ever-widening circle of stakeholders and key players

❑ *well-managed talent*, which includes

- an outstanding manager
- coaching and mentoring with quality feedback
- development and personal, as well as professional, growth
- early – and frequent – promotion and career progression
- a quality total reward package
- high earnings
- reward differentials, including bonuses, that realistically reflect outstanding performance, results and effort.

Figure 2 summarises the likely interplay of expected outcomes for the organisation and the individual as a result of effective talent management. It identifies the likely potential outcomes for the individual of an 'outstanding' company, an 'exciting' job and well-managed talent.

Build an Outstanding Company

What is an outstanding, or 'winning', company and especially one that appears, consistently, to attract – and keep – the best people? What do such organisations actually do that marks them out as the businesses top people want to join and remain with, at least for a substantial period of time?

The Organisation:

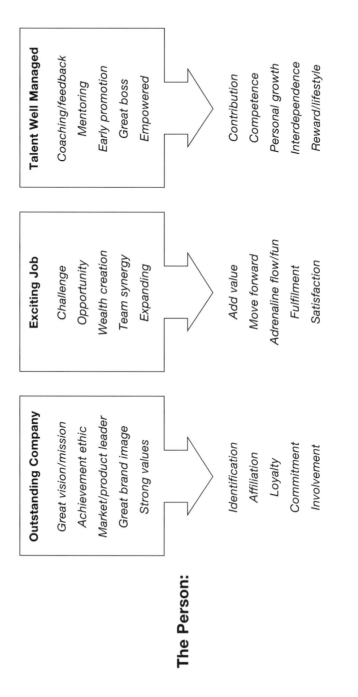

Outstanding Company	**Exciting Job**	**Talent Well Managed**
Great vision/mission	Challenge	Coaching/feedback
Achievement ethic	Opportunity	Mentoring
Market/product leader	Wealth creation	Early promotion
Great brand image	Team synergy	Great boss
Strong values	Expanding	Empowered

The Person:

Identification	Add value	Contribution
Affiliation	Move forward	Competence
Loyalty	Adrenaline flow/fun	Personal growth
Commitment	Fulfilment	Interdependence
Involvement	Satisfaction	Reward/lifestyle

FIGURE 2 Talent Management: Organisational and personal outcomes

66 *An organisation's reputation, public face and what it is seen to stand for can be the most powerful source of attraction and retention of key people.* **99**

Heading the list of potentially attractive features of any organisation is its 'public face':

☐ how it is seen in the world

☐ the sort of reputation it enjoys (what are the best and worst things people typically say about it?)

☐ what it represents or stands for – especially its *performance ethic*

☐ what obviously – and less obviously – differentiates it from other, similar organisations

☐ how the executives behave publicly and the image they portray to the world at large, in demonstrable professionalism and integrity.

An organisation's reputation, public face and what it is *seen* to stand for can be the most powerful source of attraction and retention of key people. Perhaps this can best be exemplified by a comment from a national director from the global Dutch bank, ABN AMRO. 'Here, a deal is a deal: if we agree something with a client, then we stick to it. It is a matter of integrity and it is this which keeps me with ABN AMRO.'

Wellstream Northsea has a simple, yet powerful, credo that under-pins its customer relations management:

> *We commit*
> *We deliver*
> *There are no excuses*

Secretaries and others at all levels in Wellstream show a level of consci-entiousness and concern if they feel that there is a danger of these values being short-changed in their own daily routines and work.

Attraction is so often a matter of association, or affiliation, and wanting to identify with the successful, elite image of the company or organisation (the SAS and SBS have no shortage of would-be members). We live in a status-fixated age – 'executive' homes, 'prestigious' cars, 'upmarket' this and 'top quintile' that – and high-flyers, naturally, will tend to move into the high-profile blue-chip companies. But even if you cannot become, or create, an IBM or Virgin overnight, there is a great deal that you can do to attract and develop people of talent. Any manager who can demonstrate success in at least some of the following areas, as does Tim Evitt, CEO of British Ceramic Tiles, helps to create an image and an environment that high performers are likely to want to be associated with:

☐ the conscious pursuit of recognised 'best practice'

☐ the setting and maintenance of high standards of professionalism that clearly state 'we aim to be among the best'

☐ the ability to articulate and work, day to day, to a clear vision and values that move the team and its role forward

☐ a constant searching for ways to add value to the business

☐ a personal leadership style that is based upon example, regularly creates opportunities for quality dialogues with team members and both empowers and 'enables' the release of talent

☐ the creation of an achieving, high-performing culture where talented people can readily see that they are able to make their mark, develop and grow, through their personal contribution

☐ being seen to fight, with real influence and 'clout', to overcome those organisational blockages, or political constraints, that unnecessarily impede critical individual – and collective – performance, or goal achievement.

Retention of the best people also involves all of the above – hence the need for continuity in creating a successful public face for the organisation and its leaders. Next comes the organisation's *culture*, ie:

☐ the 'felt' vision and sense of mission

☐ the principles and values it espouses and, more important, acts out on a day-to-day basis

☐ what is authentic about the way people behave, interact and transact with one another

☐ how necessary transformation is handled, communicated and progressed

☐ how the executives – and leadership – conduct themselves and how they treat less 'powerful' people within the organisation.

Culture is often defined as 'the way we do things around here', although cynics suggest it should really be 'what people do to keep the bosses off their backs' or 'what people do when they think that no one is looking'. What is done and how is often influenced by organisational size or complexity, and distance away from authority figures. As a consequence, a large or dispersed organisation may consist of several cultural layers, or 'pools', with distinct variations in behaviour, mind-sets and values.

For example, the overall notional or discernible group culture of a business might be its *meta-culture*, while at plant or division level there is likely to be a recognisable *macro-culture*, with its unique mores, values and behavioural codes. Within a major large function there may well be a distinct *tribal culture*, while at departmental, team or project level there will probably be the behavioural stereotypes of a *micro-culture*. 'Tribes' and tribal cultures, perhaps more than other cultures, can at times provide a rich source of opportunities for developing people – and, hence, creative talent management.

Tribes and Tribalism as a Source of Affiliation, Learning and Development

Usually bigger than a team as well as culturally richer, or more distinctive, tribes may include the following:

❏ a collection of local businesses with intense global co-ordination and common/interdependent goals

❏ a project team and its 'nuclear' stakeholders, eg suppliers, clients and clients' customers

❏ a large, integrated function made up of several constituent departments or sections

❏ a group of people from the same profession

❏ a complete (usually small) self-contained plant.

Working in a so-called 'virtual organisation' where boundaries are vague or non-existent may demand more than simply a *team* to create for people the necessary sense of 'we're on the move *together*, with a common purpose and a common sense of direction'. Hence the importance of the wider, unifying common culture of the 'tribe'.

Tribes can provide individuals with:

❐ shared values, beliefs and goals

❐ common identity

❐ tribal events and occasions ('gathering of the clans')

❐ crucial sense of well-being (the 'feel-good' factor).

❝ *The* company's role in the market place, *either as a product or market leader, can prove to be a major 'pull' factor.* ❞

Tribes, given effective integration and visionary leadership, provide:

❐ a sense of identity, kinship and 'family'

❐ a sense of community, with possible role relationships

❐ collaboration and commensurate commitment

❐ a feeling of affiliation and belonging

❐ a positive 'atmosphere' and sense of collective strength.

The *company's role in the market place*, either as a product or market leader, can prove to be a major 'pull' factor – again largely as a source of association and identity for someone making their way in the world. There is the added attraction of possibly being at the cutting edge of new technology and hence opportunities for the development of highly specialised skills and knowledge. Success attracts – and begets – success and so being a market or product leader tends to generate alliances and collaboration with other leading-edge and state-of-the-art businesses and influential stakeholders. Being caught up in an upwards spiral of innovation, development and success can be one of the most powerful sources of learning when managed intelligently, with acuity and acumen.

Brand image, similarly, has – like a company's public face – connotations of quality, superiority and excellence, all of which can reinforce the attractiveness and, therefore, the 'pull' and retention factors of a business. Conversely, a dismal brand image – such as that owned so reluctantly by British Leyland in the 1970s – can demoralise, demotivate and even de-skill people.

The next factor is the *professionalism, values and 'style' of the management and leadership* of the organisation. Managing and leading are inevitably such core factors in talent management that they form a key, recurring theme in the book. However, there are management and leadership issues that are relevant to explore at this stage.

Attracting Talent: Some Questions for Reflection

Ensuring that an organisation's public face, or 'brand image', is closely aligned with – and supportive of – the type of talent that is needed, involves working through the following issues:

❐ Review the organisation's mission, vision and core values – are they clear, communicable, compelling and readily identified with?

❐ Do they make people *want* to join – and remain with – the company?

❐ Will 'high-flyers', especially, get what they expect in terms of challenge, job scope, career progression/advancement and reward?

❐ What is the best way to create, develop and sustain the right 'talent mindset' amongst top management, and make it visible, 'live' and regenerating throughout the executive structure?

❐ What will the organisation's dominant top-talent and high-potential sourcing strategies be?

In order to liberate newly acquired and existing talent, remember to:

❐ recruit and deploy complementary personalities and competencies – *synergy* comes from diversity, *not* uniformity

❐ not discriminate – mix genders and cultures; the adrenaline flow increases and so does creative option generation, where the mix is rich

❐ vary but manage well the age range within a team or group, ie mix energy, drive, 'innocence', experience and wisdom

❐ give talent autonomy ('freedom within a framework') and allow people to experiment, experience, make mistakes and *learn*

❐ review regularly achievements and effort – and give honest, candid feedback; tell people what they need to do differently in order to develop, improve and meet expectations

❐ use trust as a 'cutting edge' in the effective management of time, money and physical resources, so executives give the business speed, decisiveness, boldness and the 'raw' energy necessary for competitive advantage in today's world.

Create Exciting Jobs

The second fundamental element of *building a winning environment* is developing jobs and roles that stimulate, excite and 'stretch' high performers. The achievement, or performance, ethic of a successful company needs to be experienced at the level of individual jobs, roles and projects, so that people feel directly engaged and aligned with the sharp end of the business and the results it is producing.

A recent UK survey[3] conducted by Michael Williams & Partners showed that senior executives felt that their most significant learning and development occurred as a result of:

❐ early major responsibility

❐ early leadership roles

❐ being stretched by challenging assignments

❐ extensive cross-functional, or cross-cultural, experience

❐ being allowed to take risks and fail, without 'punishment'.

Evidence from this and other research suggests that an 'exciting' and 'stimulating' job is one where there is:

❐ empowerment and high freedom and autonomy, within a job of wide scope

❐ frequent opportunity to contribute *directly* to corporate success by making significant financial impact upon results

❐ an opportunity to 'get your arms around the business', as Sir Michael Edwardes[4] used to put it

❐ regular personal challenge that 'stretches' but does not overwhelm or defeat the individual

❐ strong alignment with the primary direction and key results of the business

❏ a steady flow of new projects and ideas to become involved in and work on

❏ a talented, competent manager and stimulating colleagues to work with.

Finally, within the context of an exciting job or role there need to be frequent challenging projects, where the exercise of talent within conditions of uncertainty, risk and opportunity can produce specific end results. Typically, these might include such discrete assignments as:

❏ opening up a new dedicated business within the organisation's boundaries

❏ turning a business or business unit around

❏ improving profitability of a business by a set percentage of growth in profit/turnover/market share

❏ managing a merger strategically and/or operationally

❏ high-profile, high-value projects

❏ working in another country/culture

❏ initiating and implementing a new global role.

Well-Managed Talent

The third key aspect of *building a winning environment* focuses on four things, essentially:

❏ the manager and his or her competence and professionalism as a coach, mentor and, above all, 'enabler' who works to make things happen

❏ the coaching and mentoring processes themselves, and the feedback that is so essential to the talented person's growth and development

❏ promotion – early and often – in order to make career progression a reality (acknowledging that progression will often mean lateral moves, as well as promotion upwards, depending upon the organisation structure and roles that can be developed to accommodate the development needs of people, particularly the talented high-flyers)

❐ the total reward package, which will need to feature:

- appropriately high earnings
- differentials in salary and other benefits that realistically reflect high performance, outstanding effort and impressive results.

Like it or not, any sustained focus on talent – and its development, reward and management – inevitably raises issues of a 'meritocracy'. One characteristic of 'meritocrats' is their strong belief in – and expectation of – *reward differentials*. The interest is not solely on the rewards themselves, although they are extremely important, but also in the lifestyle offered by higher rewards. Many are likely to subscribe to the philosophy: 'work hard – play hard', and that often means play hard in ways that can be unusual, sophisticated, different and expensive.

Fundamental to the whole process of talent management is that the right conversations about a 'winning' working environment – company, job, rewards – take place, together with timely, periodic discussion about lifestyle aspirations and expectations. This is particularly so where retention of the best people is being taken seriously.

SUMMARY

This chapter identifies and explores some of the key 'pull' and 'hold' factors within the working environment of talented people. What attracts high-flyers to a particular organisation, and what keeps them there – motivated, enthusiastic, committed and delivering for a reasonable length of time? The exploration focuses on the first of the four imperatives of talent management – *build a winning environment* – and the three core factors involve the following:

- Develop an outstanding company built upon a strong, attractive achievement ethic and sound values, and a compelling vision that people will identify with.

- Create exciting jobs that will stimulate, challenge and stretch capable, energetic people. Ensure that within those jobs there is a rich variety of new experiences to test people's mettle and help them to grow, professionally and personally.

- Ensure that talent is effectively coached, mentored, given feedback and appropriately rewarded. Reward is not an end in itself – though it should be a powerful, tangible comparator. It also provides necessary access to the sorts of lifestyle that high-flyers frequently aspire to.

> ### ACTION – THEORY INTO PRACTICE
>
> - What, currently, do you see as the principal 'pull' factors in your organisation that attract people of outstanding talent?
>
> - How should these factors be further enhanced to give a true, realistic and not misleading public facelift to your organisation?
>
> - Generally in your organisation, how are jobs made 'exciting' in order to attract – and keep – the best people? For example, how much challenge, 'stretch' and opportunities for new experiences are consciously built into jobs or roles in your company?
>
> - What more should be done to make jobs genuinely more challenging and exciting for high-flyers and people of high potential?
>
> - What, specifically, could – and should – *you* be doing to make the working environment in your function more stimulating, motivating and exciting?

Endnotes

1 The now 'classic' psychological and motivational theories of, *inter alios*, Herzberg, Maslow, McClelland and McGregor.
2 Research into talent management practices was carried out by Michael Williams & Partners in 22 companies/organisations over the period 1993–2000 in Europe and North America, namely: three banks and finance groups; one insurance group; three healthcare/pharmaceutical companies; two FMCG companies; three high-tech/specialist manufacturing companies; four service companies; one consultancy; four engineering/manufacturing companies; and one business school.
3 Survey conducted by Michael Williams & Partners with over 2,000 directors, managers and knowledge workers in the USA, Canada and nine European countries, including the UK and Ireland, during the period 1994–2000.
4 EDWARDES M. *Back from the Brink*. London, Collins, 1983.

CHAPTER

What is 'Talent'?

In the battle of existence, talent is the punch; tact is the clever footwork.

Wilson Mizner

Mediocrity acknowledges nothing higher. Talent recognises genius.

Oscar Wilde

Talent: a Question of Definition and Perspective

Terms such as 'exceptionally talented', 'gifted' or 'very able', together with the concept of 'high potential', have stimulated discussion and invited argument over a great many years. An often unrealistic need for precise definitions – and the lack of consistently definitive or absolute measures – suggests that the debate will continue.

What much research seems to confirm is that IQ and other cognitive abilities, such as reasoning power and analytical thinking, are some of the most consistent core indicators of ability – when combined with factors such as drive, energy, commitment, courage and intuitive skill. Equally, a rich developmental environment would seem to be essential to stimulate intrinsic motivation and a love of learning, which Renzulli[1] calls *task commitment*.

Arising out of a distillation of research, observation and anecdotal evidence, the terms 'talent' and 'talented' in this book are used to describe those people who do one or other of the following:

❏ regularly demonstrate exceptional ability – and achievement – either over a range of activities and situations, or within a specialised and narrow field of expertise

❏ consistently indicate high competence in areas of activity that strongly suggest *transferable, comparable* ability in situations where they have yet to be tested and *proved* to be highly effective, ie *potential*.

There is in both areas of high ability – demonstrable track record *and* unproven but suspected potential – an inevitable risk of unproductive, sterile debate, with the unnecessary pursuit of over-refined definitions. Even the most validated, reliable psychometrics currently in use generate data that is essentially relative and indicative – *not definitive and absolute*. Perspective, situation and context are often the most pragmatic arbiters of performance, especially in the workaday world of business, where viable alternatives, but lack of controlled, 'laboratory' conditions, are the usual reality.

In the assessment of current or recent past performance and competence, the difficulty of isolating all the variables influencing ability – and achievement – means that judgements about talent may often, at best, be circumstantial. However, the statement engraved on a Viking ninth-century battle-axe and quoted in Samuel Smiles's[2] *Self Help* – 'I'll find a way – or I'll make one' – suggests another perspective. Such an uncompromising philosophy of competent self-sufficiency implies a strong refusal to attribute success or failure to 'circumstances'. It also suggests an absence of blame laid at others' doors. In emphasising self-reliance as a core attribute, it underlines the idea that the people who make things happen and get on do so because *they* create opportunities and circumstances, where none apparently existed. These are some of the real hallmarks of talent and potential – particularly in business. As someone once said, 'So, life gives you lemons – then make lemonade!'

Predictive validity, beyond the relative and indicative, is not – and is unlikely ever to be – 100 per cent accurate, as long as we are trying to measure human endeavour and especially people's potential, particularly in the longer term. Yet Van Lennep, a psychologist working at the University of Utrecht in the 1970s, identified what he saw as some of the consistent transferable indicators of potential whereby success in one set of conditions more or less guaranteed effectiveness in other, different environments. Summarised, these are:

☐ 'helicopter' quality, the ability to see higher and wider than the apparent confines of a particular event, problem or situation; it is also the ability to rise above detail and perceive situations contextually

☐ adaptive resourcefulness – the capacity to see through, or around, a problem, innovate and initiate effective remedial and/or exploitative action

☐ high 'common sense' and the ability to deal with everyday or orthodox issues with the minimum of waste, effort, disruption and fuss

☐ high tolerance for ambiguity, chaos, paradox and confusion, and the ability to retain a sense of focus, direction and goals, what Ray Milne[3] describes as 'managing imperfection'

☐ the capacity to operate across different cultures and 'boundaries', effectively, without becoming disoriented or de-skilled

☐ acuity and sharpness of perception, with a high degree of clarity about causal relationships in issues or problems, so that optimal appropriateness of action results.

Van Lennep's findings had their roots in research and investigatory work in companies such as Shell, Unilever and Philips in Holland, but were taken up and developed empirically in many other 'blue-chip' organisations, including BP within the UK. Experience would seem to suggest that Van Lennep's indicators are still realistic measures of leadership and management potential in business.

So far, the terms 'success' and 'successful' have been excluded from the commentary. Their necessary inclusion also raises issues of definition. What, for example, is meant by these terms in the context of applied or potential talent and outstanding achievement? Within the many arenas of talent management, 'success' may mean:

☐ consistently demonstrable achievement against – and *beyond* – job objectives

☐ coincidental, or 'bespoke', transformation of the business – or a significant part of it

❏ regularly effective identification, opening up and exploitation of wealth-creating or value-adding opportunities

❏ repeated reputational enhancement of the organisation and its core, or evolving, activities

❏ personal rapid career progression to the top or very senior executive levels of a major business or institution

❏ the ability to pick winners and create teams of diverse, complementary talents, which will regularly generate productive, contributive synergy.

❝ High-flyers who reach the top appear to be very clear about who they are and what they believe in. ❞

In their important and well-researched study of 45 'high-flying' CEOs, Cox and Cooper[4] concluded that there was obviously no one 'right' personality type typical of their sample. However, they found that *resilience* – and the ability to *learn from*, as well as *cope with*, adversity – was one crucial universal strength. This appears to derive from, and is a function of, three key factors:

❏ a strong internal locus of control

❏ a clear value system and set of beliefs

❏ a strong self-image.

High-flyers who reach the top appear to be very clear about *who they are and what they believe in*. While these are characteristics that seem to evolve and develop largely as a result of early experience, they are open to further development by effective coaching and mentoring – that is, *talent management*. As indicators of *leadership* potential and performance especially, they serve to generate a communicable confidence that has to be one of the core attributes of any executive, particularly those at the top.

Intelligent v Gifted

For the purposes of differentiation, 'intelligence', as a descriptive key element of *talent*, here refers to high IQ and what is generally termed

'brightness'. It is primarily about cognitive ability, including perceptiveness and speed of uptake. Giftedness is something more than the
analytical logic of cognition and 'high' IQ. Giftedness in its many forms,
though not in the realms of genius, appears to derive from the interplay
of *very high* IQ with other forms of very high intelligence, such as:

❏ intrapersonal (awareness of self)

❏ interpersonal (social skills)

❏ spatial ability

❏ musical skills

❏ kinaesthetic ability

❏ intuition and creativity.

The distinction between 'brightness' and giftedness emerged clearly
from research conducted in the UK in the late 1990s by the National
Association for Gifted Children. This revealed the following qualities.

Bright Children	Gifted Children
Know the answers	Ask the questions
Are interested	Are extremely curious
Pay attention	Get involved
Have good ideas	Have wild, 'silly' ideas
Work hard	Play around, but test well
Answer the questions	Question the answers
Are in the top group	Are beyond any group
Listen with interest	Show strong feelings
Learn with ease	Already know
Understand ideas	Build abstract theories
Grasp meaning	Draw inferences
Complete assignments	Initiate projects
Are receptive	Are exploratory
Copy accurately	Create new designs
Enjoy school	Enjoy learning
Absorb information	Apply information
Are good technicians	Are inventors
Memorise well	Are good at guessing
Are alert	Are keenly observant
Are pleased with own work	Are highly self-critical

While the NAGC research was conducted with children, and while
some forms of giftedness in childhood may not always persist into
adulthood (or may change along the way), the findings nevertheless
suggest some recognisable differences that mark out talented adults

from their less gifted colleagues. For example, adults of high ability typically:

❏ ask questions – to the point of demanding answers

❏ question the answers

❏ initiate, rather than follow

❏ are creative and original

❏ enjoy new experiences and learning

❏ invent and innovate

❏ apply information – rather than merely absorb it

❏ guess – and are prepared to act on intuitive 'gut feel'

❏ are usually very observant and perceptive

❏ are frequently very self-critical and push themselves hard.

More than merely implicit in the above is a strong correlation with Sternberg's[5] view that high ability involves the *development* of an individual's particular and 'natural' aptitude to exceptionally high levels. Many of the behaviours identified as being characteristic of giftedness appear to confirm the notion of continually building, developing and strengthening ability, by:

❏ questioning and active curiosity

❏ consciously enhancing and expanding understanding

❏ experimenting and experiencing as a means of learning

❏ breaking new ground and opening up new possibilities

❏ self-evaluation and consequent conscious improvement in competence.

In other words, gifted people actively work at improving and increasing their understanding and ability, so that maintaining high capability becomes, for them, a regenerative process.

Contributive Synergy: Diversity – Not Uniformity

The synergy necessary to effect transformation and move events forward stems from *diversity* – not uniformity. Crucial to effective talent management is the need, as Professor Mary Rose Greville[6] says, to *value differences* and to recognise the frequently *latent* potential that exists in teams where there is a powerful cocktail of *mixed* talents, personalities, gender and culture.

In his efforts to bring the then British Leyland 'back from the brink', Sir Michael Edwardes[7] frequently made the point that the company desperately needed complementary – not 'cloned' – competencies, experiences and personalities to help it break the mould, leave the past behind and move on. Wider, enriched knowledge bases and diverse experience enhance not only the range of perception and diagnosis, *but also the scope of prescriptive or exploitative action*. These latter strengths become very apparent when designing and running strategic and operational workshops within global (as opposed to national or 'multi-local') organisations.

Whether they are executive development courses or organisation transformation workshops, such programmes invariably generate and develop far richer and more creative solutions to problems than those from established, homogeneous cultures. While the latter tend to use convergent patterns of analysis and thinking to produce the one 'right' solution, the more heterogeneous cultures tend to brainstorm more readily and rely on *divergent* thinking to select, from many alternatives, the most appropriate, viable option.

Figure 3 shows the distinction between the two different thinking approaches to problem analysis, solution generation and decision-making typical of 'uniform' and 'diverse' cultures respectively. In talent management, one of the major practical issues is that of consciously building the appropriate mix of diversity to ensure a consistently high level of contributive and focused synergy.

The American psychologist Kolb[8] suggested that learning is a cyclical process and that it is essentially an adaptive coping cycle of:

❏ doing

❏ reviewing/reflecting

❏ coming to conclusions

❏ behaving differently, as a consequence.

1 Convergent thinking:

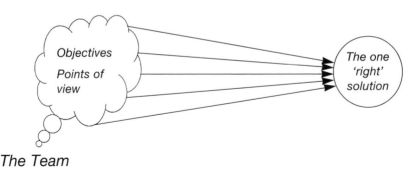

The Team

2 Divergent thinking:

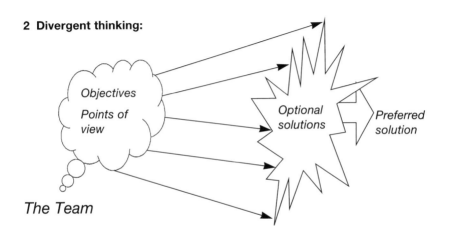

The Team

FIGURE 3 Convergent and Divergent Thinking in Problem-Solving

Adapted from Kolb's original construct as a model for developing team learning and using unique talents for optimum contributive synergy, Figure 4 suggests that learning involves:

❏ doing

❏ reviewing/reflecting

❏ making necessary 'connections' (causal relationships, inferences and conclusions)

❏ deciding what to do, as a consequence.

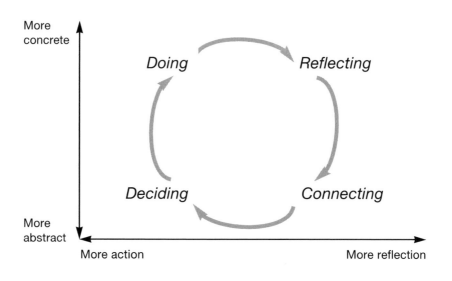

FIGURE 4 The 'Classic' Learning Cycle (Individuals)

As well as individual patterns of behaviour, there are implications for *team* talent management. One individual within a team might be a strong *natural reflector*, ideal to catalyse or lead reflection on the part of their colleagues. Another may be the *natural connector* and facilitate, better than anyone else, a clear grasp of causal relationships in a problem. A third may turn out to be the team's *natural planner* and so figure prominently as the one best equipped to 'enable' decision-making and planning to evolve most effectively. Finally, contributive synergy may be best catalysed by the team's *natural action leader*. Figures 4 and 5 both indicate the mix of talents – based upon differing learning and behavioural styles – along two axes:

❐ concrete v abstract thinking

❐ action v reflection orientation.

While these are only two variables that enrich the mix in contributive competence and synergy, they are fundamental. However, they can easily be overlooked in the day-to-day processes of developing and managing talent.

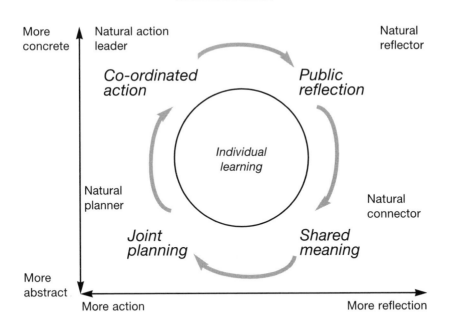

FIGURE 5 Team Learning Cycle

Emotional Intelligence – a Key Aspect of Talent and High Potential

What is currently referred to as 'emotional intelligence' – or 'EQ' – has existed for as long as people have been communicative, interactive beings, capable of awareness and feelings. Particularly in its intuitive aspects, it remains a largely untapped source of know-how, creativity and expertise. Psychologists' preoccupation with hard-nosed objectivity, unfortunately, has led to an unnecessary discounting of the centrality of 'gut feel', 'hunch' and subjective 'implicit' learning as major professional strengths. Yet in reality, and always alongside IQ, the intuitive expertise that often marks out so many successful leaders and entrepreneurs can form the basis for informed choice and decision-making.

Recent evidence[9] would seem to suggest that, in complex problem analysis, intuition and implicit learning are superior to cognitive strategies, especially where situations are ill defined and characterised by uncertainty, ambiguity or stress. While much research, particularly from the last decade, confirms the relevance of rational analysis and cognitive strategies in addressing well-defined problems and challenges, it also highlights the advantages of intuitive expertise in handling confusion and complexity. Indeed, some current research – notably that of Coulson[10] – suggests that most rational problem-solving, by definition, needs to impose order and plausibility on situations in order to work, whereas intuition or implicit learning *requires* the confusion, ambiguity and complexity typical of management to be at its most effective. Hence the 'intelligent unconscious' is re-emerging as a respectable, relevant concept in behavioural science, as intuitive awareness and competence are increasingly acknowledged as vital to success in management, leadership and business.

❝ It is the intellectual and emotional synergy *that is so vital in today's business world.* ❞

It would, of course, be completely unrealistic to discount the essential value of IQ, cognitive reasoning and rational analysis. Rather, it is the *intellectual and emotional synergy* that can be the product of combined EQ and IQ that is so vital in today's business world. The effective synthesis of 'right brain' activity with that of the left hemisphere – where rational analysis and evaluation are given the stimulus of creative insight and an instinctive sense of timing – is the essence of success in business.

EQ and its Critical Role in Leadership and Management

EQ – vision, imagination, intuition, inspiration, charisma and flair – is part of the crucial 'alchemy' in the leadership, release and management of people's contributive competence, commitment and collaboration. It is the 'Nelson touch', the enabling intervention, intuitive insight and the initiative of those leaders and managers who sense – and acknowledge – *more readily and with greater acuity than others*:

❐ productive uncertainty that is worth exploring and exploiting

❐ opportunities to move events, individuals and relationships forward

❐ what – and especially when – problems or issues need to be confronted

❐ implications and ramifications beyond the immediate 'here and now'

◻ strategic and organisational vacuums that need to be filled

◻ interpersonal bridges to be built or doors to be opened

◻ the value of immediacy, spontaneity and timing of intervention.

In the words of Rowan,[11] a journalist with *Fortune* magazine, '"hunch" is an odious word to the professional manager. It's a horse player's or stock market "plunger's" term, rife with imprecision and unpredictability.' But isn't the world of business management and organisational leadership similarly imprecise and uncertain? Clearly, in such conditions, logic, analysis and reasoned thinking *are* essential. Cognitive intelligence, diagnosis and evaluative judgement all have a crucial part to play in analysing problems, determining causal relationships and making decisions. However, as Rowan points out, *the last step to success frequently requires a daring intuitive leap to translate decisions into necessary actions – and outcomes.*

Jack Welch, CEO of GE, is arguably the greatest industrial leader–manager of recent times; in nine years he raised GE's profit value from $1.65 billion to $9.29 billion and its market value from $12 billion to $380 billion. Welch advises: 'Shun the incremental – and go for the leap.' How often, though, do fear of failure or ridicule inhibit intuitive expertise and trigger self-imposed constraints, so blocking out that 'immediate knowledge' and feeling of 'rightness' of vision and action that lie at the core of implicit know-how.

The very tools, techniques and systems of the 'information age' provide us with data, diagnosis and feedback that paradoxically feed rather than dispel such fears. Previously unencountered levels of informational sophistication can also be misused as an alibi to rationalise away the 'feel', sensing and pristine insight of intuition as unsubstantiated and irresponsible subjectivity. The intention of this chapter is not to promote the cause of unbridled emotion – far from it. Its aim is, however, to reinforce the current growing support for developing, managing and building upon the *appropriate and effective* use of EQ – especially intuition – in professional and business arenas. That EQ – particularly in conjunction with IQ – can add untold value to relationships, contributive synergy and outcomes is beyond question. *The major challenges facing management are how to identify, release, develop and use it, to optimum effect, in:*

◻ reading situations, where intuitive expertise will enhance understanding already developed through cognitive analysis

❏ developing visions that open up the scope, range and possibilities of what might be, in terms of an attainable future

❏ generating wide and more appropriate ranges of viable options and alternative strategies

❏ creatively enhancing the scope of both proactive and reactive courses of action or interventions

❏ using a more responsible, adaptive and flexible sense of timing in committing to, taking or refraining from action

❏ building more collaborative and productive working relationships (social 'chemistry') that can create the necessary levels of collaborative synergy to take people, technology, projects and organisations forward.

Intuition may take many forms – the 'Eureka' phenomenon, 'bolts from the blue' or (less respectfully) the 'GBO' (the 'glimpse of the bloody obvious') – or it may be the result of a period of reflection and incubation. In any case, it is self-evident to most practising managers that 'gut feel' or intuition has an *essential but often inexplicable* part to play in decision-making. Daniel Goleman's[12] *Emotional Intelligence* calls into serious question the traditional belief that success is primarily a matter of IQ and redefines the linkage between the two by demonstrating that so much of personal excellence is a matter of intuitive expertise and the propensity to *act* based upon the appropriate use of feelings and emotions. Although EQ is in danger of becoming a meaningless umbrella term, few would dispute that emotional 'literacy' – which is what EQ essentially is – involves the following processes and *associated competencies*:

❏ recognising our own emotions and personal 'buttons'

❏ understanding generally what triggers them

❏ having a degree of control over them and being able to 'manage' them

❏ being aware of others' emotions

❏ having the capability to influence and manage others' emotions

❏ possessing a high level of intuitive 'feel' for the potential of situations – and people's part in those situations.

Such emotional literacy opens up possibilities that analytical logic, alone, notoriously fails to, for example:

❒ stimulating and releasing productive energy

❒ engendering and building team spirit

❒ establishing rapport and goodwill

❒ strengthening interpersonal relationships

❒ stimulating vision and focus on necessary transformation

❒ inspiring people

❒ mobilising commitment and willing contributive effort.

It is this emotional literacy that makes executives like Richard Branson, Julian Richer (founder of Richer Sounds) and Tim Evitt (MD of British Ceramic Tiles) such stimulating and effective leaders and managers of talent.

Essentially, there are five key aspects to *applied* emotional intelligence, which are largely interdependent (see Table 2).

The effective integration of these five interrelated facets to EQ can add both *transformational* and *social* value to communication, quality of relationships and the nature, power and direction of human endeavour. The degree of emotional development and social maturity of the individual – factor number five – represents emotional growth as a 'whole' person.

'Flow' – EQ at its best

'Flow' is a term coined by Mihaly Csikszentmihalyi, a psychologist at Chicago University, to refer to:

❒ when you feel 'at one' with the task, or job, on hand

TABLE 2 Five Aspects of Emotional Intelligence

• emotional awareness	⎱ which, together, form the basis
• emotional integrity	⎰ of emotional 'literacy'
• emotional competence	⎱ which are essentially
• emotional synergy	⎰ emotional 'chemistry'
• emotional development and the growth of social maturity)	

- ❏ *effortless* excellence

- ❏ the ultimate harnessing of emotions in the service of performance and learning

- ❏ the positive, energised *alignment* of emotions and task

- ❏ 'peak' performance

- ❏ the stretching of previous limits

- ❏ a state of self-forgetfulness and *complete absorption* in the task, ie the opposite of anxious preoccupation

- ❏ 'masterly control' over what we are doing, when the act or task itself is pleasurable and motivating.

There are several ways to move into a state of 'flow':

- ❏ Deliberately focus sharp, intense *attention* on the task at hand (*a highly concentrated state is the essence of 'flow'*).

- ❏ Work on a task you are skilled at and engage in it at a level that taxes your skill and ability. *People tend to concentrate best when the demands upon them are a little greater than normal. ('Flow' occurs in the delicate zone between boredom and anxiety.)*

- ❏ Induce a state of calm in yourself before trying to enter the 'flow' zone (the quality of attention in 'flow', although highly focused, is relaxed).

❝ It is the experience of 'flow' that turns a job into a 'plus job'. ❞

Managing 'flow' in others is one of the most challenging, yet exciting and rewarding aspects of talent management. The 'buzz' and adrenaline add an edge to focus, direction and the pace of work. They are, in effect, a form of supercharged energy, and where this occurs between two or more people the level of productive synergy can rise immeasurably. It is the experience of 'flow' that turns a job into a 'plus job'. Where the experience occurs repeatedly, the talented individual is probably in an outstanding environment – the first imperative of talent management. Where such motivation, drive and innovative talent – that is, emotional intelligence – are being successfully harnessed, focused, engaged and managed, then an organisation can perhaps justifiably claim, 'we've started to get it right.'

SUMMARY

Within the context of this book, *talent* is seen as:

- consistently high ability – and performance – over either a wide range of activities and/or within a particular area of expertise
- high ability in areas of activity that strongly indicate transferable and comparable capability, in other fields of endeavour, even though the individual may not have yet had experience of the latter.

Talent is therefore considered to be, variously, high ability, giftedness and/or high potential.

Scholars have sought to establish two distinct but complementary facets to ability:

- various forms of cognitive intelligence
- intuitive/emotional capabilities.

Until recently, many psychologists and behavioural theorists tended to avoid serious research into non-cognitive areas, preferring the apparently more tangible and measurable areas of IQ, logical thinking and rational problem-solving behaviours. Much research carried out during the last decade, however, appears to confirm the *superiority* of so-called 'emotional intelligence', especially intuition, over more logically derived ability *when working in conditions of confusion, ambiguity and uncertainty.*

Clearly this is not an 'either–or' choice, where EQ is to be preferred to IQ as a managerial competence. Rather, the two distinctly different clusters of ability need to be able to function in synergy, in order to generate the most effective problem-solving, decision-making and management within a business. However, while IQ cannot really be developed very much within adults, many of the competencies that constitute EQ *can* be learned and greater interpersonal skills can be developed. Essentially, there are five fundamental facets to EQ:

- *emotional awareness* – of self and others
- *emotional integrity* – and personal accountability
- *emotional competence* – especially intuitive insight
- *emotional synergy* – creating productive relationships
- *emotional development* – growth as a 'whole' person.

The pioneering work of Daniel Goleman has drawn the importance of EQ to the attention of growing numbers of people, and he has identified many strong links between *emotional intelligence* and *success in business* – and in life itself. EQ strength is especially relevant in helping to deal *more effectively* with issues such as:

- overcoming fear of failure – the great constraint and impediment

- making greater use of creativity and innovation

- adapting more readily and successfully to change

- cutting through complexity and uncertainty where logical analysis seems, paradoxically, to be less effective

- inspiring, motivating and mobilising people by using vision, 'passion', drive and commitment, rather than simply rational explanation and diagnosis.

The fundamental message implicit in EQ is that logic, rational analysis and IQ alone are insufficient to guarantee success even in the 'hard' world of business. The 'head' needs the 'heart' to be fully effective. Logic needs the complementary perspectives of intuition, while rational decision-making so often requires the final creative leap to ensure successful outcomes and a move forward. On current evidence, high EQ would seem to be fundamental to leadership and management talent.

ACTION – THEORY INTO PRACTICE

1 Think about the most memorable and impressive leaders and/or managers that you have known. Name them, and, against each, identify:

- what really made them so remarkable and memorable

- which of their exceptional strengths had nothing to do with IQ

- what impact they each had upon you

- in what ways you think or act differently as a result of contact with them.

2 Of the people that you know, who might put you on their list of memorable leaders and managers?

- Why would they include you?

- How might you have influenced them (for the better)?

3 Consider three or four important decisions that you have made recently and ask yourself:

- Where did you overemphasise logic, analysis and cognitive diagnosis as the basis to decision-making and action?

- Which aspects of EQ and intuitive expertise might have proved more effective and appropriate, on reflection?

- Why did you give such emphasis to logical analysis and cognitive intelligence?

- How much did fear of failure, or wish to preserve convention and established practice, influence you?

4 Where, do you feel, do those who report to/work with you tend to rely too heavily on logic and insufficiently upon implicit learning and intuitive competence?

5 Develop personal improvement plans – with specific developmental activities – to help you and your staff/colleagues begin to recognise, acknowledge and use EQ – especially intuition – more frequently and naturally in:

- problem/situational analysis

- generating a wider range of options and alternatives

- decision-making

- identifying opportunities for improvement or transformation

- interpersonal relationships.

6 Using intuition – not logical analysis – brainstorm what feels to be the right vision and future direction of your team/department/function. Do the exercise as a group of up to 12 key players. *Then*, using logic and analytical planning, work out how you can best make the vision a reality.

7 Complete the *Emotional Intelligence Profile* on page 213. Use it as either a personal instrument for self-scoring or as a 360-degree profile to gain feedback and insights from others' perceptions of you. Work through the questions that follow the profile once you have completed your answers and scored the results. What key learning points emerge for:

- you?

- your team?

- high-performers in your team?

- your manager?

Endnotes

1 RENZULLI J. S. in Katzko, M. W. and Monks, F. J. (eds) *Nurturing Talent: Individual needs and social ability*. Assen, Netherlands, Van Gorcum, 1995.
2 SMILES S. *Self Help*. London, Penguin, 1986.

3 MILNE R. *ILO proceedings*. Prague, Ostrava and Brno, November 1969.
4 COX C. J. *and* COOPER C. L. *High Flyers: An anatomy of managerial success*. Oxford, Blackwell, 1988.
5 STERNBERG R. J., in Heller, K. A., Monks, F. J. and Passon, A. H., *Handbook of Research and Development of Giftedness and Talent*. Oxford, Pergamon Press, 1993.
6 GREVILLE M. R. *Proceedings ABN AMRO Senior Leadership Programme*. Holland, Duin & Kruidberg, 1998.
7 EDWARDES M. *Back from the Brink*. London, William Collins, 1983.
8 KOLB D. A. ET AL. *Organizational Psychology*. London, Prentice Hall, 1979.
9 CLAXTON G. 'Knowing without knowing why', *Psychologist,* May 1998.
10 COULSON M. *The Cognitive Function of Confusion*. Paper presented at British Psychological Society Conference, London, December 1995.
11 ROWAN R. *The Intuitive Manager*. Aldershot, Gower, 1987.
12 GOLEMAN D. *Emotional Intelligence*. London, Bloomsbury, 1996.

The Second, Third and Fourth Imperatives

We believe that the difference between those who treat learning as an accident and those who treat learning as a deliberate business process is the difference between those who will eventually fail and those who will succeed.

Andrew Mayo and Elizabeth Lank, *The Power of Learning*

I hate waste, and wasted human potential is the worst waste of all.

Valerie Stewart, *The David Solution*

Chapter 2 explored the first of the four imperatives of successful talent management – *create a winning environment* – in some depth. Essentially, this amounts to:

❏ creating a winning company people *want* to join

❏ developing challenging jobs people *want* to do

❏ ensuring opportunities for rewards – and lifestyles that people *aspire* to.

In this chapter, we look at the remaining three imperatives and the essential managerial interplay between them. These latter three imperatives are examined together in order to emphasise the many executive and organisational facets of what needs to be a well-orchestrated, co-ordinated corporate process – and a major strategic priority. The necessary mindsets, competencies and practices that exemplify and meet these imperatives will form the substance of succeeding chapters. Yet clearly executives acting independently and unilaterally *can* achieve some success in managing talent – both with individuals of high ability or potential, and with effective teams. However, to achieve consistent, sustained maximum impact, talent management needs to take place as a co-ordinated executive process, integrated and aligned with:

❑ corporate values and goals

❑ the direction of the business

❑ conscious transformation of the organisation.

Make Talent Management a Corporate Priority – the Second Imperative

Raising talent management to the level of a major corporate priority is far more than executive exhortation, or head office diktat. Equally, it is much more than simply the number one item on a human resources department 'wish list', however well articulated and prescribed. All of these may have a part to play in introducing or discussing the *concept* of effective talent management, but elevating the philosophy – and practices – from mere prescription to major priority involves much more.

❝ Raising talent management to the level of a major corporate priority is far more than executive exhortation. ❞

Essentially, there are three core factors in the process:

❑ Foster a talent management *mindset*.

❑ Develop the necessary talent management *skills*.

❑ Make managers *accountable* for managing talent.

Foster a talent management mindset

As the managing director[1] of a major European biotech company put it:

> I see my role primarily as the driving force behind the development of our people
> – especially the management team. Every leader's job is to develop and lead other
> leaders. My particular responsibility is to develop an outstanding Executive for the
> company.

In what he described as 'coaching the process', the CEO stated that a major objective for executives at all levels within the company was to ensure that the right discussions were constantly taking place about talent, development and potential.

The top team progressively firmed up the key values that empirically as well as ethically represented what the business stands for, in relation to the triple bottom line. Their values – termed 'gateways' (ie to the future) – have a strong element of utilitarian morality in them. Conversations with the CEO and several of his senior executives reveal nothing messianic or evangelical, but rather a healthy sense of interdependence and mutual support, expressed in ideals such as:

❐ If anything is wrong, *you* will always be the first to know.

❐ I will do all that I can to support you in your achievements – and development.

Just as the company's executives and staff demonstrate a level of social conscience significantly higher than the norm in their relationships to customers, suppliers, shareholders and the environment, so managers demonstrate a comparably high awareness of talent and the need for outstanding ability to be managed intelligently. Arriving at such a consistent and common understanding – and hence mindset – did not occur overnight. A great deal of groundwork, discussion and exploration over a period of three years took place before the executive felt sufficiently confident to say 'we're getting there now.'

United Distillers and Vintners' 'passion' for its brands and its customers represents another set of values that are 'lived' by people in that organisation. They consciously allocate some of their best people and significant resources to new brand development centres around the world to ensure that innovation continues to be a 'powerful engine' for growth in UDV.

As with any form of transformation, changing mindsets throughout an organisation's management, in order to take attitudes – and practices – further down the line, follows a 'classic' pattern of thinking, discussion and behaviour modification, as Figure 6 shows.

First, there has to be an *expressed need* (ie 'pressure') for change: a level of constructive dissatisfaction that is capable of articulating current deficiency, inadequacy or inappropriateness. *Second*, there needs to be a *vision*, reflecting what could and should be the requisite new state of affairs, based upon a clear perception of what *needs* to be changed and

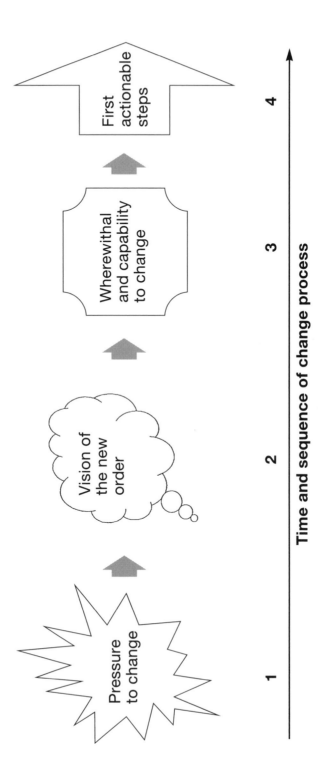

Time and sequence of change process

1   2   3   4

Pressure to change

Vision of the new order

Wherewithal and capability to change

First actionable steps

FIGURE 6   The Mechanics of Change

why. *Third*, there must be the *wherewithal* to bring about necessary change. In the case of talent management, it is the combination of:

☐ awareness and attitude, ie *mindset*

☐ competence and 'do-how'

☐ sense of personal accountability.

Finally, the *first actionable steps* need to be agreed – and taken – to begin to make the vision become the necessary reality and new, requisite state of affairs.

More specifically, the *talent management mindset* will actively acknowledge, at least, the following as crucially important:

☐ Talent is the principal source of competitive advantage.

☐ Talent comes in many different forms, some of which may not always be immediately recognisable, ie talent can be latent and may need bringing out.

☐ Talent is the most critical of a company's assets and requires at least as much managing as the physical and financial resources of the business.

☐ Talent is something to which value may be constantly – and productively – added, in the form of new knowledge, new awareness and new competencies.

☐ Talent management is an essential part of any executive's job.

☐ Talent needs to respond to and thrive upon appropriate challenge, ie challenge that stimulates and 'stretches', but does not overwhelm or defeat.

☐ Talent criteria and standards need to be agreed, confirmed and understood, so that people are clear about what is and is not 'talent', in terms of an organisation and its business.

Develop the necessary talent management skills

The real skills in managing talent are not those of being able to follow, manipulate or 'work' the current human resource systems and reporting procedures. Nor do they involve pious hopes, platitudes or opiates, to calm nerves, raise false expectations and buy a temporary, uneasy peace from ambitious, but frustrated 'unpromotables'. While a manager's 'political' repertoire and stock-in-trade may include dispensing bromides, making soothing noises and boxing cleverly, talent management is based upon an authenticity and mutual understanding that can only come from *frequent candid dialogue*. Skills in questioning, probing, exploring – *and creating discovery* – are among the most critical competencies in initiating, conducting and developing highly productive dialogue and debate.

In today's world of 'virtual organisations', networked businesses and increasing global activity, face-to-face *quality* discussions are becoming an even greater rarity. This is especially so with discussions about talent and its development, intelligent use and management. Developing skill in discussion and dialogue is a highly personal matter where individual style, sensitivity and 'chemistry', rather than mere technique, are crucial to success. Techniques and tools, however, can help significantly *in developing style, sharpening awareness and fostering the necessary alchemy* that, together, make for effective discussions about performance, development, improvement and growth – the very stuff of talent management.

❝ In today's world of 'virtual organisations', face-to-face quality discussions are becoming an even greater rarity. ❞

Figure 7 illustrates the EAR technique of questioning – and *listening* – which can both stimulate and control the flow, direction and, most important of all, the *outcomes* of dialogue.

While real life is never as simple as a theoretical concept, the EAR model is useful in that it focuses on the *reflective* mode of questioning and listening. Experience suggests that this is the least used, but most effective, means of developing dialogue and debate – particularly about performance and how best to develop and improve it. The move from executive 'tell' style, to 'reflective', review-explore-and-discover mode, shifts the ownership of the problem or issue – and of the subsequent solutions and action – from the manager to the job-holder.

The EAR model emphasises the significance of *style versatility* in order to move appropriately around and also 'shape' leader–colleague and manager–subordinate relationships. The range of versatility inherent in the model runs from 'closed', high autocracy to strongly empowering, 'open' styles of leadership, management and interaction with others.

The letter 'E' of the mnemonic EAR indicates *executive*, or essentially autocratic and authoritarian styles in dealing with others. This is not intended to be pejorative or critical terminology, but a description of

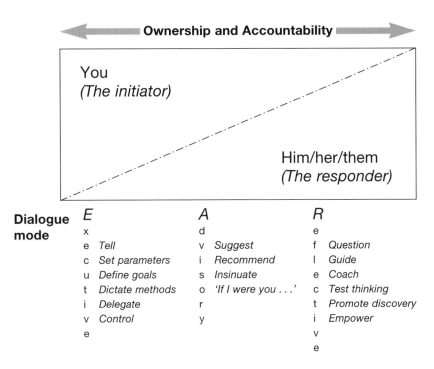

FIGURE 7 The EAR Approach to Developing Dialogue

styles that may reflect the reality of particular situations. Executive styles are viewed as the product of what are primarily mandatory conditions – as well as the natural or adaptive responses of more tough-minded individuals. They are therefore often likely to be necessary, legitimate or fitting responses to crisis or other urgent, dominating imperatives, as well as being a 'natural' predisposition towards autocracy.

The letter 'A' of EAR represents what are really *advisory* styles of leadership, or interaction, which make use of what typically falls into the broad behavioural category of 'advice', namely:

❑ non-mandatory prescriptions for success or problem avoidance/resolution

❑ suggestions for improvement, change or remedy

❑ recommendations (usually for *action*, ie 'why don't you do. . .?').

Much advice is likely to be based on the coach's or leader's personal experience, interpretations, wants or expectations.

Finally, the 'R' summarises the *reflective* styles of questioning and listening, so essential to effective coaching and mentoring – and, indeed, mobilising leadership styles. Figure 7 shows the relationship between those three fundamentally different style categories and their varying impact upon the awareness, responsibility, sense of ownership and learning of those being managed, led and coached. Clearly, the model omits all the intermediate shades of 'grey' and the dynamics of style 'switch' or inconsistency, characteristic of so many people. Using two dimensions only, its purpose is simply to convey the idea of *fundamental* style difference and some of the likely hallmarks of each.

The quality of questioning, listening and exploration fundamental to the *effective* practice of the *reflective* style forms the interactive foundation of coaching. Using essentially – but not exclusively – 'open' questions, derived from Kiplings's[2] 'six honest serving-men': 'what', 'where', 'when', 'how', 'why' and 'who' – the reflective style is likely to stimulate necessary *investigation, exploration, conclusion and learning* far more effectively than commands, directives or advice.

It is a powerful tool for defining the scope and extent of empowerment in the context of 'freedom within a framework', by the effective use of open questions, such as:

❏ 'What do you see as the critical priorities?'

❏ 'What else is of crucial importance here?'

❏ 'What are your most viable options?'

Moving the dialogue on to the 'what-are-you-going-to-*do*?' stage are the questions that explore the necessary *sequence* of intended and necessary action, such as:

❏ 'What will you do about "X"?'

❏ 'What will you do next?'

❏ 'And then?'

The technique can also be used retrospectively using the same sequence and beginning with, 'what did you actually do about "X"?' – and so on.

Questioning about three stages of sequential *action* is an effective way of confirming not only what was done – and why (given the appropriate one-word question) – but also of identifying whether the individual:

❒ is quite clear about the issue under review and necessary actions taken

❒ may be pulling the wool over the questioner's eyes

❒ is confused or uncertain about what happened or what to do

❒ is lying or deliberately misrepresenting facts and distorting reality.

The open questions help to shape and control the direction and flow of the dialogue without unnecessarily constraining people. Rather, they are used to focus thinking on the 'musts' and serve to promote discovery:

❒ 'What alternatives should we consider?'

❒ 'What would be a less expensive/more effective way to do this?'

❒ 'How could we really add value here?'

❒ 'Suppose we did that – what would be the worst that could happen?'

❒ 'If it did go wrong, how much could that cost us?'

❒ 'What possibilities would this open up for us?'

❒ 'You've described what it would look like if well done. Suppose we aimed for an outstanding job – what might that look like?'

A second model, shown in Figure 8, reveals how progression up a hierarchy of communication, social intimacy and interaction can move dialogue from routine conversation ('Good morning. How are you?') to 'sparking' and creative synergy, where the exchanges between people become highly contributive, productive and fulfilling to those directly involved.

Levels 4 and above in the hierarchy of communication and relationships represent areas of *personal uniqueness*, culminating in the fruitful, mutually stimulating dialogues characteristic of level 6 – 'peak communication'. At level 6, interaction and transactions between people are free and uninhibited, where there is high candour, honesty and personal authenticity. Such discussions, at this level of spontaneity and openness, typically generate:

❒ high joint or collective 'flow' (see Chapter 3)

❒ mutual intellectual honesty and freedom from 'political' games

❒ absence of hidden agenda

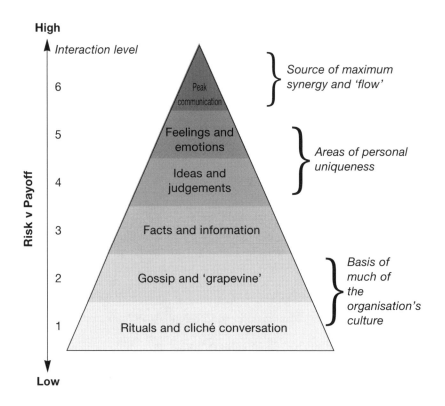

FIGURE 8 Hierarchy of Interaction

❒ the building on – and adding of value – to others' contributions

❒ natural, productive 'brainstorming' and creative resourcefulness

❒ a far richer range of options and wider scope for action and solutions.

❝ It is impossible to contrive, or force, where there is little or no interpersonal chemistry. ❞

Peak communication is a feature of the particular 'chemistry' that can exist between two people, or within a small, close-knit team, and is capable of generating perceptions and outcomes way beyond solely individual effort. Spontaneity, sense of timing, high sensitivity to others and being on the same – or complementary – wavelengths as the parties to the dialogue are all part of the intellectual and emotional alchemy from which can emerge peak communication and creative synergy. It is impossible to contrive, or force, where there is little or no interpersonal chemistry between those working together.

However, as was indicated above, learned techniques and acquired communications skills *can* help to facilitate necessary productive dialogues, though they may lack the 'spark' of genuine peak communication. Here are just three examples of communication tools and techniques that can be developed and used, in order to raise the quality of conversation and dialogue between people, and particularly on issues of performance improvement, development and use of skills, role enhancement and personal growth.

Listening with your whole body
Focus the discussion on 'you', not 'I':

- Focus attention on the *other* person and their thoughts, ideas, values, wants and concerns.
- Concentrate on intentions and outcomes for the other person.
- Look at the other person instead of looking away or around.
- Naturally match, or 'mirror', the other person's posture.
- Use 'you'- not 'I'-centred words.
- Use language patterns that match those of the other person, without submerging your own identity.

Accept the other person's uniqueness
Differences are inevitable, legitimate and perfectly natural:

- Recognise and capitalise upon the differences between you.
- Value the differences and show respect for them.
- Show interest and ask questions about the other person's values, beliefs, expectations and priorities.
- Explore the differences to find common ground and a mutually acceptable way forward.

Give objective feedback, free from threat or innuendo
Feedback, feedback and more feedback is crucial to effective talent management:

- ❐ Separate the issue from the individual. Focus on the 'crime' (if it is one) and not on the 'criminal'.

- ❐ Build rapport and mutual understanding, using the tools and techniques described above.

- ❐ Stick to the facts and avoid value judgements.

- ❐ Break major issues down into manageable parts that don't overwhelm, divert or confuse.

- ❐ Work from the general (context) to the particular (specifics) and back again, to help understanding.

- ❐ Don't create dramas out of issues – keep things in perspective.

- ❐ Ensure feedback is relevant, specific and objective – not peripheral, woolly or personal.

- ❐ Focus on what is important to the other person and their need for change, development and improvement.

- ❐ Put yourself in their shoes. How are they likely to view you and your feedback?

- ❐ How do you come across to them? Hear yourself giving feedback – any warning notes?

- ❐ What will they find hard to accept in your feedback? What might they be afraid of or anxious about? How can you make your feedback more positive, but still achieve your goals, by getting your point across in a more appropriate way?

Make managers accountable for managing talent

If talent is to be actively acknowledged as an organisation's most important and critical asset, then it follows that its management is *automatically* a major accountability of all line executives. Reality, as we know from experience, is somewhat different. Surveys into human resource management repeatedly confirm that talent and high potential are generally far less effectively utilised and managed than are physical and financial resources. When questioned by the author, during a survey on the management of talent and *high potential*, one senior executive with a major motor manufacturer said, indignantly, 'Hypertension? Dammit, I've got no one here with hypertension!'

Why, when executives are becoming increasingly sophisticated and management is a far more focused process than hitherto, does the paradox persist? Why do so many organisations continue to waste, squander and fail to invest sufficiently in their most crucial asset – especially the one most capable of creating competitive advantage for them?

In many instances, evidence[3] suggests that it is *not* – as is often supposed – a matter of lack of will, but rather a question *lack of talent management know-how*. Identifying high potential, managing talent and using people of talent to greater effect frequently emerge among the top three major concerns of executives. Well-intentioned and otherwise experienced, highly competent CEOs and directors will admit to a strong need to 'do something' about managing talent, but often see the process as being one of: 'Which course do you think we should send him/her on?' So long as human hope 'springs eternal', it seems, there will always be a search, somewhere, for panaceas and cure-alls as issues of talent management continue to be 'exported', rather than dealt with 'at home'.

There are, of course, two sides to the talent coin. It is equally important that individuals take responsibility for – and ownership of – their own learning and development. Without self-development, there can be little real management or professional development. Even where there is a 'system' of regular objective-setting, performance review and assessment, there is frequently insufficient rigour – and creativity – in the measurement of *applied* ability as a major determinant of outputs, outcomes and results. For executives to be realistically held accountable for the effective management of talent, they need to have the critical know-how of how to:

❏ agree and set clear performance objectives and the principal outcomes required of a job

❏ identify what the key competencies are that are necessary to produce requisite and agreed results

❏ identify gaps in competence and performance expectations in well-defined, relevant and objective terms

❏ recognise the true causal links in both good and poor performance, as a basis for realistically establishing an individual's professional, managerial and personal development needs

❏ deploy and employ high capability and unique talent in the most effective and productive ways

❏ coach and mentor, in order to

- bring people up to speed, where necessary
- help people to develop, grow and fulfil their real potential

❒ evolve realistic and relevant personal development plans for people, including both on- and off-job learning experiences

❒ enrich and enhance roles, or jobs, in order to challenge and 'stretch' individuals – especially for their longer-term and continuing development

❒ structure and 'engineer' the most appropriate career *progression* – and not always promotion, where *lateral* fast-tracking may be a more viable option – for especially talented people and those of high potential.

Given the above knowledge, understanding and skill, ownership of the challenges and priorities of talent management naturally and logically becomes an essential executive accountability.

❝ *Acting as stimulus, catalyst and keeper of the king's conscience should be a highly professional human resources function.* **❞**

Among the more junior ranks of management, that accountability evolves primarily as an *operational* one, concerned with developing and managing talented individuals and teams. At more senior executive levels, the accountability assumes strategic significance to include succession, company transformation and corporate growth. The CEO's role is to lead, stimulate and orchestrate the process, understanding what is involved and what needs to be done to take the business forward as a whole. As Tichy[4] affirms, the leader's job – at whatever level of leadership – is to develop other leaders who, in turn, will lead and manage the business tomorrow.

Acting as stimulus, catalyst and keeper of the king's conscience should be a highly professional human resources function. To be credible and a significant contributory force within the business, the HR function must have influence and impact within the highest executive echelons and power bases. As an influential, credible partner in the process of talent management, the HR professional primarily helps to:

❒ stimulate awareness, concern, responsibility and necessary action

❒ educate executives in both necessary know-how and 'do-how'

- ❏ challenge and question conventional wisdom and 'old' thinking about managing ability and high potential

- ❏ keep executives up to date with current best practice in talent management

- ❏ set the pattern and example by working to the same criteria and para-meters as both line and other specialist functional executives

- ❏ wherever possible, 'live' and practise – and be seen to practise – the values as well as the techniques of talent management.

Create the Means to Identify and Select Outstanding Talent – the Third Imperative

The third imperative, at its most elemental, amounts to:

- ❏ knowing what talent you need for the business

- ❏ being able to recognise it when you meet it

- ❏ going for it – and getting it.

In Chapter 3, we gave generic descriptions to outstanding talent and to high potential. Within the context of a particular organisation or enter-prise, necessary uniqueness will be given to the generic definitions – normally spelled out as specific competencies, together with personal attributes.

Talented people already within the organisation are most likely to be recognised as such on the strength of track record and existing contri-bution. Even so, there is still margin for error here, and subjective assessments of a particular individual may vary considerably between those evaluating his or her competence and capability. Where new or would-be recruits are involved, the risk of making wrong decisions in selection is far higher. Intelligent, articulate and plausible people may well fool equally intelligent but untrained interviewers and so, often disastrously, gain unwarranted entry to an organisation. Not until it is too late is the expensive mistake discovered, that the contents don't at all match the attractive packaging. As an American CEO remarked,[5] 'The most dangerous figure of all is the glib, fast-tracker with his (or her!) quality bullshit.'

Selection and Placement – Reducing the Margin of Error

Still something of a minefield, where mistakes can be both costly and painful, selection and placement, especially of highly talented people, is undertaken with varying degrees of competence and success. Techniques of selection and placement differ immensely – as do the skills in their application. In a significant survey conducted by the (then) Institute of Personnel and Development and published as a report in October 1998, it was found that UK companies used the selection processes listed in Table 3.

What is of concern is the apparently heavy reliance upon the notoriously subjective selection interview, without sufficient objectively derived back-up data and information. Well-conducted individual – and panel – interviews *are* a valid selection tool, but unfortunately the number of horror stories confirms that many are undertaken unprofessionally and incompetently. As Angela Baron, employee resourcing adviser at the Chartered Institute of Personnel and Development (CIPD), says,[6] 'Untrained interviewers who hold unstructured interviews might just as well be tossing a coin.' The CIPD has done a great deal over many years to raise the standards of professionalism in all aspects of talent management – including recruitment and selection techniques – but unfortunately many of the unconverted remain unassailable and in a position to make the critical selection and placement decisions.

TABLE 3 Selection Processes

Process	Used by (%)
Individual interview	82
CVs	61
Application form	59
Covering letter	47
Panel interview	32
Group interview	26
Work sample	22
Aptitude test	18
Personality profile	18
Biodata	4
Open day	3
Computer-assisted selection	3
Assessment centre	2
Graphology	1

Increasingly, however, industry-specific recruitment consultancies are being used as more and more organisations follow the trend in outsourcing. The professionals amongst these are both thorough and ethical, and can greatly reduce the margin of error in selection. Here too, however, there are rather too many 'cowboys' who add to the misery of misplacement, through gross incompetence and irresponsibility. In a helpful, cogent article, 'Ready, aim, hire', which appeared in the July 1999 edition of the Institute of Directors' journal, *Director*, Maureen Moody[7] underlines the crucial need for the following:

1 Professional selection interviews, which use well-structured, 'open' questions and where the same questions are used consistently for all candidates – the 'EAR' model of interaction (Figure 7) relies upon open questions in the reflective mode of dialogue, such as: 'Tell me how you have added value to the business in your current role'; 'On reflection, given your time over again, what would you have done differently to achieve greater impact?'; 'What are the most important things you would tell your replacement to help them move into the role with maximum initial effect?'; 'What has been the most significant learning for you in your current role?'; 'What are the greatest challenges for you in moving from your present job to the role you have applied for with us?'

Though developed by John Munro Fraser at the University of Aston in its original form in the 1960s, the 'Five-Fold Grading' selection technique,[8] still provides a relevant framework for an effective, structured interview in today's world. Under each heading, the interviewer needs to develop appropriate open questions, to lead the interviewee through the areas that will provide the necessary biographical data:

❑ *Impact on others*: Appearance, turnout, speech, manner, health and first impressions (the latter are generally made within the first 40 or so seconds of meeting someone).

❑ *Acquired knowledge*: General education – to what level, professional/vocational education and work experience, to date, both direct and indirect professional experience, including level of accountability, size of budget and decision-making.

❑ *Innate abilities*: General intelligence – verbal, mathematical and spatial intelligence. Perceptiveness, intuition and 'EQ'.

☐ *Motivation:* Level of objectives; realism and consistency in follow-ing them up; achievements in relation to opportunities. Here *patterns* of opportunity and achievement, over a period of time, are often an important indicator and predictor of likely future behaviours.

☐ *Adjustment:* Acceptability to others, sense of personal account-ability; reliability; capacity to take leadership roles; ability to cope, especially under pressure (what constitutes 'pressure' for this individual?).

2 Outsourcing to comparably professional recruitment specialists – particularly those who specialise in selected industries and who understand the need for 'culture fit' between candidate and organi-sation. Increasingly, headhunting and the use of recruitment agencies are becoming the norm in the acquisition of talent.

3 Appropriate back-up and alternative data and information – derived from well-designed and structured *assessment centres* where psycho-metric profiling, replicated or actual work tasks and group interviews are used. On their own, without back-up information, selection interviews may have little predictive validity in identifying how a newcomer may perform in the role applied for.

The assessment centre provides many different opportunities for trained observers to see candidates in action in a carefully structured variety of relevant circumstances, and so provides a more compre-hensive picture of new applicants than does an interview alone. The IPD survey (see page 68), which identifies only 2 per cent of respon-dent organisations as using assessment centres in selection, suggests that there is still far too much hit-and-miss in the selection and placement of talent within UK companies. Specifically, in the search for people of high potential and – as yet undiscovered – talent, we have made extensive use of development/assessment centres with several of our clients, both in the UK and abroad.

4 Wide ranges of screening techniques to test aptitudes and to estab-lish personal preferences at a sufficiently early stage in the selection process.

5 Refinement and increased professionalism of traditional tools and techniques in those organisations, especially, that are too small to justify the often high cost of external professional headhunters and recruitment consultancies.

The Changing Expectations of Talented People

❝ *Today's high performers need to be both valued and involved.* ❞

People's expectations – and ambitions – have changed significantly within the last few years, thanks to:

❐ more knowledge-based business (information technology, higher education levels, more thinking and creativity on the job, more team-work)

❐ social transformations (more freedom on the job, ageing of the overall population, entry of women into the workforce at the most senior and technological professional levels)

❐ economic evolution (creation of a global market requiring the integration of cultural differences).

Today's high performers need to be both valued and involved. New *talented* employees, especially, expect:

❐ to know more about what is happening in the organisation

- who is doing what?
- new objectives?
- new priorities?
- are changes in the structure of the corporation planned?
- new strategies?
- threats and problems?
- visions and new direction?

❐ to understand why leaders have made decisions

- why not another decision?
- what is behind the decision?
- were there other options?
- what are the implications of the decision made?

❐ to contribute their own ideas and ability in order to participate in the elaboration of the vision or agenda for change

- what could I be tomorrow?
- how can I help build a future I believe in?
- what about the vision of the organisation?

❏ to feel important and have a meaningful role to play within the corporation

- who am I within the organisation?
- do I count?
- do I contribute and how do I contribute more?
- am I receiving the recognition and respect that I desire?
- do I have a fair chance to grow and develop as a person?

As Pierre Casse, former Professor of Organisational Behaviour at IMD, Lausanne, says, 'People are not resources and resent being treated as such. They are not pieces of equipment to move around according to needs. Contrary to what some managers claim, people are not "Human Capital".'

Some successful businesses, such as Baxter Healthcare, Club Méditerranée and Hoffman La Roche, expressly recognise leadership as the art of managing people's talents – not simply a means of 'getting things done, through other people'. In making this concept a reality, such organisations are increasingly taking the following steps:

❏ Organisations are taking more *risks with inexperience* and allowing people to take on challenges and new roles that they have not encountered before. In doing this, they allow people to learn from failure as well as from success as part of their planned, managed development and career progression through the company.

❏ Organisations are creating specific *developmental roles* that, while making a significant contribution to the business, allow people to learn, develop and grow through the medium of work itself. Feedback on decisions and performance play a significant part in the developmental process. In the more enlightened companies, the feedback is provided by a carefully selected and *trained cadre of coaches* who represent a pool of experience, reflection, stimulus and guidance for people of outstanding talent and high potential.

❏ Organisations are taking initiatives to *remove, or move aside, 'dead wood'* to enable committed, accountable and talented people to contribute more fully and productively to the business as barriers and blockages disappear.

The Fourth Imperative – Engage Talent and Develop It

Closely bound up with the philosophy – and actions – triggered by the third imperative are the know-how and do-how of the fourth and final imperative of talent management. Essentially, the fourth imperative stimulates and seeks to drive both the use and development of people of outstanding ability. Typically, it involves:

❑ engaging talent with the goals and direction of the organisation, so that people of high ability are able to contribute their unique strengths to the success of the business. Tina Brown – the dynamic former editor of such top magazines as *Tatler*, *Vanity Fair* and, more recently, the *New Yorker* – uncompromisingly cuts through others' angst and protests in order to engage and place the people she knows that the business needs: 'I just take talent where I find it.'

❑ moving and promoting talented people frequently and, especially early in their careers, giving them as much relevant experience as possible

❑ confronting issues of turnover, loss and retention among outstanding performers and people of high potential – and taking realistic action to prolong stimulating career progression within the organisation. (They also recognise that, today, it may mean career progression – via lateral, cross-functional or global moves – as well as promotion and upwards movement through the organisation.)

❑ giving regular feedback and both coaching – which is essentially job, role- or task-specific – *and* mentoring, which is primarily aimed at the individual's longer-term development and growth, irrespective of current role.

❑ breaking the reward rules, where appropriate and necessary, to ensure that contributive talent is properly recognised and realistically rewarded. High performers are likely to show less patience than most with over-rigid, illogical reward systems, managed by inflexible and overconformist bureaucrats. The market place for talent and the 'going rate' represent far more realistic determinants of reward levels than do the so-called salary policies of some organisations. Many of

these 'policies' have been hallowed by little more than the passage of
time, or are the result of some long-forgotten quirk that may have
been relevant in the past, but no longer reflects current reality.

❐ ensuring that planned, or projected, development does take place
and does not merely remain on some well-intentioned manager's
wish-list. Personal development plans, jointly agreed and drawn up,
must reflect *real* training and development needs. They also need to
be built up around challenging assignments, which stimulate,
'stretch' and test people – as well as providing critical learning and
growth for them. According to identified development needs, they
might include the following learning experiences:

- 360-degree verbal and psychometric profile feedback on specific
  areas of activity and behaviour; from superiors, subordinates and
  colleagues

- jointly preparing an 'essential reading list' and working through
  selected texts, or articles, summarising and presenting to a panel
  a synopsis of each or one, or an overall view from the collected
  readings. This can then lead into a question and answer session
  with the panel

- undertaking two major projects from the list in Chapter 2 (see
  page 31)

- within the context of the corporate vision or mission statement,
  agreeing with manager and team members a vision, based upon
  values, members' aspirations, and market conditions, for the func-
  tion/department/current major projects

- introducing a highly involving process for continuous improvement within the function or team. They can then ensure that it is
  developed, implemented and used jointly within the team/func-
  tion where it is to be adopted.

One of the most comprehensive source books of suggestions and ideas
for both personal and professional development is the *Successful
Manager's Handbook*,[9] published by Personnel Decisions International
and linked to their very effective PROFILOR 360-degree assessment
tool. The PROFILOR currently measures almost 40 dimensions of
managerial and professional competence in addition to nine derived
'second order' factors, including *leadership, self-management, motivation,
thinking* and so on. Such source material can help prevent reinvention
of the wheel when drawing up personal development plans. Its very

comprehensiveness and detail allows people to build up a series of valuable learning experiences, which can be tailored to a particular organisation's – or individual's – needs.

Talent management, like management itself, is an art – albeit one of the 'possible' – where success appears to be largely influenced by the fulfilment of key imperatives. Sir John Harvey-Jones,[10] describing management, makes the point that 'because it is an art, there are no limits to its development, no limits as to how far one can develop oneself and no limits to individuality and originality in our practice of it'.

> 66 *Successful talent management is the outcome of the effective interplay of the arts of managing and leading.* 99

As Figure 9 suggests, successful talent management is the outcome of the effective interplay of the arts of managing *and* leading. The four imperatives need the structure, parameters, planning and co-ordination that are essentially sound *management* – in other words, the necessary executive orchestration or choreography – to give control, consistency and stability to the process. Equally, *leadership* provides the stimulus, inspiration and personal encouragement that inject challenges, creativity and commitment into the development, intelligent use and retention of outstanding ability.

Stemming from the interplay and balance between managing and leading is the likelihood of the synergy essential to 'breathe life' into the management and *mobilisation* of talent. If there is any 'magic' in management, then it must have its roots in the processes of motivating, focusing and engaging human brains and abilities, in the successful pursuit of significant, worthwhile endeavour.

Eberhard Van Koerber, the dynamic and visionary Head of ABB, Europe, affirms that 'It's the soft investment that makes us competitive. It's making use of brains that are 90 per cent underutilised. People who don't understand this have no access to the solution of our poor competitiveness in Western Europe.' In his typically very telling way, Professor Tom Cannon[11] underpins the concept of 'soft investment' when he states: 'Today's increasing professionalism is a vindication of all the people who said we had to improve the quality of management.' Learning itself needs to be invested with far more significance than hitherto if the quality of leadership and management in Britain is to develop at a rate at least as good as that of the best of our competitors. As Tom Cannon says, 'Management is so demanding that it requires commitment to life-long learning.'

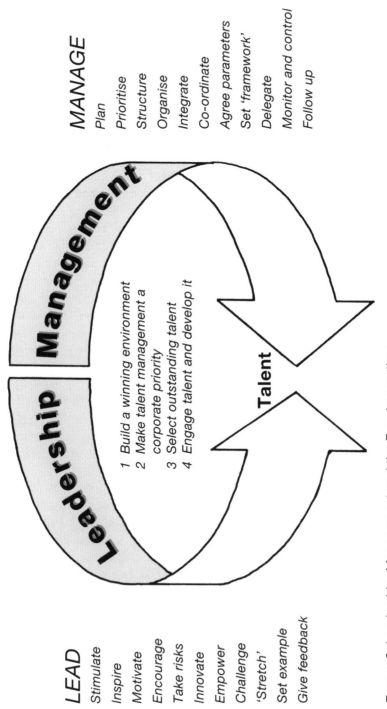

LEAD

Stimulate
Inspire
Motivate
Encourage
Take risks
Innovate
Empower
Challenge
'Stretch'
Set example
Give feedback

MANAGE

Plan
Prioritise
Structure
Organise
Integrate
Co-ordinate
Agree parameters
Set 'framework'
Delegate
Monitor and control
Follow up

Leadership | Management

1 Build a winning environment
2 Make talent management a
  corporate priority
3 Select outstanding talent
4 Engage talent and develop it

Talent

FIGURE 9 Leadership, Management and the Four Imperatives

SUMMARY

Given that management and, particularly, *individual leaders and managers*, are demonstrably trying to fulfil the first imperative – *build a winning environment* – the remaining three imperatives become even more critical. *Make talent management a critical priority*, the second imperative, essentially involves three co-ordinated actions to create necessary corporate critical mass of:

- awareness
- accountability
- commitment to action.

Those three actions are:

- establish a talent mindset
- build talent management skills, at all levels
- make individual managers personally accountable.

All three may require very different 'triggers', stimuli and supportive action, before they begin to become a reality. Typically, however, in addition to discussion, coaching, training and head office policy statement, the impetus for change (see Figure 6) necessary to make talent management a critical corporate priority is more likely to arise out of dedicated:

- top management team workshops
- board away-days and 'retreats'
- task- and process-focused workshops with the board and key external stakeholders, possibly catalysed by the contribution of a 'global' or key outside resource from a credible business school or consultancy
- close follow-up and follow-through involving internal 'watchdog' monitoring and feedback.

All four imperatives – and especially this second one – derive from and thrive upon *appropriate beliefs and values* about:

- customers and clients
- products and services
- competitive advantage
- the organisation's own people.

These are the values that underpin commitment to the 'triple bottom line'.

Talent management *is* a critical and therefore essential part of any leader or manager's role. Growing professionalism in management appears to reflect not so much a lack of commitment to the effective managing of talent but rather *absence of the necessary know-how*. Not only much of this chapter, but also subsequent chapters deal with the key skills necessary to manage talent more appropriately.

Creating the means to identify and select outstanding talent – the third imperative – involves the disciplines and techniques that reinforce competent:

- selection interviewing

- assessment centres

- participation of candidates in the selection process

- creation of development roles and opportunities for early promotion.

The fourth imperative – *engage talent and develop it* – requires managers to:

- develop skills in giving feedback, mentoring and coaching

- be prepared to cut through and replace inappropriate reward systems in order to give people of talent the *realistic* reward levels they expect for the lifestyles to which they aspire

- engage people of outstanding talent and high potential with the key goals and objectives of often dramatically transforming organisations

- move their best people around frequently, and at a sufficiently early stage in their careers

- see career progression – like organisational transformation itself – as a *continuous*, challenging interplay between uncertainty, on the one hand, and multiple choice and opportunity on the other

- consider talent management as a critical, inescapable challenge that, ultimately, holds the key to much of an organisation's likely success – and survival in the market place.

At the very core of both leadership and management – which, essentially, are complementary processes – *lies the personal accountability of individual executives* for focusing, mobilising and co-ordinating the brains and abilities of, especially, their key players in the effective pursuit of legitimate business endeavour.

ACTION – THEORY INTO PRACTICE

- Involve appropriate members of the board/executive of your organisation in discussions about the design and development of a workshop/'retreat' programme for top management that would begin the process of raising talent management to the level of a critical corporate priority. You will need to consider the following questions:

  - Should you involve internal and external human resource professionals as enablers/catalysts?

  - What specific outcomes will you pursue via such an event?

  - What strategies for follow-up/follow-through will be agreed, explored, defined and initiated at the workshop?

- What do you see as the principal talent management skills and 'know-how' that need to be developed/improved within the different levels of your organisation? What would be an effective strategy and succession of actions to build up the necessary competence in talent management within your business?

- How are the more sensitive and 'political' issues of breaking the reward rules, promoting talented people earlier and more frequently, and removing 'dead wood' going to best be addressed and worked through within your organisation? If linked to major organisation transformation and/or changed commercial strategy, how would you reinforce that linkage to ensure that appropriate action will be taken on such crucial issues? Create executive 'vehicles'/systems that will ensure that 'political' blockages will be effectively countered.

Endnotes

1 RENSING V. *Proceedings of Mobilizing People Program, IMD*. Lausanne, October 1997.

2 KIPLING R. 'The elephant's child'. *Just So Stories*. Harmondsworth, Penguin, [1902] 2000.

3 Surveys into talent management conducted by the author, 1993–2000.

4 TICHY N. *The Leadership Engine*. London, HarperCollins, 1997.

5 SMILEY T. *Proceedings of IMI Senior Management Program*. Geneva, May 1988.

6 BARON A., in Moody, M. 'Ready, aim, hire', *Director*, July 1999.

7 MOODY M. 'Ready, aim, hire'. *Director*, July 1999.

---

8   MUNRO FRASER J. *Employment Interviewing.* MacDonald & Evans, 1966.
9   DAVIS B. L., HELLERVIK L. W., SHEARD J. L., SKUBE C. J. *and* GEBELEIN S. H. *Successful Manager's Handbook.* Wadhurst, Atlantic Books, 1996.
10 HARVEY-JONES J. SIR. *Making It Happen.* Collins, 1988.
11 CANNON T., in Watts, S., 'Career directors have a charter to learn how to do their job'. *Sunday Telegraph*, 18 July 1999.

Managing Knowledge –
More than a Fad

The perpetual questions for us are: 'What have we learned today?'
and 'How are we going to put that learning to use?'
Dr Paul White, CEO, Warman International

Vaclav Havel, president of the Czech Republic, has described the current era as 'an age when so much is uncertain, yet so much is possible'. In this information age of rapid change, paradox, but seemingly limitless opportunity, the intelligent development, processing and use of knowledge becomes paramount. More than ever before, with so many organisations evolving as global players, knowledge at all levels within the business – so-called 'intellectual capital' – emerges as the primary asset of an enterprise.

As Peter Drucker[1] states in *The New Realities*, 'Knowledge has become the capital of a developed economy.' Knowledge – and the effective transfer and use of knowledge – is becoming increasingly critical to competitive edge in business and to what Professor Tom Cannon[2] defines as 'Getting to the future first – before the competition does'.

Von Krogh and Roos[3] make the point that competitive advantage is the *raison d'être* of business. An organisation could be said to have competitive advantage when it:

❐ develops and implements unique, productive strategies, not being *concurrently* implemented by its competitors

❑ capitalises, pre-emptively, upon opportunities within the environments that its competitors have still to exploit

❑ consistently outperforms its rivals with better products and/or better services

❑ has – and exploits more intelligently than its rivals – sheer good luck

❑ acquires, develops and *uses superior knowledge* to

  ● ensure the four points above

  ● forestall rivals' attempts to erode or 'capture' its competitive advantage

  ● maintain superiority – and uniqueness – of resources, strategies and its competitively advantageous knowledge.

Two Forms of Knowledge – and Knowledge Transfer

❝ *The central purpose and effort of talent management is to find, develop and intelligently use outstanding ability.* ❞

The central purpose and effort of talent management is to find, develop and intelligently use outstanding ability and to fulfil high potential to the optimum longer-term advantage of the business – and the individual. Building and releasing that talent, in turn, presupposes that the acquisition, transfer and application of knowledge are also effectively managed, and that *high intelligence is appropriately mobilised.* Nonaka and Takeuchi[4] in particular have drawn attention to two fundamentally different – yet complementary – forms of knowledge: *explicit knowledge* and *tacit knowledge.*

As Figure 10 shows, *explicit knowledge* is essentially that knowledge and understanding that derives from both *formally and informally* generated, transmitted and disseminated information, via the organisational infrastructure of:

❑ management information systems

❑ 'official' communication channels and corporate media

❑ functions, goals and roles.

Typically, sources of explicit knowledge are those associated with traditional, formalised and structured processes of information and knowledge transfer, such as:

❏ publicised corporate philosophy, with its explicit, or implicit, values

❏ formal policy statements

❏ mission statements

❏ defined and declared goals, including job objectives

❏ formalised strategies

❏ board/head office communications

❏ structured/formalised briefings.

Tacit knowledge, by contrast, is the information and derived understanding that is acquired, internalised and used (or not used) by individuals. It may be (but often is not) transmitted, transferred to and shared with other individuals or groups. Primarily, tacit knowledge amounts to:

❏ the results and outcomes of personal discrimination and reflection

❏ perceptions and interpretations of direct and indirect experience

❏ objectively and subjectively derived 'mental models' – including those of human kind

❏ the result of asking questions and engaging in dialogues and debates with others

❏ unique learning and 'gut feel', which derive from intuition, or emerge creatively, as the result of insight and imagination.

Figure 10 confirms the differences between 'organisational' explicit knowledge and *personal tacit knowledge* and, in a sense, implies a need to use comparably different means of transferring and developing the two kinds of knowledge. Explicit knowledge so often derives from a 'given' world, defined in terms of technical, economic and commercial parameters. It is a world very much governed – or at least influenced – by financial and statistical imperatives. While mandatory boundaries focus thinking and decision-making, they nevertheless tend also to 'condition' and constrain perception, judgement and the believed scope for action.

1 Explicit Knowledge

Organisational and 'official' knowledge:

- Knowledge of a 'given' world
- Shared stereotypes and knowledge
- Universal and objective knowledge
- Illusory knowledge and 'party line'
- Probability judgements

- Logic and cognition

- Organisation specific

- Role/goal-dependent learning

2 Tacit Knowledge

Knowledge created from personal learning:

- Exclusive/specialist knowledge
- Personal/collaborative discovery
- Global knowledge
- Unique intuitive competence
- Insight and personal/joint exploration
- Creative ability and original thinking
- Intellectual 'openness' and freedom
- Mindset, ie *motivated* learning

FIGURE 10 Explicit and Tacit Knowledge

Explicit knowledge, too, is frequently strongly influenced by what Irving Janis[5] terms 'group think', where shared (but not questioned) stereotypes and *illusory* unity, superiority and invincibility tend to proliferate as expressions in such phrases as:

❑ 'Well, we all know how accountants would see this.'

❑ 'We're a really great team – all for one and one for all.'

❑ 'We're the best – we're unbeatable: the competition doesn't stand a chance.'

❑ 'If men are from Mars and women are from Venus, then customers must be from hell!'

❑ 'You can forget ideas like that, Smithy. Nice guys don't win and you know what the boss says about always being number one.'

Thus, though usually organisation-dependent, goal-specific and directed towards achieving identified results, *explicit* knowledge tends to lack context and discrimination. While it may seek to identify and explore the 'what-ifs' of decision-making, the tendency to rationalise lack of creativity, constrained thinking and risk- aversion as 'objectively based cautious optimism', or a 'carefully considered view' can be very strong. Fear of failure – the great managerial 'bogeyman' – can have a paralysing effect upon even highly intelligent people and, therefore, the information and knowledge that they seek – and transfer to others. As

Robert Frost, the American poet, wryly remarked, 'The brain is a wonderful organ. It starts working the moment we get up in a morning and doesn't stop until we get to the office!'

Fear of failure and reluctance to move out of comfort zones, or break through boundaries and self-inflicted constraints, too often results in information that is 'safe', conformist and aimed at preserving either the prevailing 'party line' or status quo. While much of the 'official' information from which explicit knowledge derives *is* legitimate, objective and essential, it is also frequently 'sanitised', censored or simply too 'local', and therefore lacking wider context, perspective and *intelligence*.

Crucial to both explicit and tacit knowledge is what Von Krogh and Roos term 'scarce knowledge', that is *knowledge about lack of knowledge*. Knowing what we don't know is fundamental to learning. It is thus crucial to the process of knowledge transfer, as well as *engaged* knowledge acquisition. In their excellent book *The Knowledge-Creating Company*, Nonaka and Takeuchi state: 'The key to learning and knowledge creation lies in the mobilisation and conversion of tacit knowledge' – which is the very essence of talent management, particularly the focused activation of high ability and competence.

The mobilisation and transfer of tacit knowledge lends itself more to what Von Krogh and Roos[6] term *new perspective processes* (as opposed to traditional/conventional information and knowledge transfer processes). These processes are discriminatory, context-sensitive and essentially co-operative. Tacit knowledge, which may be acquired individually or collectively through study, reflection, experimentation and debate or discussion, emerges from working, doing, achieving and simply *being*. New perspective knowledge creation and transfer:

❐ is based upon the individual's ability to discriminate and make relevant situational or contextual distinctions

❐ involves *collaborative* exploration and experimentation; this may be between organisations, stakeholders – such as suppliers and customers or customers' customers – across multi-disciplinary functions and teams, or between individuals, working and experimenting co-operatively, on issues or projects where collaboration and productive synergy are essential to successful enterprise.

❝ *New perspective knowledge generation and transfer are essentially the mobilisation of intelligence – not merely knowledge management.* ❞

In effect, new perspective knowledge generation and transfer are essentially the *mobilisation of intelligence* – not merely knowledge management. It is the more 'organic', less rigid, new perspective forms of knowledge transfer – and talent management – that are likely to stimulate, and, in turn, be stimulated by both 'flow' (see Chapter 4) and 'peak communication', described in Figure 8 (see page 62), that are essential to productive innovation and creativity.

The 10 Imperatives of Knowledge Management

1 Value – and use – diversity, not uniformity, of knowledge

As we saw in Chapter 3, the greatest synergy – and, hence, *potential for knowledge creation and transfer* – comes from collaborative *diversity* and not uniformity. Thus, the richer the 'mix' in the knowledge transfer network, the greater the scope for knowledge acquisition, sharing and development – particularly where there is competently 'managed' productive collaboration, between critical sources of information, knowledge and learning. Key elements of *diversity* of perspective, perception, experience and knowledge include:

❐ role/function

❐ gender

❐ race

❐ culture

❐ age.

2 Managing knowledge transfer and learning

Acquiring knowledge, developing learning and building both competence and necessary confidence – via individual reflection, collective sharing and knowledge transfer – are heavily dependent within the workplace upon *intelligently managed*:

❐ encouragement to explore, discover and experiment – especially in problem-solving and decision-making

❐ opportunities to test out ideas and conceptual 'models', or theories, with day-to-day realities

❏ 'safe' opportunities to take risks and initiatives and be allowed to fail, without 'punishment', and where relevant lessons can be drawn from failure through productive feedback, analysis and discussion

❏ challenging *relevant* work assignments or projects that are aligned with significant business objectives – including transformation – and where learning goals may be both clearly defined and also allowed to emerge empirically

❏ regular feedback and personalised coaching, with *'quality' dialogues* about performance, development, job enrichment and career progression

❏ internal and external sources of information and learning, which are available to be opened up, explored and used by the learner

❏ opportunities for reflection – including 'away-days' – whereby learners consciously think through work issues *with colleagues* in order to share and transfer learning with people who are also involved in the same situation; a mentor, acting in the role of facilitator, can often 'trigger' the flow of ideas and discussions, but primarily his or her role is to 'kick-start' – and subsequently guide

  • personal reflection and self-awareness
  • exploration of personal experience
  • learner initiatives and solutions
  • the process of discovery.

Helping people to see things differently – in the sense of 'more appropriately and productively' – is one of the key arts of both coaching and mentoring.

3 Develop knowledge acquisition and transfer among 'high-flyers'

If, as it certainly appears, the world of business is becoming increasingly *knowledge-driven*, then it would also seem that one critical aspect of talent management is the intelligence, knowledge and expertise that high-performing key people, especially, possess. Developing and managing their knowledge acquisition and its transfer, between them and other high-flyers, emerges as a vital 'enabling' function in the conscious management of talent. The transfer of knowledge amongst people of high talent is not merely a process to be confined to key players *within* the organisation. *Rather, it should be a means of creating appropriately wider networks that stimulate synergy and knowledge transfer between internal 'stars and shapers' and comparable individuals – or groups –* outside *the organisation.* Such cross-fertilisation and productive intellectual collaboration can add immeasurable value to internal thinking, expertise and practice. Typical external sources of collaborative knowledge transfer – and build-up of vital 'business intelligence' – might include:

❑ major academics from universities or business schools who are capable of imparting unique and leading-edge thinking

❑ selected consultants who are familiar with *state-of-the-art* tools and techniques – not merely those representing 'state of the ark' (with both consultants and academics, a crucial competency is being able to distinguish between fad and valid innovation, and between change for change's sake and necessary, critical progress)

❑ leading specialists, or experts, from government, professional bodies, or relevant scientific/technological institutions, who are able to provide credible knowledge about significant trends, tendencies and likely future direction of importance to a business

❑ key clients and customers who can bring immediacy and crucial relevance to a company's customer relations management strategies

❑ leading and successful figures from the business world who can credibly exemplify current 'best practice' by virtue of track record and personal example.

4 Recognise that there is a 'hierarchy' of knowledge and competence

One problem in explicit knowledge is that, perhaps, too many people tend to operate at the level of unconscious incompetence – the state of blissful and painless ignorance, where personal stress levels are significantly lower (see Figure 11). At the lowest level of the 'competence hierarchy' – *unconscious incompetence* – people *do not know what they don't know* and, therefore, fail to recognise the consequences of that ignorance. What they don't know – and don't recognise – may well represent knowledge that is fundamental, in particular, to emerging or changing conditions in the business. Unconscious incompetence – and hence ignorance of the real state of affairs – is often expressed in management by comments such as:

- ❐ 'If it ain't broke – don't fix it.'

- ❐ 'Let sleeping dogs lie.'

- ❐ 'That's news to me.'

- ❐ 'I can't see the point.'

- ❐ 'That sounds great – let's do it!'

- ❐ 'Get rid of him!'

At this level of incompetence, decision-making varies from the sublime to the disastrous. In the absence of sufficient facts, contextual knowledge and informed perspective, ignorance of cause and effect, or important implications, may so easily lead to quite inappropriate decisions and actions.

Next in the hierarchy comes *conscious incompetence*, where the individual is only too aware of their lack of knowledge, skill and ability – both to understand and to do. The awareness of ignorance – and, therefore, possible lack of fittingness for the demands of a job or role *may well be accompanied by a significant upsurge in stress*. Stress, so frequently, is a response to 'crises of addition, or subtraction', where the individual has to learn to cope with such changes as:

- ❐ new responsibilities and tasks, for which they have not been properly equipped

- ❐ extra work over and above an already demanding schedule, and where coping mechanisms have been over-taxed

- ❐ increased headcount with new, unknown staff, with unfamiliar problems or challenges

- ❐ reduced roles and slashed budgets

- ❐ diminished levels of responsibility with consequent loss of status or power.

All of the above introduce elements of moving into the unknown, unfamiliar and possibly hitherto unencountered – and *hence apprehension about a felt lack of knowledge, skill and personal capability*.

The third level in the hierarchy – that of *conscious competence* – may bring apprehension and anxiety, because the degree of cognition and conscious effort to become knowledgeable and competent may be accompanied by *acquisitive striving* and a tendency to try too hard, which is noticeably absent from the 'effortless superiority' characteristic of the highest level of capability, *unconscious competence*. This last stage in the hierarchy represents a level of competence that is more or less automatic. Long-held skills and knowledge lead to familiar patterns of coping and working, which place little strain upon the individual. On well-trodden ground, the individual appears to act *instinctively*, such is the level of practised assimilation of knowledge, skill and experience

In a changing world, where radically different challenges are encountered and where tasks may be far more complex, then a stage of capability – and delivery – beyond 'unconscious competence' is called for. *In essence, this level of super-competence is 'mastery', which in one form or another represents the outstanding capability of talented people.*

Commensurate with the classical competence hierarchy is the progression from 'raw recruit' to 'professional mastery' identified in Figure 12. This also draws attention to the likely problems of stress and role-strain that frequently characterise the knowledge acquisition, learning and development stages in personal growth.

5 Develop professionalism amongst talented high performers

The implications for talent management, in the progressive acquisition of knowledge, understanding and capability, are significant, wide-ranging and may even be critical. For example, the period of developing professionalism (the centre band in Figure 12) may involve the manager or director facilitating learning and so managing talent by:

❏ establishing what key knowledge is not available to/possessed by the individual

❏ identifying any blockages that prevent the flow and transfer of requisite knowledge to the individual

❏ seeking new, more effective ways to leverage information and knowledge – both explicit *and* tacit knowledge

❏ encouraging initiatives to add value to information and knowledge through networking and collaborative working, likely to foster 'peak communication' and productive synergy between people

❏ enhancing and widening the ways in which knowledge can be

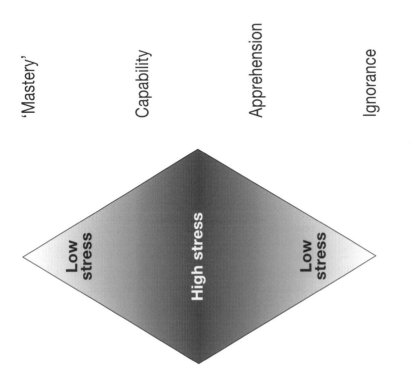

Complex knowledge and competence
Very high competence across boundaries, roles and
relationships. High use of EQ. Breaking new ground.

Unconscious competence
Operating on 'automatic pilot'
Acquired, long-established capability
Using familiar knowledge and skills
Working in familiar roles, with familiar rules and goals

Conscious competence
I know about that. I understand that.
I can do that.

Conscious incompetence
I know I can't do that. I don't understand.
I recognise my lack of capacity/capability.

Unconscious incompetence
Ignorance is bliss.
I don't know what I don't know.

'Mastery'

Capability

Apprehension

Ignorance

Low
stress

High stress

Low
stress

FIGURE 11 Knowledge, Competence and Stress

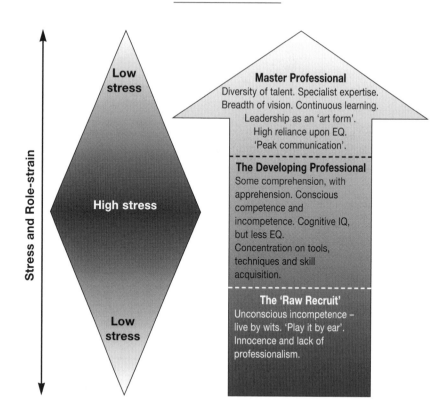

FIGURE 12 Progression from 'Raw Recruit' to Professional 'Mastery'

acquired and effective learning can take place, through a planned variety of practical, experimental, reflective and conceptual learning opportunities

❑ encouraging experimentation and higher levels of risk-taking in order to learn, develop and grow, through 'boundary-busting', adopting more radical approaches and generally raising their game in decision-making – and action

❑ encouraging and actively supporting talented people, by building upon initiative, decision-making and the individual's need to use more EQ in order to capitalise more fully upon their high IQ

❑ putting together highly talented people, under competent, comparably talented leaders, to increase understanding of issues, problems and their likely solutions by generating *collaborative* outcomes

❒ actively reducing the inhibiting effects of fear of failure by giving talented people much more *coached exposure* – with effective feedback and quality time devoted to 'learning' dialogues and knowledge transfer with top executives and leading professionals, inside and outside the organisation

❒ ensuring that, at this developmental stage in career progression, challenges 'fit' the individual and stimulate, motivate and engage his or her talent and commitment – but do not 'swamp', submerge or de-skill them with unrealistically tough and unattainable goals.

At the 'master professional' level, many of the above interventions will, similarly, apply. The difference is that they will be increasingly initiated by individuals *themselves*, rather than as the result of superiors' interventions.

6 Identify the blockages to knowledge transfer within the business

❝ 'Need' has often been determined by negative discrimination. ❞

Traditionally, knowledge has tended to be viewed as a largely 'static' resource, differentiated by function or specialism and distributed according to level and position in the hierarchy, as well as by job title or role. The conventional basis for distribution of information – and knowledge and skill – has widely been 'need to know'. 'Need' has often been coloured and determined by negative discrimination rather than by positive differentiation, as these quotations from discussions with clients suggest:

❒ *'They are just supervisors, Mr Williams; we don't give information of that sort to people like that'* (where essential cost information and detailed manufacturing processes were deliberately withheld from the supervisors responsible for deciding manufacturing options and best practice).

❒ *'If we told them that, they'd most likely go blabbing to our major competitors'* (referring to marketing surveys and product development information that sales managers could have made direct use of in their approaches to key account customers).

In one steel tube manufacturing company, constant confusion was caused by the production departments and *some* of their satellite functions always expressing tube sizes as *internal* diameters, while the marketing, sales and technical support functions only talked in terms of *outside* diameters. Variations on tube wall thicknesses ran into hundreds, with resultant chaos for people inside the organisation, as well as to customers and customers' customers. The basis of differentiation was, unbelievably, 'we've always done it like that.' With unnecessarily differentiated and discriminately distributed information, the possibilities for ambiguity, conflicting interpretations, confusion – and costly error – can be almost limitless.

Reducing such confusion, ensuring *unequivocal* information and knowledge transfer and sharing common – or complementary – meaning are critical issues in knowledge management. Furthermore, much knowledge that does appear to be unequivocal and 'transparently clear' is often taken as an objective representation of a given state of affairs, rather than being recognised as largely subjective and observer-dependent, as Von Krogh and Roos[7] found in their extensive studies of knowledge management.

7 Check the accuracy, reliability and validity of information and knowledge

One powerful characteristic of knowledge should be its potential for creating *new* knowledge, which suggests that verifying the accuracy and therefore validity of information is another key function of knowledge management. To do this realistically and with maximum objectivity, it would seem appropriate to *check and validate* crucial information and knowledge by:

❏ separating true knowledge from perceptions, value judgements and *appeals to authority*, such as

- 'Everyone knows that's the case.'
- 'Nobody would touch that idea with a barge pole.'
- 'It's always been like that, in my experience.'

❏ where the use of absolutes like 'everyone', 'nobody', 'always', or 'never' distorts and misrepresents reality; such corruption of logic and objective truth simply may not be picked up by the unsuspecting, harassed, busy or overworked

❏ testing out information and knowledge with appropriate sources *outside* the organisation who are politically and commercially neutral, or who, equally, may have a marked need to establish objectivity, such as customers, suppliers and even competitors

❏ testing out explicit, organisational-level knowledge with individual tacit, interpreted understanding – particularly that of successful high performers or individuals of recognised high potential, who have consistently demonstrated sound judgement and effective personal knowledge management

❏ monitoring data-collection methods – as well as the processes of information interpretation – in order to identify where misrepresentation of information, or the uncritical acceptance of spurious facts and figures, arises within the system

❏ ensuring that crucial expertise and specialist information and knowledge are appropriately interpreted and disseminated for non-experts, especially where the latter need to use, transfer, and/or add value to expert knowledge, 'down the line', in their functions or roles; this is especially critical in multi-disciplinary project team-working

❏ creating sufficient 'public' arenas and collaborative events, where information and knowledge can be constantly validated, in the course of work itself, by people from a representative multiplicity of functions and/or projects.

A more 'organic' view of knowledge creation, transfer and management, which fits better with networked information age enterprises, departs from traditional views of information and knowledge by considering knowledge as essentially the outcome of creativity, innovation and experimentation. In this context, knowledge emerges as the result of defining, exploring and overcoming challenges, frequently as the result of collaborative, team effort and high intellectual and emotional synergy.

8 Check knowledge for context- and culture-dependency

Knowledge generation is seen as the result of making distinctions between different situations or sets of conditions, ie it is the result, variously, of analysis, selection and distinction. Where it is essentially context-dependent and contextually sensitive, it may not be readily and directly transferable because of the degree of uniqueness in one given situation compared with others. Knowledge may be culturally and historically dependent – determined largely by what has gone before, mythology or simply *'the way we've always done it here'*. Thus it often represents a parochial view of the world, based primarily on internally generated and derived information – not external, objective data.

Typical of 'organisational' knowledge, with its distinctly 'tribal' flavour, is the 'group think' of Irving Janis, described earlier (see page 84). Group think, with its half-truths, distortion of facts and unrealistic exaggeration, makes a mockery not only of objective information, logic and truth, but also of people's capacity to think, evaluate and judge for themselves. Yet it remains a political reality and exerts a powerful pressure to conform in most organisations.

As Williams and Hodgson state,[8]

> In adopting a truly strategic perspective the executive is working with a curious double standard. In one way, he is challenging the reality and relevance of taken-for-granted assumptions. In another way, he has to support and even create the myths which feed organisational identity. . .The perceptions of the executive really determine the nature of the questions he is able to ask. By stimulating the range and even the audacity of questioning, the perceptual field is opened up.

The realities of the 'total' world in which an organisation operates are far greater and richer than the myths, be they negative or positive. The negative aspects of company mythology are those that diminish the organisation's hold on reality. They are, as Hodgson describes, the blindness and fantasy that run away with the organisation's resources and energy. Typically, they include the sacred cows that are often respected unquestioningly. They can be the very stuff of a lemming-like rush over some unforeseen cliff. The positive side of myth is what the organisation stands for, such as its values in relation to its products, services, people and customers.

9 Recognise your role in managing knowledge and intelligence

One hallmark of functional maturity is the recognition that highly effective people are neither entirely 'born' nor 'made'. The reality is that they are continuous learners, who largely develop themselves. In effect, they reinforce the old maxim: *'There is no personal development, without self-development.'* Increasingly, in the information age, key knowledge management skills emerge as the ability to:

◻ gain access to and acquire relevant information, and transform it into knowledge – especially critical knowledge

◻ add value to both information and to knowledge, to enhance their relevance, contribution and potential

◻ transfer knowledge, to stimulate necessary learning and growth, in both people's competence and confidence

◻ stimulate openness and, hence, receptivity to information, knowledge and learning by cutting through the historical and cultural idiosyncrasies, emotional blocks and political 'mine fields' that might otherwise impede or corrupt information flow, knowledge-sharing and transfer; in other words, recognise the continuing reality that knowledge is power – and perhaps increasingly so, in today's information-driven world

◻ understand that, ultimately, it is knowledge and intelligence that leaders and managers are responsible for eliciting, developing, selling and managing.

10 Recognise the realities of knowledge generation and transfer

❝ Within mobilised, collaborative activity, people need a quality of information and knowledge that reflects a given reality. ❞

Within mobilised, collaborative activity, people need a quality of information and knowledge that reflects a given reality. The *management* of knowledge, therefore, needs to take into account seven critical factors:

◻ Much information – and knowledge – develops primarily as the result of collaborative effort, especially where there is high productive task synergy.

◻ The mind has an almost infinite variety of ways in which it is able to create individual representations – and misrepresentations – of reality.

◻ The nature and quality of *learning* – the consequence of information and knowledge – is reflected in changed behaviours, changed outcomes and changed levels of knowledge for future actions.

◻ The transfer of knowledge is a crucial process in co-operative endeavour, such as

- team-working
- cross-functional activities
- stakeholder collaboration, generally.

❏ Openness is critical to information and knowledge transfer; Hamel and Prahalad[9] argue that 'transparency' between the parties involved is critical for necessary learning to take place in collaborative enterprise.

❏ People have varying capacities and abilities to receive, process and internalise learning and accordingly modify their behaviour. Their existing bank of knowledge, the pressure on them to take in new information and knowledge and previous relevant experience are all determinants in the quality of their receptivity to new learning and their ability to unlearn old messages.

❏ The other side of the personal coin is the individual's ability – and preparedness – to disseminate knowledge, especially that which they perceive to be an advantageous source of personal power.

The knowledge database needs to consist of individuals' names, specific knowledge – especially 'quality' knowledge – possessed, the context of that knowledge/competency and the most effective means of transferring, sharing and *adding value* to that knowledge/competency.

Finally, there remains the managerial issue – how best to mobilise and *use* knowledge, even where there are high levels of co-operative transfer and exchange. Exploiting knowledge potential – particularly as a source of *collective* learning – is where leadership and management take on the quality of an art form. It is at this stage of knowledge management that *leadership*, capable of transforming, integrating and mobilising human effort, becomes the major determinant of successful, competitively advantaged enterprise.

SUMMARY

Knowledge – 'intellectual capital' – and the effective transfer of knowledge is the critical wherewithal of both gaining and sustaining competitive advantage. If, as Von Krogh and Roos argue, competitive advantage is the *raison d'être* of a company, then it follows that the management of knowledge must ultimately be a manager's most important contribution to the continuing success of the business. For many years, psychologists and leading figures in the field of organisational behaviour have made the distinction between two types of knowledge:

- *explicit knowledge*, with its proceduralised forms of organisational information generation and knowledge transfer

- *tacit knowledge*, the outcome of personal perception, discrimination and reflection.

It is the focused management of tacit knowledge, especially, that lies at the root of knowledge management and, thus, the effective mobilisation of intelligence and talent.

Knowledge, as a key element of functioning competence, traditionally exists at five levels:

4. Unconscious competence – low stress
3. Conscious competence – high stress
2. Conscious incompetence – high stress
1. Unconscious incompetence – low stress.

Above these four levels is a fifth stage of outstanding knowledge and competence, 'mastery'.

Much of effective knowledge generalisation and transfer is a collective and collaborative process, functioning within – and across – work teams or groups. In today's information-driven business, where continual transformation is the norm, knowledge can no longer be viewed as a 'static' resource differentiated primarily by status, position, role and function. Rather, information, knowledge and learning need to be created, transferred and shared throughout the business. Here, openness and receptivity are critical behaviours that managers need to encourage and support. Knowledge creates knowledge, and the generation, transfer and successful exploitation of that knowledge is fundamental to the processes of mobilising and managing talent.

ACTION – THEORY INTO PRACTICE

1 What are the myths – latent or conscious – that characterise management style and behaviour in your organisation?

- What are the negative aspects?

- To what extent do they impede/corrupt effective knowledge, knowledge transfer and learning?

- What are the positive legends and values?

- How do these give 'edge' and impetus to knowledge, knowledge transfer and learning?

2 How would you like to see knowledge management improved within:

- your organisation?

- your function/department?

Given significant improvement, as you define it, what would be the most important outcomes for:

- the organisation?

- your area of responsibility?

3 What specific actions do you need to take to work through the issues identified in 1 and 2 above?

4 Develop a detailed proposal for setting up a 'knowledge audit' for the areas you control:

- Ensure that the database contains specific facts about knowledge/competencies possessed.

- Give appropriate contextual information, where relevant.

- Confirm key means of transferring, sharing and adding value to 'quality' knowledge.

Endnotes

1 DRUCKER P. *The New Realities*. London, Mandarin, 1990.

2 CANNON T., in Watts, S., 'Career directors have a charter to learn how to do their job'. *Sunday Telegraph*, 18 July 1999.

3 VON KROGH G. and ROOS J. *Managing Knowledge – Perspectives on co-operation and competition*. London, Sage, 1996.

4 NONAKA I. *and* TAKEUCHI H. *The Knowledge-Creating Company: How Japanese companies create the dynamics of innovation*. Oxford, Oxford University Press, 1995.

5 JANIS I. *Victims of Groupthink*. Boston, MA, Houghton Mifflin, 1972.

6 VON KROGH G. *and* ROOS J. *Managing Knowledge – Perspectives on co-operation and competition*. London, Sage, 1996.

7 *Ibid.*

8 WILLIAMS M. R. and HODGSON A. *Proceedings, Strategic Management Development in BL Cars*. Internal policy document, 1977.

9 HAMEL G. *and* PRAHALAD C. K. *Competing for the Future*. Cambridge, MA, Harvard Business School Press, 1994.

CHAPTER

'Enabling' Leadership – The Basis of Talent Management

If you want to build a ship, do not bring men together to fell timber, prepare tools, assign tasks and think about easing work ... Rather, teach your men the longing for the wide, open sea.

Antoine de Saint-Exupéry

Enabling: Leading and Managing *from behind*

The Marquis de Lafayette, a soldiers' general who helped the Americans to remove the British in the War of Independence, led his troops with the belief, 'I am their leader – therefore I must follow them.' In the world of business, 'enabling' leadership is essentially the same as that practised by Lafayette. As Senge[1] indicates in his very relevant book, *The Dance of Change*, enabling styles of leadership seek to transfer power to those doing the work and, consequently, focus on developing:

❑ learning, knowledge and capability

❑ freedom to take necessary initiatives

❑ personal ownership and engagement

❑ commitment, rather than mere compliance

❑ confidence to take decisions and to act.

In the author's own research, involving over 2,000 managers and knowledge workers in the USA, Canada, as well as in nine countries in Europe, including the UK and Ireland,[2] one question asked of respondents was, 'Under what conditions were you most motivated and productive at work?' Irrespective of nationality or culture, the most frequently cited conditions were:

❑ the work undertaken was personally challenging (over 90 per cent)

❑ the work was significant to the business (over 90 per cent)

❑ considerable responsibility was involved (over 80 per cent)

❑ I was in a leadership/influencing role (over 70 per cent)

❑ I was engaged in cross-functional activity (over 70 per cent).

The clear message to executives and leaders in their roles as enablers, coaches and mentors would, therefore, seem to be: *Help us to make work a learning journey and make that journey challenging, relevant, exciting – and fun. We, for our part, will learn, develop and grow in our commitment and contribution to the business.* Such a shift from traditional forms of authoritarian leadership involves functioning less in the role of a leader as *commander*, but more in the role of a leader as a *servant*.

The former role is often restricted and confined by an overriding fear of failure, a need to respond to superiors' real – or assumed – wishes, whims and wants and, hence, leads to many self-imposed constraints, adopted in the interests of a hassle-free life. The role of 'servant', by contrast, creates a good deal of autonomy and initiative, 'freedom within a framework'. The 'commander' tends to function according to the dictates of rank and hierarchy, while the 'servant' works according to the demands of the situation and the needs of those involved in it. Theirs is an *authoritative* – rather than authoritarian – role, based upon the power of wisdom and competence, not the authority of position or status. The leader's authority – and influence – emerges not simply from explicit knowledge, command and instruction, but largely from the appropriate interweaving of his or her:

❑ tacit knowledge, wisdom and competence

❑ feelings and spirit

❑ values and beliefs

❑ authenticity and credibility as a person.

As Figure 13 suggests, they work freely across what is primarily a *hierarchy of stimuli* to create – and capitalise upon – a growing quality of communication and interaction with others. By *leading from behind* – and so using a wider range of communication channels – *they* give more than they take, they open up rather than close down and they encourage, or challenge, instead of dominate and drive. Their essentially 'catalysing' and facilitating style is central to the success of the team, but since the leaders do not obviously take control or lead from the front, the kudos and personal satisfaction that come with success are more readily experienced and 'owned' by team members themselves.

> 66 *The critical leadership competencies and styles are emerging as those that can access, transfer and mobilise knowledge.* 99

Seen in the context of today's world, much of what has passed for traditional, authoritarian management appears as a form of 'upfront puppetry'. It may serve to gratify a need for personal power, or flatter the macho image some people have of themselves, but it generally proves to be a poor means of identifying, releasing and managing talent. In her book *In the Age of the Smart Machine*, Shoshanna Zuboff[3] makes the point that the days of the manager as 'jungle fighter' are really over. Increasingly, in the information age, with its attendant social and commercial transformation, the critical leadership competencies and styles are emerging as those that can access, transfer and mobilise knowledge – particularly people's so-called 'tacit knowledge' – as well as willingness to contribute. As organisations transform themselves in response to the imperatives of the information revolution and a dramatically changing market place, inflexible hierarchies and 'silo'

Nature of interaction (stimulus)	Quality of interaction (response)
1 Cognitive	*Connects intellectually*
2 Emotional/Feelings	*Engages feelings and needs*
3 Energy/Charisma	*Hooks hopes and aspirations*
4 Insight/Wisdom	*Releases potential and talents*

FIGURE 13 The Nature and Quality of Interaction

management thinking are, necessarily, giving way to more organic, adaptable structures and managerial mindsets.

Enabling styles of management and leadership, which acknowledge the crucial value of talent – especially knowledge-based competencies – ratify the place of the manager or leader as a key player at the 'hub', rather than the 'head', of a business unit, team or project[4]. Such a shift in role necessarily involves the need to develop fundamentally different styles of both leading and managing, as Figure 14 shows.

Clearly, there will always be occasions when decisive leadership and management are needed, when someone has to say: 'We do it this way and in this time scale.' In conditions of crisis, for example, the ability to take immediate control and issue clear, unambiguous instructions in order to mobilise co-ordinated effort rapidly and effectively may be paramount. It is thus not simply an *either–or* choice about style, but essentially a *'both–and'* issue, whereby leaders are able to adopt and operate with versatility according to changing circumstances.

Increasingly, however, the need is for leaders who can source, release and mobilise intelligent enterprise, creativity and committed goodwill in the pursuit of goals and outcomes that are going to ensure competitive advantage in the long term for a business. Above and beyond that, there is the question of integrating and meeting the demands of the *triple* bottom line – commercial, ecological and social – referred to earlier. Heroic overload, the 'alone-I-did-it' mindset, where there is minimal delegation – and even less *empowerment* of others – belongs to another time and place.

Enabling Leadership: a Four-Function Process

Figures 7 and 8 in Chapter 4 give clues as to the techniques essential to successful enabling leadership, which itself relies heavily upon *quality one-to-one dialogues* for its effectiveness. Personal *networking*, where oral communication is critical in building up contacts, relationships and mutual support, is similarly vital to moving ideas – and necessary action – forward. Patrick Dixon[5] refers to such networks – involving people both inside and external to the business – as *'ideas factories'*. Within the context of enabling leadership, such ideas factories are crucial to foster and reinforce:

❐ knowledge generation

❐ knowledge transfer

1 Traditional hierarchy

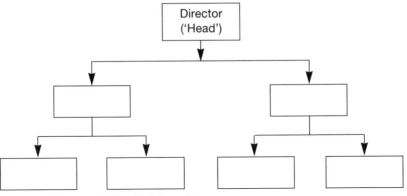

1 Director/manager is 'head' of the unit
2 'Cascade' communication of information
3 Head initiates ideas, decisions and action
4 Head directs and controls
5 Focus on 'bottom line' and tangible results
6 Head tells subordinates what to do
7 Knowledge (explicit) transmitted 'officially'

2 Adaptive, responsive structure

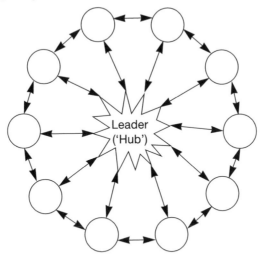

1 Leader becomes 'hub' of the team
2 'Networking', using contributive competence
3 Leader facilitates ideas, decisions and action
4 Leader enables others to be effective
5 Emphasis on values as well as results
6 Leader stimulates and builds shared vision/goals
7 Tacit knowledge transferred and mobilised

FIGURE 14 Enabling Leadership – 'Hub', not 'Head'

❐ exploration of ideas and issues

❐ valid option generation

❐ creative, productive synergy

❐ bases of essential collaboration

❐ project and cross-functional styles of working

❐ collective action to clear bottlenecks, which, as in bottles themselves, tend to occur at the top.

Beyond tools and techniques, however, the richly varied arena that is talent management depends for its success upon four, often interrelated, activities that make up the process of *enabling leadership*. These are:

❐ **coaching** – this is primarily job-, task-, role- or project-specific, usually within a given context

❐ **mentoring** – this is aimed at the longer-term education and development of the individual

❐ **empowering** – this is directed towards creating enough 'freedom within a framework' to use talent, to the full, in goal achievement

❐ **sponsoring** – this is aimed at promoting awareness of and opening up opportunities for people of talent and potential, to enable them to make the most appropriate contribution to the business.

Figure 15 illustrates the four critical activities that together constitute the directed, dedicated process of enabling, intervention and support essential to the orchestrated management of talent. Each is explored in more depth, using appropriate models to illustrate techniques and methods, in subsequent chapters. They are introduced at this stage to show something of the broad spectrum of integrated *leadership* actions that make up much of talent management. As a managed process of dedicated enabling, there is a high level of interplay and co-ordination between the four activities.

Many directors and managers, concerned with identifying, developing and using talent, still tend to think within outdated frames of reference and see vertical movement against predictable vacancies as the principal way to progress people of potential and high ability through

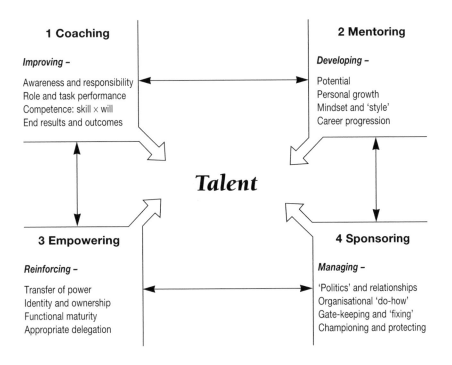

FIGURE 15 Managing Talent: Four Key Functions

the business. Unbelievably, even at the start of the twenty-first century there are still executives who believe that: Talent management = management training = 'Send him/her on a course'.

Clearly, anachronistic perceptions about what talent management really is in today's world and a genuine lack of necessary know-how as to the scope, opportunities and techniques of selecting, deploying and developing high achievers, continue to limit the thinking and action essential to managing talented people. As the operations manager[6] of a large, high-tech manufacturing company stated at an in-house workshop on talent management:

> I have two outstanding young men who we could so easily lose to the competition, but I just can't see any likely positions coming vacant in the near future. I really don't know how I'm going to be able to hold them if they are headhunted.

The four key imperatives of talent management (see Figure 1, Chapter 1), together with the four areas of leadership response identified in Figure 15, are intended to deal effectively with the issues and feeling of impotence expressed by the operations manager. *Moreover, they provide the framework to link talent management strategies to the business strategies of the organisation.* The four imperatives and four managerial responses seek, too, to reaffirm the emerging shift from 'old style' thinking about placement, training and development, to current, 'new paradigm' practices in talent management. The broad differences in approach are summarised in Table 4.

Enabling: More Than Competence – a *Mindset*

The universal shift from 'industrial age' managerial thinking and practices to a necessarily very different 'information society' *leadership* mindset has seen the management of knowledge and talent evolve as critical competences, at all levels, within businesses. The significant move away from manufacturing, in the USA and Europe towards largely service-based economies has led to the rapid proliferation of 'knowledge workers' and informed specialists, for whom traditional authoritarian leadership is inappropriate and counter-productive.

During the last decade, especially, there has also been extensive globalisation of businesses, with attendant 'world class' aspirations and standards. As a consequence, organisations have tended to develop more 'organic', adaptive structures, which enable talented people from different functions – or locations – to operate collectively and generate the productive synergy critical to competitive advantage, technologically and commercially. As Kanter[7] has pointed out, in the 'global village' success is not merely a matter of competitive advantage, but it also involves *collaborative* advantage, requiring people who can initiate and manage appropriate strategic and operational alliances and partnerships.

❝ *'Enabling' leadership and management are essentially about doing what is needed to source, develop and leverage talent for the benefit of the business.* ❞

Along with increasing uncertainty, less predictability and the often contradictory imperatives that characterise the information age, there is seemingly limitless opportunity and challenge – which is where 'enabling', as a way of managing talent and leading capable people, enters the picture. As Figure 14 indicates, 'enabling' leadership and management are essentially about doing *what* is *needed* to source,

TABLE 4 Old Style v New Paradigm Practices

Old-Style 'Human Resources' Thinking	New Paradigm Talent Management
1 Promotion is essentially a matter of 'upwards' movement through the hierarchy.	1 *Career progression necessarily encompasses wide-ranging and frequent lateral moves.*
2 Promotion is often within a particular function or 'silo'.	2 *Progression deliberately takes place across functional – and other – boundaries.*
3 Promotion is usually to one new role at a time.	3 *Progression is likely to include several concurrent roles at any one time.*
4 High emphasis is placed upon developing experience within one country or domain.	4 *There is wide exposure to a variety of international roles and global experiences.*
5 Caution in placement is emphasised, ie 'Promote when ready and not before.'	5 *There is more risk and readiness to experiment, ie 'Promote early and take a calculated chance.'*
6 Selection/promotion is very subjective and often traits-based.	6 *Selection/promotion is more objective and based upon perceived competencies.*
7 Fixed salary bands are for job 'levels', with less scope for flexible differential, ie a 'rate for the job' mentality.	7 *Increasing 'rate-busting' and use of more flexible differentials reward contributive talent appropriately.*
8 Development emphasises training and 'teaching'.	8 *Development is a matter of coaching, mentoring and learning from experience.*
9 There is general 'blanket' training, across the organisation, ie a 'scattergun' approach.	9 *Greater focus is on selective development to maximise longer-term pay-off to the business.*
10 Development is generally a low-priority or even peripheral activity.	10 *Organisations, increasingly aware of the 'war' for talent, acknowledge its management as a priority.*

develop and leverage talent for the benefit of the business – and the fulfilment and continuing growth of those contributing to its success.

The four generic bases to enabling leadership in Figure 15 – *coaching, mentoring, empowering and sponsorship* – need to develop beyond competence into an *art form*. Moreover, enabling is a dynamic combination and *interweaving* of those arts, where there is no one unique, 'right' prescription or formula. Thus, there are few limits to the practice and development of enabling as a leadership art – other than the often self-imposed constraints brought on by fear of failure, or a reluctance to challenge 'sacred cows' and test established boundaries to the full.

Enabling, as a process that is central to helping people do and achieve the requisite, is often about encouraging them to move out of comfort zones, to think differently, *to discover solutions for themselves* and to experiment, where higher degrees of risk may well be involved. In the context of interventions aimed at releasing and mobilising talent to achieve competitive advantage, enabling needs to be undertaken by those who are themselves prepared to raise their own game and move forward into the 'land of I don't know', as Richard Leider[8] described breaking out of the emotional safety and 'insulation' of the status quo.

Stepping out of the comfort zone, with its attendant security – however illusory that may be – and moving into new roles that may be largely unmapped territory is rather like abandoning familiar, firm ground and walking into a swamp. The 'alligators' are the multiplicity of risks that are typically identified with fear of failure, threats to career – or simply ridicule. Figure 16, developed from an original and comparable model of Roger Plant[9] in *Managing Change and Making it Stick*, shows something of the dynamics and challenges involved in moving out of a comfort zone into the many swamps that typify necessary change and transformation within a business and its interaction with its environment.

The comfort zone itself tends to be determined by two key factors that together define the horizons and limits. One (the vertical axis) is the individual's *breadth of perception* and the degree to which a person views the world parochially and in a narrow local context or with the much higher, wider and, therefore, 'helicopter' perspective typical of a more global mindset. The second determinant is the *time frame* in which the individual views and considers life and the imperatives and decisions that determine its course (horizontal axis). Linked to both vertical and horizontal axes is the individual's capacity for appropriate *adaptability and versatility*, eg the ability to 'think global and act local' (vertical axis) or to manage the future by acting today (horizontal axis).

Empowering becomes a crucial leadership skill in helping somebody to move from familiar ground into the 'land of I don't know'. However, empowerment has its obvious limitations and will only be effective when linked to clear-cut delegation, appropriate coaching and, on occasions, what Buchanan and Boddy[10] refer to as the 'backstage activities' of politically sensitive sponsorship, in the form of door opening, bridge-building and/or promotional lobbying with key stakeholders.

Preparing people, by developing their competence and their confidence, for the journey into new arenas and what may be largely unmapped or unfamiliar territory should be something that the sensitised and aware enabling leader will tend to do as a matter of course. The personal 'radar' of the enabling leader functions through a combination of acuity, sensitivity and adaptive timing. Reality, in many

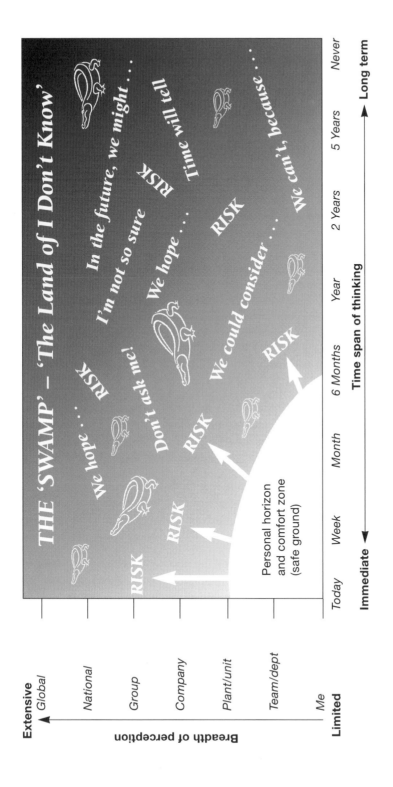

FIGURE 16 Thinking and Acting – Personal horizons

organisations, is that there are not enough trained leaders with the requisite levels of awareness and competence to play the role of effective enabler or facilitator. This remains a significant, if not critical, challenge in a number of businesses. If ever there were an 'ideal' time for competence in enabling and for enabling leaders, then this is it, as we learn to recognise and deal with the imperatives of the information age.

The current conditions of high turbulence, ambiguity and continuous transformation are more likely to intensify in pace and complexity and not diminish, and as a consequence there is a high need for enabling leaders who possess, at least, the following competences and strengths:

❐ the ability to recognise, diagnose and help in *catalysing* solutions or satisfactory outcomes to complex, multifaceted problems

❐ the ability to give cogent definition to and 'map out' *evolving* situations and to identify the potential and opportunities *within* change and turbulence, ie a capacity to identify likely *productive uncertainty in whatever form it may emerge*

❐ integrative thinking, which is capable of creating or synthesising a new unity out of paradox and apparent contradiction – what McCaskey[11] refers to as 'Janusian thinking', ie thinking akin to the Roman god Janus, who supposedly possessed the gift of being able to look in different directions at the same time

❐ a clear perception and understanding of what is *mandatory* and what is *discretionary* in a particular project or task, and hence the ability to focus and mobilise others' initiatives and contributive effort for optimal outcomes

❐ sensitivity in recognising when to use loose or tight rein to trigger appropriate motivation, response, energy release and commitment in others, ie an intelligent flexibility and *acuity* in both leadership style and enabling interventions

❐ high awareness of themselves and others – and thus interpersonal skills that encourage, stimulate and inspire, as opposed to styles that diminish, threaten, inhibit and demotivate

❐ strong personal credibility derived from courage, track record, demonstrable competence, integrity and perceived organisational 'clout' – especially the ability to use the power afforded by transforming

❝ *Twenty-first century managers are not expected to be all-knowing gurus nor peddlers of panaceas.* **❞**

organisations, as fluidity allows opportunities to be seized and capitalised upon

❏ the necessary 'political' acumen and, consequently, the capability for *anticipating and dealing with* the politics typical of organisations and functional, hierarchical activity

❏ the ability to make sense of and derive optimum use of the increasingly sophisticated management information systems that underpin the functioning of the business – especially in its form as 'virtual organisation'

❏ a developed mindset which accepts that radical change is increasingly coming to be the new norm in business life.

Twenty-first century managers are not expected to be all-knowing gurus nor peddlers of panaceas who are there to supply all the 'answers'. Rather, their role as enabler is to *help others to help themselves* by creating an environment – and personal relationships with those who report to them – where *exploration, personal discovery and continuous learning* are triggered as a result of:

❏ probing the understanding of context, scope and potential of both existing and new challenges

❏ providing questions – and time – for reflection

❏ prompting appropriate causal analysis, diagnosis and evaluation, as necessary preliminaries to solution generation

❏ stimulating the generation and exploration of viable options, alternative scenarios, pathways and courses of action

❏ initiating the processes of generating, building and sharing of collective visions and aspirations about and for the business, or its constituent functions and projects – *a 'felt' sense of mission is both more relevant and real than a perfectly worded mission statement on the wall in the company's reception*

❏ helping people to focus and align their thinking, actions and contributions, where appropriate – especially within rapidly changing environments

❐ encouraging people to commit to necessary action, when talking has eventually become a secondary, supportive process

❐ operating, generally, with 'ears and eyes on' – but largely 'hands off' – to provide the necessary 'freedom within a framework' and the contextual thinking to put issues of *power, ownership and personal accountability* into a realistic perspective.

Sourcing, selecting and placing those executives who will make effective enablers and then training and developing them to fulfil the role of leader remains a major challenge in most organisations.

One Company's Approach

One company that is successfully addressing the problem – as a critical part of a major cultural transformation – is First Quench, a new business formed out of the merger of Victoria Wine and Threshers, two major high street beverage-retailing companies. Under the leadership of former managing director Jerry Walton, the company embarked on a series of major strategic and operational initiatives aimed at radically transforming the organisation, its *culture* and its approach to its customers. The various initiatives and programmes, which deal with different but interrelated facets of the business – managerial mindset, core values and competences, shopping experience for customers and working environments for shop teams – are well co-ordinated and 'choreographed', and consciously interwoven for optimum impact upon the business, its people and its markets. High emphasis is expressly put on the importance of enabling styles of management and leadership – especially the significance of mentoring and coaching – in growing and retaining talent within the company.

Four simple but powerful values form the basis of First Quench's philosophy and *day-to-day* lifestyle:

❐ **boldness** – *energy, breaking the mould, determination, courage, risk-taking*

❐ **trust** – *reliability, letting people get on with it, recognising expertise, enabling*

❐ **integrity** – *honesty, straightforwardness, respect, fairness*

❐ **involving** – *understanding the impact of your actions, good communication, collaboration, support.*

The four First Quench values make an interesting comparison with those that underpin day-to-day operations at Wellstream, quoted in Chapter 1:

Trust	Integrity
Clarity	Tenacity

Under a wide cultural and behavioural umbrella known as 'Alchemy' (ie the 'alchemy of change and transformation'), the programme of reform and renewal is having a dramatic impact upon attitudes, mindsets and practices throughout the company. Even after only 12 months, the widespread positive effects are very apparent. From the board down to the retail outlets, the essentially 'human', aspirational and cultural change messages have been exceptionally well received and responded to, with high enthusiasm, energy and commitment.

Within such an energised and motivated environment, the effective management of talent and the development of enabling rather than authoritarian styles of leadership emerge as a natural and almost inevitable consequence, as individuals at many levels in the business begin to initiate necessary changes themselves. Explicit knowledge is coming to be seen as a servant to – not a dictator of – tacit knowledge, while knowledge transfer is emerging in a similarly 'organic' way, as a critical but equally natural process throughout the business. Thus, successful enabling requires a mindset, preferably a collective one, that demonstrably believes in the intelligent mobilising of talent as the primary means of achieving entrepreneurial success. This emerges as one of the cornerstones of culture transformation at First Quench.

In positive, essentially employee-friendly transformation programmes, such as that at First Quench, where change is *consciously related to people's own work ambitions and aspirations*, mobilising talent becomes a wider issue involving many, rather than simply small numbers of obvious 'high-flyers'. In the longer term, much of the pay-off of 'Alchemy' and its supporting change programmes is likely to be the brainpower, initiative and focused energy released – and leveraged – as a result of leadership that *actively lives* the values of the new culture, day by day, establishing a high level of say–do credibility, personal example and trust. In such a climate, fear of failure becomes much less of a 'life-threatening' issue or universal inhibitor, as people experience approval for having the courage to experiment, take risks and pursue initiatives.

In businesses less enlightened than First Quench, it is still the enabling skills and mindsets of individual executives that begin – and underpin – the process of transformation in talent management. Developing and implementing the policies and practices of successful talent management is comparable to the process of building successful product or service brands, in any field. This requires organisations to:

❏ build in quality, based upon best practice

❏ build superior service, based upon continuous anticipation of 'customer' needs

❏ get there first – take the initiatives to make things happen

❏ create uniqueness and seek differentiation – especially of experience, reward and development

❏ innovate, innovate and innovate again (*remember the operations manager of the high-tech manufacturing company, quoted above, who really did not know how to develop, progress and retain his best people*)

❏ communicate strongly, clearly and frequently, so that people understand what you are offering them and what you need from them

❏ build in a passionate conviction and commitment for what you are doing and the benefits or opportunities it can give (*remember Saint-Exupéry's words at the outset of this chapter – and allow for the fact that he wrote in less gender-conscious times!*).

The pay-off and return are generally proportional to the intelligent thought and energy put into discovering, understanding and meeting customers' needs. So it is with talent management, where the 'customers' are the organisation's *own* people.

SUMMARY

In today's businesses, where there are increasing numbers of 'knowledge workers' and informed specialists, leadership should be the means of serving the needs of such people – not simply acting as a driving force, pushing or dragging people into action. Undoubtedly, there are times when leaders *must* lead from the front – though that is often a matter of leading by example. However, essentially enabling, or facilitating, styles of leadership, aimed at acting as a necessary catalyst to trigger and mobilise commitment and effort, are much more in demand in information age companies. The shift from 'head' to 'hub' of the unit, team or network represents a necessary and critical change of emphasis in both leadership role and style in today's more flexible and often 'vertical' organisations.

Four key activities are fundamental to enabling, facilitating styles of leadership and management. They are:

- **coaching** – job-, role- and project-specific guidance and support

- **mentoring** – concerned with 'life' issues in personal growth and career progression

- **empowering** – aimed at transferring power to those charged with doing the work

- **sponsoring** – which is about opening doors and opportunities for those with talent to guide them through the 'political minefields' that characterise much of organisational life.

While such enabling processes can stand alone as effective support activities, it is usually the intelligent and appropriate interweaving of them all that is likely to make the greatest impact in the longer-term successful management of an organisation's talent and potential. Not only is enabling leadership aimed at developing – and capitalising – upon outstanding know-how, do-how and specialist expertise, it also becomes the means of encouraging people to move out of the questionable safety of organisational 'wombs' and comfort zones. The role of enabler is, therefore, very dependent upon the facilitating leader's own 'say–do' credibility and professional integrity.

Research conducted by the author and others[12] reinforces the need to develop motivation of opportunities within work itself as a critical means of stimulating learning and releasing 'adrenaline' within people. Consistently, irrespective of country, culture or job function, five factors – especially within the individual's role or job – serve as vital triggers to outstanding performance given requisite levels of intelligence and competence:

- challenging work that 'stretches' the individual

- work that is significant and important to the success of the business

- a high level of responsibility for the job-holder

- adequate opportunity to lead and/or exert necessary influence

- work that involves cross-functional and cross-boundary relationships and activities.

The research – as well as practical experience – sends out clear messages to those responsible for leading and managing others about the job conditions they need to 'engineer' in order for people of talent, particularly, to contribute to the best of their high ability.

ACTION – THEORY INTO PRACTICE

- Together with each member of your team, where you consider there will be appropriate pay-off, develop a significantly enriched version of their *current* role to create higher levels of opportunity for them, to experience each of the five 'adrenaline' factors identified in this chapter and summarised on page 117.

- How will you ensure continuity of these stimuli, acting in the role of enabler to those whose roles/jobs have been enriched?

- What do the results say about you as an 'enabling leader'?

Endnotes

1   SENGE P. *The Dance of Change*. London, Nicholas Brealey, 1999.

2   WILLIAMS M. R. *Enabling – beyond empowering*. London, Thorogood, 1998.

3   ZUBOFF S. *In the Age of the Smart Machine*. London, Heinemann, 1988.

4   HARTLEY L. P. *The Go-between*. Harmondsworth, Penguin Books, 1999.

5   DIXON P. *Futurewise: Six faces of global change*. London, HarperCollins, 1998.

6   *Proceedings, Workshop on Managing Talent*, at a high-tech client company, run by the author, November 1999.

7   KANTER R. M. *World Class*. London, Simon & Schuster, 1996.

8   LEIDER R., in White, R.P., Hodgson, P. and Crainer, S. *The Future of Leadership: A white water revolution*. London, Pitman, 1996.

9   PLANT R. *Managing Change and Making it Stick*. London, Fontana, 1991.

10 BUCHANAN D. *and* BODDY D. *The Expertise of the Change Agent*. London, Prentice Hall, 1992.

11 McCASKEY M. B. in *Proceedings, High Potential Professionals Program*. Theseus Institute, January 1998.

12 Author's research, 1994–2000.

CHAPTER

Talent Management – The Coaching Leader

Give a person a fish and you feed him for a day. Show him how to fish and you help him to feed himself for life.

Chinese Proverb

Current Context of Coaching

While hierarchies look set to continue in one shape or another in most organisations, they are likely to be found, increasingly, in more 'organic' and adaptable forms, frequently based around project teams, networks and virtual organisations. Information age managers will spend increasing amounts of time building dedicated teams and focused multidisciplinary groups, constantly dismantling or reforming them. They are likely to move quickly and freely from one project to the next, in the roles of change agent, catalyst, initiator of change and contributing team member.

New 'clusters' of competences are emerging as the mindsets and skills necessary to work effectively in much more adaptive and organic arenas. These competences include:

❏ unique, or scarce, differentiated competences, frequently technical and specialist – *critical to taking the business forward into new fields*

❏ the ability to mediate effectively across different functions and disciplines *in order to mobilise collaborative effort and synergy*

- the ability and commitment to take ownership of one's own unit or domain – *constantly adding value to it and running it, in effect, as a successful, interdependent 'business'*

- the skills and readiness to act as a competent team player within a project

- group, network or other team – *by playing roles that support the collective endeavour and add to others' contributions.*

66 *The timescale in which managers – and others – must prove themselves is shrinking significantly.* **99**

The timescale in which managers – and others – must prove themselves is shrinking significantly, hence the importance of the 'bespoke', personal attention of coaching as a means of developing people in transforming environments. The value of more specific and tailor-made development is further underlined by the growing acceptance that:

- Building on identified strengths and *unique* competences is likely to be more productive than 'blanket', or hit-and-miss, training interventions.

- Some competences and aptitudes are largely genetic and difficult to develop. As Terry Lunn[1], former personnel director of Joshua Tetley once said, 'Don't try to teach the pig to sing: it annoys the pig and wastes your time.'

- Coaching, increasingly – and especially when a feature of a focused personal mentoring programme – is coming to be seen as a more effective developmental process in people's learning and career progression. Megginson,[2] Pedlar and Boydell[3] and others have, for many years, differentiated between, and given definition to, the separate but complementary processes of coaching and mentoring. Particularly relevant is Megginson's view that coaching is likely to contribute more to people's development *within* specific stages, whereas mentoring aims for a continuity of learning and growth and so seeks to develop individuals through the transitions *between* stages in their career.

In this context, coaching tends to be role-, job- or project-specific, aimed at improving task performance and, therefore, the development that underpins such improvement. By contrast, mentoring is both wider and more fundamental in scope, concerned with building a life-long career. A largely eclectic and, therefore, more diffuse process, mentoring is what Gareth Lewis[4] describes as an 'added value activity'. Concerned with the longer-term development and growth of people, mentoring may encompass many other, often apparently unrelated, learning experiences, as well as specific elements of dedicated coaching. Seen in a perspective above and beyond the utilitarian and practical, mentoring can become what Clare Freeman[5] defines, with acuity and insight, as 'a celebration of the uniqueness of the individual'.

Coaching: Learning – Not Teaching

Some teaching and instruction are inevitable in coaching. The transfer of knowledge – and 'do-how' – from one individual to another will only be possible in some circumstances by telling, showing and instructing. Yet in the world of business and management, where performance and achievement may depend upon the interplay of so many variables – often outside the control of the individual – coaching is much more a question of helping people to see things differently.

The opportunities for coaching people and improving their contributive effectiveness are almost limitless, provided that managers are prepared to think in creative, expansive and opportunistic terms. For example, coaching projects for directors, managers and knowledge workers, taken from the author's client organisations,[6] include:

❑ shaping new learning experiences and developing appropriate new skills, as a pair or team, where mutual support reinforces new competence and confidence

❑ learning to adapt to and capitalise upon change and transformation in the way the business conducts its affairs in the market place

❑ using – and enhancing – the opportunities afforded by new, emerging organisational structure and roles

❑ benchmarking the best current comparative – and competitive – business and managerial practices

❑ learning via involvement in mergers, acquisitions, management buy-outs and multi-stakeholder alliances

❒ consciously 'unlearning' old skills and ways of doing things so as to develop new, more appropriate ones

❒ using co-coaching techniques, whereby individuals with a particular and needed expertise from one function regularly 'shadow' those from another department – and coach them on the job

❒ giving people challenging, cross-functional and multidisciplinary assignments to lead, develop and manage

❒ putting together a specialist task force and running it to deal with and resolve, satisfactorily, a significant organisational blockage or major process inefficiency.

As Marcel Proust said, 'The real art of discovery is not to visit new lands but to see existing ones with different eyes.' It is thus likely to involve:

❒ stimulating awareness and reflection about an issue

❒ crystallising responsibility and accountability for results

❒ triggering the generation and exploration of options, ideas and likely solutions

❒ prompting risk, benefit and outcome evaluation

❒ encouraging commitment to the first actionable steps to be taken

❒ helping people to take ownership of issues – and their outcomes.

Beliefs rooted in traditional, passive and teacher-dependent learning that coaching leaders frequently have to confront and counter are:

❒ The 'teacher' knows the *answers*.

❒ The teacher will tell us what we have to do, ie he or she represents a surrogate 'parent'.

❒ When we do it, we must get it right, otherwise the teacher will be displeased and might 'punish' us.

❒ Ownership and responsibility for the success (or otherwise) of learning and learning outcomes rests with the teacher.

Coaching, aimed primarily at facilitating learning, is, by contrast, based upon the following beliefs and expectations:

❑ It is principally about helping people to recognise the *reality* of an adult workaday world.

❑ Motivation to learn, face challenges, take risks and commit to action comes from *within* the individual – motivation is not some exclusive balm with which managers anoint and bless their people.

❑ The coaching process tends to follow, both in sequence and logic, the classical learning cycle (see Figure 4, Chapter 3). At each stage of what David Kolb[7] defined as a primarily cyclical learning process, the coach's role is critical in stimulating and guiding

- awareness
- learning
- understanding
- skill development
- confidence.

❑ Coaching seeks to enhance others' awareness, understanding and competence through the *conscious exploration* of different

- perspectives
- contexts
- parameters
- imperatives.

❑ Coaching is, coincidentally, a process aimed at increasing people's

- sense of responsibility
- ownership of issues
- personal accountability for results and outcomes
- commitment to learning and improvement.

❑ It recognises the need – and opportunity – for people *to make choices*. In exercising their discretion, individuals may act in ways different from, or even alien to, the coach's style, approach and expectations.

❑ Coaching focuses upon how people can develop and implement *their own*

- ideas
- answers
- solutions

- tactics
- strategies.

66 *Honest coaching – where empowerment may well be a reality – requires the coach to give up some control.* **99**

❏ Honest coaching – where empowerment may well be a reality – requires the coach to give up some control so that others have the requisite autonomy and freedom to take necessary decisions and action.

❏ Coaching is not a one-way street but a critical element in a relationship where there is mutual trust, respect and support, founded upon constructive feedback and dialogue.

Coach – the 'Head' and 'Heart' of Coaching

Based upon the acronym COACH[8] is a model developed empirically with UK and US clients that highlights the complementary management and leadership ('head' and 'heart') aspects of coaching. Questions that can be asked with regard to each of 10 aspects of coaching are identified in Figure 17. The model comprises two interrelated facets to the coaching process:

❏ building structure

❏ building ownership.

The questions posed in the left-hand column are intended to lend *structure* to the coaching dialogue – especially to those discussions that are about taking *necessary decisions and action*, such as:

❏ clarifying goals and outcomes

❏ establishing 'why' action is necessary or unnecessary

❏ agreeing parameters, or criteria, for outcomes and results, eg deadlines, consequences and other imperatives

❏ determining priorities, sequences and monitoring and control processes

Building structure
(Management)

Building ownership
(Leadership)

Confirm
- What do we need to discuss?
- Why do we need to discuss this?
- What do we want out of the discussion?
- What are the consequences of not discussing it?
- What's in it for you?

Collaborate
- *Who do you want/need to work with?*
- *How will you secure their active support?*
- *What 'ownership' will you give them?*
- *What if you don't get co-operation?*
- *What back-up/support do you need from me?*

Objectives
- What do you need/want to achieve?
- What are your deadlines?
- What are your short-/long-term goals?
- How attainable and realistic are they?
- What challenge are you building in?

Opportunities
- *What opportunities do you see here?*
- *What is the potential for growth?*
- *What options do you have?*
- *How can you best exploit opportunity?*
- *How will you sell it to others?*

Actions
- What actions do you want to take?
- What actions do you need to take?
- What happens if you take no action?
- What are the consequences of action?
- What will you do next?

Aspirations
- *How does this fit in with your plans?*
- *What do you see as career opportunities here?*
- *What learning is there for you?*
- *Where is the 'adrenaline' here?*
- *How will you sustain the adrenaline?*

Control
- What are the key parameters?
- How will your performance be measured?
- How will you monitor progress?
- Who approves or sanctions your actions?
- What is the bottom line?

Change
- *What must/can you change?*
- *Why change it?*
- *How do you build upon change?*
- *What happens if you don't change it?*
- *How will you get people out of their comfort zones?*
- *What is the next likely change after the current one?*

Head
- Think! Is this what is really needed?
- Think! Is there a better way?
- Think! Are your objectives right?
- Think! Contingency plans?
- Think! Follow-up and follow-through?

Heart
- *What do you really like about this?*
- *Is there anything else you would rather be doing?*
- *How do you feel about this?*
- *How will you fight for it?*
- *Will you really achieve all this?*

FIGURE 17 Coaching – Building structure and ownership

❐ reflecting upon relevance, realism and appropriateness of plans and actions

❐ confirming the key 'what-ifs' and necessary preventive, contingency and follow-up actions.

The left-hand column focuses principally on *task* issues in order to confirm the objectives and results required and the actions, in sequence, necessary to achieve them. By contrast, the *complementary* questions of the right-hand column cover largely *process* matters and the *learning opportunities* afforded by taking planned, well-thought-through decisions and action, such as:

❑ securing and building ownership and commitment to objectives and the actions necessary to achieve them

❑ identifying the scope and potential for development and growth, of oneself, one's role and contribution and of the business – *that is, adding value personally as well as organisationally*

❑ linking task performance and goal achievement to personal ambitions and career development *by relating work and its outcomes to lifestyle aspirations*

❑ exploring the significance of involvement in transformation, experimentation and adaptation to changing conditions and imperatives

❑ establishing the emotional alignment, motivation and sense of fulfilment of the individual by engaging fully with organisational roles and goals.

The combination of the 'head' and 'heart' questions is intended to generate coaching dialogues that create productive, stimulating *synergy* between those coaching and those being coached – but also to 'turbocharge' the adrenaline flow in people as they begin to see their roles and contributions through new eyes and with new opportunities and challenges opening up for them.

Turning Learning into Necessary *Action*

Coaching is a very personal – and *interpersonal* – matter and there is no universally 'right' or 'best' approach. Even within the closest and most collaborative of working relationships, people will not 'get it right' every time. A common blockage to effective coaching is what Professor Tom Bateman[9] terms 'self-sabotage'. Somewhat in the form of a 'self-inflicted wound', it may happen where discussion and even potentially productive dialogue take place, where information and knowledge may well be passed on and processed, but where requisite action and follow-through simply do not happen – hence the importance of follow-up and follow-through in coaching.

Professor Jim Dowd, of the IMD Business School in Lausanne,[10] makes the critical point that *knowledge is not behaviour* and that there is a world of difference between *knowing* something and *doing* what that knowledge confirms should be done. Many coaching conversations are full of good intentions, but unless these discussions are translated into relevant, necessary and effective action the process can become a sterile, unproductive exercise, where the main outcomes are disappointment, frustration, disillusion and longer-term resentment, with mutual loss of credibility.

Obviously, there *are* development needs that are primarily issues of increased awareness and where the acquisition of information and knowledge is the essential coaching goal. Even in such cases, however, the requisite learning outcomes frequently become matters of *changed behaviours and, therefore, adaptive responses*. This is especially so in environments where there is more or less continual transformation, with consequent ambiguity, uncertainty and emergent opportunities.

More often than not, coaching is about how best to reach specific goals – which are something more than wishes, hopes, desires and dreams. Essentially, a goal represents a focused, true *intention* to achieve requisite outcomes – and is usually defined in specific terms. An agreed, declared goal is a clear decision *to take action and succeed*. Achievement and success are not simply matters of the intellect, or analysis and talk; they are, ultimately, the results of the interplay of determination, drive and persistence – with a high measure of courage thrown in. They require goodwill, dedication and the readiness of people to make all-important time available.

Achievement is normally underpinned by a necessary sequence of related activities or stages where the competence, insight, experience – and time – of the coaching manager are critical factors in ensuring success in learning and task outcomes for those being coached. One useful model was evolved empirically, by the students, during coaching sessions on a major international leadership programme on *Mobilizing People*, run at the IMD Business School, Lausanne. The coaching process is viewed as a crucial preliminary step leading to effective action built round the sequential structure of the '3 As': Allow, Act and Adapt.

Allow

Within the spirit and context of 'freedom within a framework', the coach's task is to:

☐ confirm imperatives and parameters that allow for optimal empowerment, ownership and freedom to act

☐ encourage risk-taking and experimentation and progressively develop in the person being coached the restless creativity and constructive dissatisfaction leading to practices of, 'If it ain't broke – break it and re-fix it'

☐ help in creating opportunities – and arenas – where people may challenge, and be challenged, over issues of change v the status quo

☐ create environments where it is safe to say 'I don't know' or 'I don't understand'

☐ setbacks are seen as necessary forms of learning, adaptation and growth

☐ develop acceptance of the reality that there is usually more than one effective way to reach a goal or produce necessary outcomes.

Act

At the action stage, the coach's role includes:

☐ helping to stimulate awareness of the scope, possibilities and potential for action

☐ encouraging exploration of the areas of *productive uncertainty*

☐ injecting the necessary concern for reflection, preparation, pace, timing, direction and follow-through, so that actions have the optimum chances of success

☐ keeping a practised hand near to the tiller, but giving maximum ownership and involvement to others in the formulation and initiation of action

☐ recognising that crossing the bridge from talk to action is a crucial source of learning for both coach and coached.

Adapt

Essential *coached adaptation* is about finding answers, together, to the following questions:

❐ So what have we learned about ourselves, each other and how we can work better together?

❐ What do you/I need to *do* differently as a consequence of this experience and these results?

❐ What *development* actions/inputs are going to help us to acquire the new skills, knowledge, understanding and behaviours that we need to be successful?

❐ Who else do we involve in the change/development process? What other sources of valid feedback, or support, would help most here?

❐ What might impede/impair adaptation and development, and how do we best deal with that?

The Coaching Process: Style and Techniques

As a process, coaching depends upon:

❐ a clear identification of people's achievements, aspirations and job/role ambitions

❐ an equally clear definition of specific training, development and hence coaching needs, in relation to task and role demands

❐ agreed improvement or 'stretch' benchmarks and challenges

❐ constant movement from the general to the specific – and back again – to create, explore and understand the context, scope and potential of situations, as well as the detail and specifics

❐ a unique combination of *empathy*, which enables the coach to identify sufficiently closely with people's needs, fears and expectations and the *detachment* to think objectively and to rise above arbitrary, subjective or selfish improvement criteria; *there is no room for evangelical, over-zealous or ignorant managers who are essentially feeding their own egos in coaching others*

❏ the quality, relevance and open format of questions designed to stimulate, provoke and explore thinking, reflection and discovery; these
need to be followed by more probing questions aimed at changing
the focus from wide angle to zoom lens – see Figure 18 (developed
from Figure 7 in Chapter 4).

Table 5 sets out the different stages of the coaching process.

The coaching sequence described in Table 5 can also be illustrated
diagrammatically as a hierarchy of activities, each aimed at stimulating,
encouraging or triggering an appropriate response – *intellectual and
emotional* – from the individual being coached (see Figure 19).
Intuition, passion, imagination, ingenuity and courage (the 'EQ
factors') are stimulated to provide the necessary 'engine' for their cognitive and analytical counterparts in the coaching process of moving from
dialogue to requisite decision-making and action.

Coaching – the Development Plan

The development plan, which emerges during coaching, is not a definitive, 'one-off' experience but rather a 'rolling' and constantly evolving
response to continually identified needs. It is essentially a map of a
learning journey, which helps the individual to:

❏ learn

❏ develop

❏ adapt

❏ grow.

There also needs to be built into the development plan a continuous
alignment between the needs of the individual and what is important
for the success of the business. Coaching, then, is essentially about
focused and directional learning, which is why specific and *bespoke*
learning opportunities are an essential feature of the development plan.
While formal courses, if carefully selected, *may* be highly relevant, there
is still too much widespread loose thinking about ill-defined development needs, resulting in remedies and prescriptions that, even today,
reflect attitudes of:

❏ 'he needs training – send him on a course'

TABLE 5 Coaching Sequence

The coaching sequence	Specific *actions*
7 Follow-up, follow-through – capitalise upon achievements *Promote follow-through*	• *Monitor progress with the individual* • *Check on-target and up to standard* • *Agree remedial/exploitative action*
6 Summarise and review *Promote reflection*	• *Ask individual to summarise points of discussion – ensure understanding and agreement* • *Note action points and agree start date and key 'milestones'*
5 Authorise and empower *Stimulate autonomy and interdependence*	• *Give authority and responsibility to make and take decisions* • *Ensure financial and administrative responsibility control is clear*
4 Agree the parameters and delegate *Stimulate ownership*	• *Establish deadlines and agree monitoring process between you both* • *Set aside dates and times to review progress* • *Identify job/task or role 'boundaries'*
3 Confirm current situation and alternative scenarios *Promote discovery*	• *Listen actively – ask questions, using EAR model* • *Draw out consequences* • *Share your experiences* • *Promote learning and 'ownership'*

2 Agree outcomes, goals and objectives
Stimulate responsibility
	• *Longer-term goals and objectives*
	• *Sessional goals and objectives*
	• *Goals should be*
	  – *achievable*
	  – *measurable*
	  – *specific*
	  – *challenging*
	  – *realistic*

1 Agree the issues for development
 	
Stimulate awareness and interest
	• *Identify specific improvements*
	  – *What can you delegate?*
	  – *What do they need to know?*

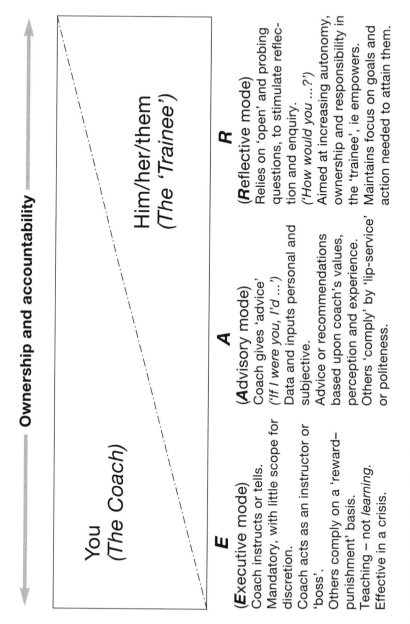

Ownership and accountability

You
(The Coach)

Him/her/them
(The 'Trainee')

Coaching mode

E

(**E**xecutive mode)
Coach instructs or tells.
Mandatory, with little scope for discretion.
Coach acts as an instructor or 'boss'.
Others comply on a 'reward–punishment' basis.
Teaching – not *learning*.
Effective in a crisis.

A

(**A**dvisory mode)
Coach gives 'advice'
('If I were you, I'd ...')
Data and inputs personal and subjective.
Advice or recommendations based upon coach's values, perception and experience.
Others 'comply' by 'lip-service' or politeness.

R

(**R**eflective mode)
Relies on 'open' and probing questions, to stimulate reflection and enquiry.
('How would you ...?')
Aimed at increasing autonomy, ownership and responsibility in the 'trainee', ie empowers.
Maintains focus on goals and action needed to attain them.

FIGURE 18 The EAR Model in Coaching Dialogue

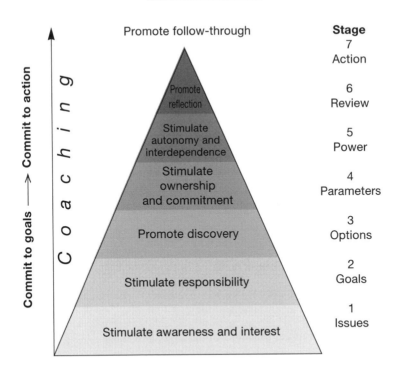

FIGURE 19 The Coaching Process

❑ 'they'll soon sort her out – book a place for her on their next programme.'

Learning is different for different people. Moreover, according to the stimuli, circumstances and development need, the same individual is likely to learn in differing ways, over a period of time. At different times, learning may be a matter of:

❑ reflection

❑ conceptualisation

❑ pragmatically working out of ideas

❑ direct experience of an activity.

❝ The development plan needs to reflect the richness and variety of the different learning modes. ❞

Accordingly, the development plan needs to reflect the richness and variety of the different learning modes, in ways that are appropriate to a particular individual's perceived learning needs 'mix'. Rich, varied and *relevant* learning experiences also need to be accompanied by review and appropriate feedback, in order to stimulate and consolidate new or enhanced insights, awareness and skill development.

As we saw in Chapter 6 (see page 102), responses to questions like 'Under what conditions were you most motivated and productive at work?' sent out clear messages to those leading and coaching others to make the journey stimulating, relevant and 'stretching'. People learn, develop and *grow*, for example, when they:

❒ switch from line to staff roles, and vice versa

❒ are given significant but achievable bottom-line responsibility

❒ set up and run project and cross-functional teams or task forces

❒ delegate to and empower others, in key areas of activity, and learn to allow others to make mistakes and learn from them

❒ take on global assignments and/or move to another country and culture

❒ set up and manage internal and external networks to progress a particular theme – for example, increasing competitive advantage, adding value for customers or significantly improving customer relations management

❒ consciously develop and enhance the contributive performance of a team whose motivation, effectiveness and results have been in decline for some time.

These are simply seven assignments that possess enormous potential for learning and development, but also may make substantial contributions to business performance and organisational transformation. They are typical, however, of the almost infinite learning and growth possibilities that can be formalised and set up within virtually every organisation, provided that those in the role of coach are prepared to commit energy, innovation and time to their people as well as to next month's figures.

SUMMARY

This chapter focuses on one of the cornerstones of talent management – coaching. This is primarily a process aimed at stimulating:

- awareness of what needs to be developed or changed

- learning that is seen as fundamental to effective, focused development

- an enhanced sense of personal responsibility for improving performance and results.

Though some degree of tutoring or instruction may, at times, be inevitable, the essential focus of coaching is upon learning. This can be difficult for both the coach and the person being coached, if one or both have really only had previous experience of largely passive learning, where the key relationships have been those of 'teacher' and 'pupil'. The coach's role is to help the other person to *take responsibility* for their own learning, development and performance improvement – *not* 'teach' and provide the 'answers'.

The coaching process is made up of three elements:

1 Techniques, which include:

- identifying and defining areas for improvement

- relating the individual's development to the needs of the business

- constantly moving between the general and the specific to relate detail to context, environment and the wider picture

- the coach's competence and interpersonal skills

- the crucial issue of *listening*.

2 Structure and sequence, which range through the following activities:

- clarifying improvement goals

- establishing context and alternative scenarios

- agreeing parameters of requisite improvement and development

- delegating and setting dates for review

- authorising and empowering ('freedom within a framework')

- summarising and reviewing agreements about improvement, change and development

- follow-up and follow-through on action taken and results obtained.

3 The coach's style, including:

- approach to developing dialogue and, therefore, the basis of the coaching relationship

- questioning and listening

- balancing of 'head' and 'heart' approaches in order to relate and align people's aspirations and ambitions, more fully and appropriately, with the demands of what is often *a changing* or transforming business.

Professor Jim Dowd's dictum[11] that *knowledge is not behaviour* reinforces the need for coaching to be a process that stimulates and *ensures* necessary improvement and development *action*. Fundamental to coaching is the 'learning journey' of those being coached, where the 'destinations' are essentially *interim* development and improvement goals. The learning journey is, above all, a continuous process that needs constant 'remapping' and refocusing as businesses and people learn to develop and grow together. Critical to the directional effectiveness and relevance of the journey and its progressive outcomes, at each stage along the way, are the competence, commitment and managerial professionalism of the coach.

The ability to make doing, learning and development *challenging, stimulating and compelling* is fundamental to the success of coaching, as a means of bringing about necessary change, improvement and growth – both in the individual and within the business of which he or she is an essential member.

ACTION – THEORY INTO PRACTICE

- Please complete the *Talent Coaching Profile* on page 231. Wherever possible, use it as a 360-degree instrument and work through the *Action Points* at the end.

- Developing Coaching Skills – A 'Coaching Challenge' Workshop (developed from a model originally designed at IMD, Business School, Lausanne for the 'Mobilizing People' Programme) (see page 234).

Endnotes

1 LUNN T., in *Sunday Times* regular feature on Management, in the early 1980s.

2 MEGGINSON D. 'Instructor, coach, mentor: three ways of helping for managers'. *MEAD Journal*. Vol. 19, Part 1. Spring 1988.

3 PEDLAR M. *and* BOYDELL T. *Managing Yourself*. London, Fontana, 1985.

4 LEWIS G. *The Mentoring Manager*. London, Institute of Personnel and Development/Pitman, 1996.

5 FREEMAN C. 'Mentoring for personal growth, organisations and people'. *MEAD Journal*. October 1994.

6 Coaching projects for directors taken from author's client organisations.

7 KOLB D. A. ET AL. *Organizational Psychology: Perspectives for managers*. London, Prentice Hall, 1979.

8 COACH model developed by Michael Williams & Partners with UK and US clients, 1995–6.

9 BATEMAN T. *Proceedings, Mobilizing People Program, IMD Business School*. Lausanne, October 1997.

10 DOWD J. D. *Proceedings, Mobilizing People Program, IMD Business School*. Lausanne, October 1997.

11 *Ibid*.

Mentoring and Sponsoring Talent

There are two people who are crucial to your career progression: get yourself a good mentor and a sponsor who has influence and clout.
Keith Paxman, formerly Director of Personnel,
Stewards & Lloyds Ltd

You cannot create experience – you must undergo it.
Albert Camus

Mentoring: More Than 'Coaching'

In contrast to coaching, mentoring creates a synthesis of learning, from many sources and over a significantly longer timescale. Using the analogy of a photographic zoom lens, coaching represents the close-up function – specific and focused upon detail – while mentoring is more akin to the whole zoom capability, with extensive use of the wide-angle facility.

Coaching is primarily aimed at developing competence, confidence and personal responsibility within the parameters of a particular task, role or project. The learning journeys involved, therefore, tend to be sharply focused and largely short term, although they may well become *additive* learning experiences aimed at clearly defined longer-term development and improvement.

> **❝ Mentoring is essentially an additive and often open-ended learning process. ❞**

By contrast, mentoring is *essentially an additive and often open-ended* learning process, which, in the words of Williams,[1] is:

- directed towards an individual's longer-term development and growth, within the broader perspective and possibility of continuity, offered by that person's potential – not simply the more specific scope afforded by improvement in the job performance

- fundamentally deeper in scope and so both generates and builds upon a variety of learning and developmental experiences

- essentially an eclectic and inclusive developmental process, rather than a highly selective or discriminating approach to both learning and the choice of learning opportunities and experiences; mentoring focuses more on the development of the 'whole' person and so can accommodate or relate to other, often apparently unrelated but specific learning – as Gareth Lewis[2] observes in his very useful book *The Mentoring Manager*, 'In this sense, it [mentoring] is an 'added-value' activity'

- more inclined to draw upon a far greater range and choice of learning *sources*, which in turn may lead to other fortuitous and hitherto unexpected openings and opportunities for extending and enhancing an individual's talents and development, since '*learning begets learning*'

- sometimes involved with learning and development, which, in the profit-conscious world of business, may appear to be only marginally relevant to the individual's current role and performance needs; its credibility, continuing support – and success – therefore, depend upon mentors who possess

  - clear, well-focused visions of opportunities and likely alternative scenarios
  - realistic longer-term perceptions of people's potential
  - developed and informed awareness of how the world is changing and what emerging imperatives are critical
  - creative understanding of the ways in which career patterns are moving within the changing business world

- the ability to sense and give definition to as yet untapped potential or previously untested talent
- the courage to break out of conventional wisdom and take intelligent risks in promoting, developing and using talent.

Though still too rare in most organisations, such people are at the very heart of effective mentoring and, therefore, intelligent talent management.

If coaching is primarily about helping people to see and do things *differently, mentoring is about investing human potential and uniqueness with major significance and relevance.* Ian McMonagle, a talented consultant operating out of Tynemouth, has evolved a relevant and practical model (Figure 20) that effectively links coaching and mentoring to the core skill of listening and also, more importantly, to one another, as a *progression* in:

❐ the increasing scope of talent management

❐ the breadth and depth of the learning perspectives involved

❐ commitment to the learning relationship between mentor and 'learner'.

Viewed in the context of the model, mentoring, with coaching as an inherent element, becomes tantamount to helping people manage – and use – their todays better, in order to shape their tomorrows.

Identifying and Mentoring Talent and Potential

As explained at the beginning of Chapter 3, *within* the context of this book talent is taken to mean: *exceptional* ability and achievement that is *regularly* demonstrated across either a range of situations or tasks, or within a more specialised and narrower field of expertise. Potential is viewed as consistent high ability in activities that indicate *comparable and transferable* competence in situations not as yet encountered by the individual.

Talent, then, may be considered as demonstrable outstanding ability that leads to *realised* high performance and results, in any number of relevant fields of activity. Potential is, in a sense, latent or *unrealised* talent that, although deemed to be transferable, is often difficult to prove or measure realistically. In young people, especially, where the

FIGURE 20 Listening, Coaching and Mentoring

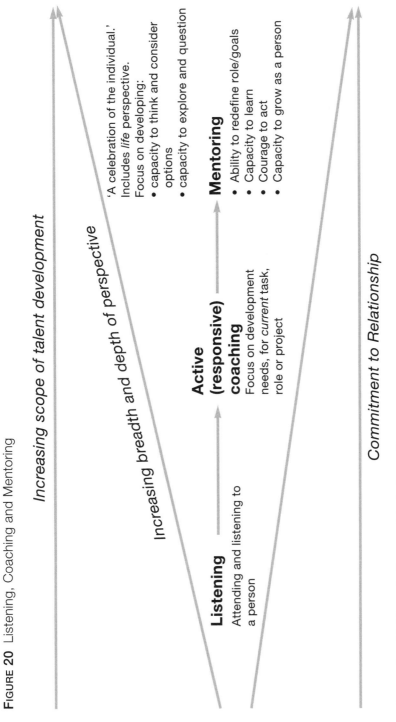

Increasing scope of talent development

Increasing breadth and depth of perspective

Listening
Attending and listening to a person

Active (responsive) coaching
Focus on development needs, for *current* task, role or project

Mentoring
Ability to redefine role/goals
• Capacity to learn
• Courage to act
• Capacity to grow as a person

'A celebration of the individual.'
Includes *life* perspective.
Focus on developing:
• capacity to think and consider options
• capacity to explore and question

Commitment to Relationship

Source: Ian McMonagle Partnership (adapted)

period of greatest maturation is normally between the ages of 18 and 28, 'ultimate' potential may be virtually impossible to define and give shape to.

In formative periods, particularly, where major development and growth may be taking place, the concept of a series of 'horizons' in potential may represent the most relevant and realistic way of considering the likely transformation of an individual and hence significant improvement in their mindset, competence and confidence. The mentoring of evolving talent and progressively realised potential takes the form of the process illustrated in Figure 21, where successive stages of personal development and growth each represent a transition from the 'me as I am right now' to the 'me as I could be in X months'/years' time' (what might be described as the 'plus me').

The assessment of an individual's current talent is expressed as the 'me as I am right now', which is a summary of key relevant strengths – and weaknesses ('areas for development'). As a matter of 'functional maturity' (can do – will do), the strengths and areas for development need to be seen as matters of both skill and will, so that confidence and commitment are identified as 'plusses' and 'minuses', against agreed expectations, just as much as competence needs to be.

Horizons in potential, which represent the milestones against which to plan development action, are usually best expressed in months rather than years. Time spans, however, will depend upon individual circumstances, such as:

❏ the age of the individual

❏ the rate of organisational change

❏ the pace of technological advances

❏ changing policies and strategies

❏ fast-track (or otherwise) pace of career progression.

Typically, however, the gap between horizons is likely to vary between 12 and 30 months, which acts as both a necessary stimulus and 'speedometer' to the mentoring development process.

Confirming the 'current' strengths and areas for development – and the mentoring of each emerging 'plus me' – is usually most effectively carried out through the developing individual to regular role or job enrichment, as illustrated in Figure 22. Experience of working in the field, both as manager and consultant, seems to suggest that the

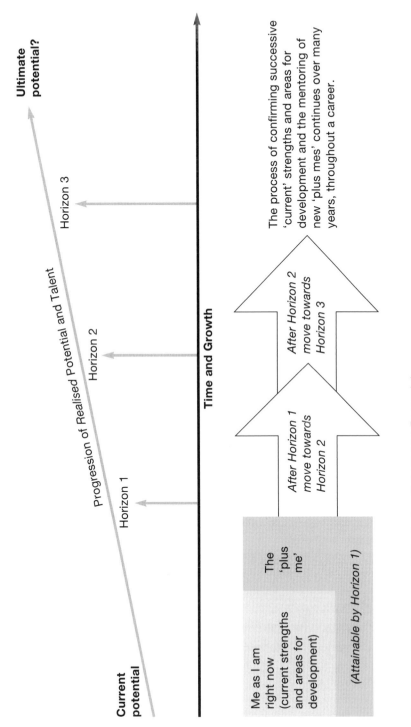

Current potential

Progression of Realised Potential and Talent

Horizon 1   Horizon 2   Horizon 3

Ultimate potential?

Time and Growth

Me as I am right now (current strengths and areas for development)

The 'plus me'

(Attainable by Horizon 1)

After Horizon 1 move towards Horizon 2

After Horizon 2 move towards Horizon 3

The process of confirming successive 'current' strengths and areas for development and the mentoring of new 'plus mes' continues over many years, throughout a career.

FIGURE 21 Confirming and Mentoring Talent and Potential

common enrichment linkage between the *role as it is* and the *role as it could be* (the 'plus role') needs to focus on three critical aspects of work:

- ❑ what I enjoy doing, ie what starts – and keeps – the adrenaline pumping

- ❑ what I do well, ie contributions to wider success, as well as self-fulfilment, via the exercising of growing competences – and the experience of 'flow'

- ❑ challenges that test and 'stretch' me, but that are not so overwhelming that they demotivate or de-skill me.

The linked '*plus me*'/'*plus role*' model suggests that, at times, there will be a rather fine line between coaching and mentoring. However, the *overall* time frames, learning goals and commitments are greater than simply the 'next' horizon. As essentially moving targets, the horizons tend to ensure a continuity of *evolving* learning and development, where the additive nature of mentoring is more apparent.

Mentoring with the 'Plus Me'/'Plus Role' Model

The process begins with a dialogue between the mentor and the person being developed, and typically follows the pattern set out below:

- ❑ The 'trainee' produces a written 'stocktake' of his or her perceived *current major strengths and weaknesses*. (The mentor can also compile his or her own perception of the trainee's strengths and weaknesses for the purpose of comparison and discussion.)

- ❑ Together they agree the likely next 'horizon' date, for example 20 months' ahead.

- ❑ Either individually, or jointly, they agree what the *attainable* 'plus me' of the person being mentored should look like by the horizon date, in terms of

  - ● new strengths and levels of competence to be acquired

  - ● existing strengths that should be built upon and developed

  - ● skill levels that must be raised.

- ❑ The discussion then moves from the 'plus me' to the 'plus role' or 'plus job' and how it should be enriched in order to

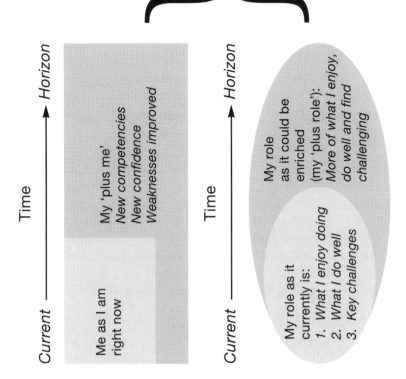

Mentoring regularly interrelates the two 'moving targets' of the 'plus me' and the 'plus job', as a major basis for the continuous development, performance improvement and long-term fulfilment of potential of the individual.

MENTORING

Time —————— → Horizon

Current —————

My 'plus me'
New competencies
New confidence
Weaknesses improved

Me as I am
right now

Time —————— → Horizon

Current —————

My role
as it could be
enriched
(my 'plus role'):
More of what I enjoy,
do well and find
challenging

My role as it
currently is:
1. *What I enjoy doing*
2. *What I do well*
3. *Key challenges*

FIGURE 22 Mentoring: Relating the 'plus me' to the 'plus role'

- increase the scope – and contribution – of the role for the benefit of the business, especially in terms of adding value and improving competitive and collaborative advantage
- create more learning and developmental opportunities.

❏ Together, they confirm what within the *current* role the trainee

- excels at
- contributes significantly and uniquely to the business
- enjoys doing and so derives 'adrenaline flow'
- finds particularly challenging and 'stretching'.

❏ Jointly, the mentor and the individual under development explore how the four facets of the current role listed above might be enhanced and expanded, through role modification and/or job enrichment and so developed as a 'bigger' or deeper 'plus role', which gives the job-holder increased scope both to grow and to contribute.

❏ Both then agree – and confirm – what training, coaching, mentoring and 'enabling' will be needed during the period up to the next horizon date, in order to

- meet the defined development goals of the individual, identified through his or her 'plus me'
- ensure the necessary changes and enrichment to evolve the agreed 'plus role' and its greater scope and contributions
- sustain the continuity of learning necessary to grow into the new 'plus me' and the evolving new 'plus role'.

❏ Finally, both agree and draw up the necessary *development action plan* to facilitate and sanction the 'learning journey' through to the horizon date.

The first actionable steps and key milestones need to be specific and spelled out in sufficient detail to initiate movement – and commitment – in the right direction.

Subsequently, much of the plan will need to be sufficiently responsive to evolving circumstances – *without losing sight of the key learning and developmental goals* – hence the critical importance of:

❏ regular feedback

❏ agreed and adhered-to review dates.

One major strength of this model – apparent over the many years of its evolving use – is that it is very person-specific and provides opportunities to build in many motivational and personal elements into the individual's development – and growth – and the progressive enrichment of his or her contribution to the business.

The 'plus role' element, especially, allows those responsible for managing talent to understand more clearly:

❏ how people view their role and contribution

❏ what they see as the major opportunities and 'blocks' within their current and enhanced roles

❏ what they perceive to be the principal thrust of their role, within the wider context of the business and its market place

❏ whether or not they are appropriately aligned and engaged with the transformation and direction of the business, ie are they really managing today *in order to get to the future as effectively as possible*, or are they largely doing what amounts to 'yesterday's job'?

The model shown in Figures 21 and 22 helps to develop the necessary talent management mindset that recognises the synergy that can exist between coaching and mentoring, and which provides the necessary leadership 'engine' to ensure:

❏ the optimum appropriate development of the individual

❏ realistic matching – and realignment – of career progression to the progressive recognition and acknowledgement of people's talent and potential

❏ well-managed – and well-led – learning as a critical determinant of organisational as well as individual development, and ultimately the success of the business.

Beyond the Bottom Line – Mentoring for the Future

In the more task- or project-specific role of coach, the manager frequently needs to ask the questions:

- What?

- When?

- Who?

- How?

- What if?

These are by no means the sole prerogative of the coach and are frequently part of the stock-in-trade of the mentor as well. Yet above all, the role of the mentor is to stimulate *purposive reflection* by asking the questions '*Why?*' and '*Why not?*' Its focus is often more diffuse than that of coaching, and is directed beyond *immediate* solutions and results, towards change, transformation and growth. In the longer term, mentoring is one of the most critical and powerful influences in managing talent.

The progressive move to more challenging, opportunistic and 'bespoke' work experiences is akin to shifting away from climbing the traditional career 'ladders' to scaling, clambering over and scrambling through a 3-D climbing frame. The holes, chutes, tunnels, slides and obstacles built into this much more complex frame present a far greater range of challenges, opportunities and experiences than any ordinary ladder. Mentoring, then, is primarily about:

- creating valid and relevant learning opportunities for talented people to help them align with the business, yet grow and fulfil their unique potential as individuals

- providing regular stimulus and feedback on performance – and development – to generate necessary awareness and sense of personal responsibility in the individual

- triggering adrenaline and passion, along with the directional sense and focused aspiration that a developed personal vision can provide as a necessary basis to motivated career pathfinding and progression

- helping people to see and do things differently (like coaching)

- a *continuous* process of helping people to develop themselves

- being a way of leading and managing others that *actively and expressly* acknowledges the effective management, development and deployment of people as a crucial managerial responsibility.

What Makes a 'Good' Mentor?

❝ *Current 'best' practice involves building pools of coaches and mentors on whom the company can rely.* ❞

As with so much leadership and management, there is no *one* 'right' style or approach to mentoring. Research from PDI[3] was conducted amongst both US and European companies in the period 1996–8 and sought to differentiate between state of the art and state of the practice in talent management. It confirmed that current 'best' practice involves *building pools of coaches and mentors on whom the company can rely* – with the obvious recognition that not every manager or leader is, *de facto*, a 'good' mentor. Further research into mentoring practices within client companies in the USA, UK and much of Western Europe indicates that the most effective mentors possess certain essential *empathic* competences that distinguish them from the less capable and sensitive, namely:

❐ an ability to recognise and work with the other person's truth and being

❐ a capacity to work with others *with commitment*, – intellectually, emotionally and even spiritually – and to range over these various channels of communication and interaction appropriately as the relationship develops

❐ a readiness to pose challenges – and accept possible failure – without 'punishment', threat or overcritical judgement

❐ the ability to convey confidence, trust and belief in others and their ideas

❐ a mature outlook and balanced life philosophy, where *respect* for others is apparent

❐ an ability to stimulate and motivate those whom they mentor to

   ● take, exploit and develop the opportunities of ownership, autonomy and personal accountability that empowerment offers

   ● keep open and develop, for themselves and for others, opportunities for learning in as many forms as possible

   ● communicate with clarity and impact, so striking the right chords with people

- act with necessary courage and determination to make sure that what should happen does happen

❐ be capable of creating what Morris, Meed and Sverson[4] term '*co-operative self-sufficiency*', where mature self-reliance is able to alternate, appropriately, with collaborative mutual effort and enterprise

❐ possess 'social radar', with the capacity to trigger and sustain 'peak communication' with others and to generate and release productive synergy and creativity.

As Bennis, Parikh and Lessem[5] affirm in *Beyond Leadership*, today's 'new paradigm' manager is primarily acting in the role of *transformational leader*. He or she is not a developer first and foremost, but a revolutionary. In such a role, the leader acts as an explorer or adventurer – not merely a traveller, and even less a passenger – and, in so doing, commits to a journey of 'truly heroic proportion'.

In a world where certainty and the accurate, assured prediction of a future state of affairs is becoming a more and more unrealistic expectation, the mentor needs to provide the intellectual – and emotional – stimulus and visionary frameworks to promote exploration of:

❐ the evolving and responsive *sense of direction* for an organisation, its business and its people

❐ opportunities to see – and give – sharper definition to *potential* and '*productive uncertainty*'

❐ scope to *imagine and think through possible alternative* transformation goals and strategies

❐ the opportunity to integrate disparate and even seemingly contradictory aspects of the business, by creating a *possible new unity* from apparent paradoxes, ie helping people to conceptualise the business and to see interdependence where none may have been apparent before

❐ the need to crystallise purpose and direction, and so to provide a source of coherence and motivation for people

❐ an accurate reflection of current realities.

Far more than simply a 'jumble of superlatives', a vision needs to crystallise and grow out of a feel for an organisation's roots and traditions and out of its current activities, as well as serving as the desired future state and shape of the business. As Dr Carol O'Connor[6] says, 'Vision is the quality which allows us to see potential and imagine how this can transform everyday life.'

In the information age, visionary competence and the ability to create, communicate and share a picture, based upon an ambitious but realistic sense of the future of an organisation, will remain one of the major strengths of effective leaders, especially in the role of mentor. Warren Bennis and Burt Nanus[7] emphasise the centrality of envisioning as a core *leadership* competence in the following way:

> If there is a spark of genius in the leadership function at all, it must lie in this transcending ability . . . to assemble out of the variety of image, signals, forecasts and alternatives – a clearly articulated vision of the future that is at once simple, easily understood, clearly desirable and energising.

Vision is more than an end in itself: it provides context and perspective for the strategies of the organisation and the endeavours of people. In times of pressure, change and uncertainty, it can also act as a rallying point, especially where it is underpinned with strong shared values and beliefs. Increasingly, it would seem, the world is becoming a place where there is less certainty, little security, but almost limitless choice and opportunity. Hand in hand with most opportunity goes risk – especially in what are essentially arenas of *productive uncertainty*. In such conditions, particularly, *opportunity* may well:

❒ emerge unexpectedly, or suddenly, calling for swift, decisive and courageous action

❒ appear 'in disguise' and not always be immediately recognisable

❒ occur haphazardly, randomly or fortuitously and, therefore, not in logical sequence or familiar patterns

❒ arrive as a 'one-off' or short-term aberration, so catching people off guard or unprepared

❒ involve considerable change and 'hassle'.

Arriving on the scene in any of these forms, opportunity can so easily generate in people:

❒ fear, risk aversion and resistance to leaving comfort zones

❒ preservation and protection of the status quo

❐ anxiety and the inertia of doubt, suspicion and defensiveness

❐ self-inflicted and often imagined constraints or obstacles to moving forward.

Vision, derived from the powerful and optimistic synergy of sophisticated information, respect for knowledge and strategic competence – as well as realistically crystallised aspiration – represents one of the most effective ways of 'creating' the future, in conditions of uncertainty. To be fully effective, however, such visionary and organic work styles need to be linked by the reciprocal professional rights and obligations of shared ownership and *interdependence* within the wider organisation. At strategic and operational levels, such forms of adaptable working are in a state of post-revolutionary *evolution*, where the need (and opportunities) for continuous learning and the development of knowledge are paramount.

❝ At their most fundamental, organisations represent the interplay of people, power and politics. ❞

In such arenas, opportunities exist, too, for new *counter-productive boundaries*, elitism, exclusion and other dysfunctional behaviours. New identities, new, often assumed, territorial rights and new (often equally assumed) authority can create major disruptive or even destructive forces within 'flatter', networked and more 'organic' organisations. Hirschhorn and Gilmore[8] describe the origins, form and outcomes of many of these new boundaries that may emerge in the so-called 'boundaryless' company. They make the point that, though previous work roles, boundaries and rigid hierarchies – as defined by the formal organisation structure – might have changed to provide for more adaptive working, the old differences in authority, competence and talent have not necessarily just disappeared. *At their most fundamental, organisations represent the interplay of people, power and politics.* As people struggle to define and enact new roles for themselves within more flexible organisations, self-preservation, protection of territory and power play will all continue to make their presence felt.

The challenges, therefore, facing visionary leaders include not only mentoring talented individuals and *enabling* well-motivated interdependent teams to work even more effectively, but to work through – and catalyse – solutions to the psychological, political, role and identity boundaries that beg such questions as:

❏ Who is now in charge of what and in charge of whom?

❏ Who now does what and in which circumstances?

❏ Who is accountable for what?

❏ Who, exactly, are 'we' and who is/isn't part of 'us'?

❏ So, what's in it for me/us?

Dramatic remapping and repositioning of traditional or existing functional and hierarchical boundaries has taken place – and will continue to occur – in businesses and organisations. This is an inevitable outcome of continuous organisational transformation and adaptation. The processes of mentoring and thus 'enabling' in such conditions become more:

❏ complex and less readily understood

❏ dependent upon an understanding of what transformation is about within a particular organisation and its strategic/operational arenas

❏ reliant upon a variety of – and synergy between – *different* disciplines

❏ the responsibility of an 'enabling team' – not simply that of one manager or leader, where there are both mentors and sponsors working in collaboration

❏ one in which people themselves have both accountability and ownership of coaching, mentoring and sponsoring.

Sponsoring Talent

As Horace Walpole once said, 'They who cannot perform great things themselves may yet have satisfaction in doing justice to those who can.' In faster-transforming and more complex organisational structures and hierarchies, sponsorship would seem to be one means of short-circuiting the uncertainty of serendipity, which seems to characterise the development, use and management of talent in some companies. If management's objective is to ensure the optimum deployment of talent, where and when it is needed most, four – often interdependent – aspects of sponsorship emerge. They are:

❏ championing

❐ protecting

❐ gatekeeping

❐ organisational 'do-how'.

1 *Championing*

'Championing', as a key element of sponsorship, is the promotional complement to the encouraging, supportive development of mentoring. Like the kindred sponsoring activities of *protecting* and *gatekeeping*, championing underlines the frequently necessary roles of 'guardian' or 'patron', which can be so critical to publicising and capitalising upon the talent that coaching and mentoring develop. Essentially, championing is a process aimed at securing appropriate recognition of people whose talents and potential need to be better used and managed for the good of the organisation and its business. Typically, championing may involve:

❐ identifying and highlighting people of talent and potential

❐ publicising, promoting and *advancing* such competences and strengths within the right circles and spheres of influence across the organisation

❐ identifying likely instances of person–role 'fit' within the business and drawing top management's attention to such potential matches

❐ seeking out appropriate career-progress opportunities for specific people within the business

❐ generating interest and, above all, a *'talent management mindset'* amongst key players in the business, about likely protégés and high performers

❐ generally providing *active* and appropriate 'patronage', with its implications of facilitative, authoritative organisational support.

2 *Protecting*

Whereas 'championing' is primarily a promotional activity involving 'push', patronage and the enthusing of likely 'buyers' of talent within the business, *protecting* essentially engages the 'guardian angel' role that managers may need to play to advance protégés through organisational minefields and power play. 'Protecting' is typically likely to involve:

❏ acting as a strategic or operational 'umbrella', under which people may take appropriate action, with comparative freedom, safety and impunity

❏ going 'out on a limb' on behalf of a protégé, in order to give active support as well as 'protection'

❏ creating 'safe havens' of relevant support around the organisation in order to reinforce influence and power bases, eg 'Talk with Jim and Bart about this. I think you'll find that they would back a proposal like that'

❏ creating an environment of adequate security within which protégés may contribute with optimum impact and 'grow' as people of talent and potential.

❝ Both championing and protecting are important elements in the overall process of talent management. ❞

Both championing and protecting are important elements in the overall process of *talent management* since, jointly, they are dedicated leadership interventions aimed at:

❏ taking people with requisite contributory talent forward – into roles and relationships where they can be more productive and optimally aligned with corporate direction

❏ increasing people's visibility and accessibility within the organisation – and its operational environment

❏ providing such individuals – and teams – with sufficient legitimisation, support and ratification to be able to deliver effectively

❏ creating the necessary functional, cross-functional and hierarchical support to make things happen that otherwise might not occur successfully

❏ establishing professional patronage and sponsorship as legitimate, critical and appropriate alternatives to nepotism, the 'old boy network' and mere 'halo effect', in succession planning, career progression and the management of talent generally.

Championing and *protecting* help in creating teams and groups of *the richest possible mixes of talent*, in ways that are more adaptive – and responsive – to the constantly changing needs of the business.

3 *Gatekeeping*

Within the context of talent management, 'gatekeeping' consists principally of interventions by sponsors that typically:

❑ open doors and make accessible to talented individuals key people of influence, who are capable of using their talents and contributions to the business; they may be within or outside the organisation, but are usually central to its continuing success and development

❑ build necessary 'bridges' in relationships, between protégés and key players, to facilitate growth and strengthening of appropriate productive interaction between the two – in effect, a 'matchmaking' role

❑ help to remove barriers of status, rank, distance and accessibility that otherwise might impede – or even make impossible – contact between those being sponsored and those who might use, develop and progress them further in their careers.

Gatekeeping, like so much of sponsoring and, indeed, talent management, relies heavily on such competences as:

❑ networking skills and the development of wide-ranging networks, both inside and outside the business

❑ high 'political' acumen and awareness in relevant strategic as well as operational arenas of the business

❑ diplomatic skills and social acuity appropriate to the spheres of actual and intended influence, ie the ability to play the roles of 'diplomat' or even 'elder statesman' rather just 'politician'

❑ sufficient personal – and professional – credibility and 'clout' to be accepted and respected by those whose patronage, support and backing are being solicited

❑ adequate and appropriate standing, based upon *power competence* derived from formal role authority as well as expertise, style and connections.

4 *Organisational 'do-how'*

Organisational 'do-how' may have connotations of backstage activity, or *'facipulation'* – a term coined by Tom Cummings of Leading Ventures to describe manipulative facilitation – since sponsorship may, necessarily, include finding ways through organisational politics and pecking orders. Conflicting vested interests, assumed and real territorial 'rights', and issues of status, position and hence *power*, may all work against the advancement of what is seen as threatening talent, energy and ambition. Changing the status quo, transforming the organisation and its business, 'boundary-busting' and injecting a new order of things – however necessary – while seen as essential by the agents of change, may be viewed by the 'establishment' as heresy, revolution or insurrection and, therefore, activities to be resisted at all costs.

Where the aim of sponsorship is to deploy transformational talent where it is likely to be most effective, organisational 'do-how' of the highest order may be vital to secure *bridgeheads of change*, within the business, to enable the change agents to function with optimum effect and outcomes. Like so much of talent management, sponsorship seeks to replace the uncertainty of serendipity with conscious, effective strategy, while recognising that 'adhocery' and resourceful adaptation are also essential to the successful deployment of talent within a transforming business.

Organisational 'do-how', then, is primarily about:

☐ the effective use of *power competence* in dealing with the blockages within the organisation, ie the preparedness and *ability* to use organisational 'clout'

☐ high levels of political awareness and the ability to 'read' situations, in terms of *realpolitik*, as well as moral, ethical or 'ideal' standards; it is in the area of political sensitivity that women can sometimes be significantly more effective than men: as Margaret Thatcher said, '*If you want somebody to talk in politics, get a man; if you want somebody to take action, get a woman*'

☐ networking skills and lobbying, where 'networking' is defined as '*the ability to secure necessary goodwill and backing, from others, primarily by means of direct, and/or indirect, oral communication*'; lobbying and networking may need to take place both within and without the organisation in order to open doors for talented people

☐ acuity and well-developed *skill* in what Buchanan and Boddy[9] term 'backstage activity', where informed opportunism, developing coalitions, creating pressure groups and securing the support of influential and power figures are typical 'political' strategies needed to underpin the sponsoring and advancement of people

❏ understanding how the business functions as a whole, how the constituent 'domains' interact, and to whom to go for specific information, backing or influence

❝ Ignoring the growing 'information culture' of business, by inappropriately short-circuiting the information systems, can prove counter-productive in businesses. ❞

❏ understanding the management information systems (MISs) and the roles of key 'knowledge workers' who generate, process and transmit information that is fundamental to the functioning of the business (Figure 23 shows, in terms of 'organisational architecture', the *increasing degree of dependence* that businesses now have upon the continuous flow of critical management information); ignoring the growing 'information culture' of business, by inappropriately short-circuiting the information systems, can prove counterproductive in businesses where

- *information systems* are central to creative decision-making and integrative control
- *information networks* are necessary to collect, share and disseminate the information required
- increasing numbers of *information workers*, who are skilled in IT, information analysis and screen-based visualisation, underpin the functioning of the MIS
- *information cultures* evolve necessarily to transfer and share information and reflect upon its significance, rather than simply arguing about 'facts' *per se*, and to add value to information, *via collective, cross-functional or multi-stakeholder activity.*

In developing and using vital organisational know-how, the common-sense philosophy of Reg Revans[10] remains, as ever, highly appropriate, namely to establish:

❏ who *knows* about the problem

❏ who *cares* about it

❏ who *can do* something about it.

Out of these contacts, which Revans terms 'temporary coalitions of power', emerges the *start* of an effective organisational support basis for:

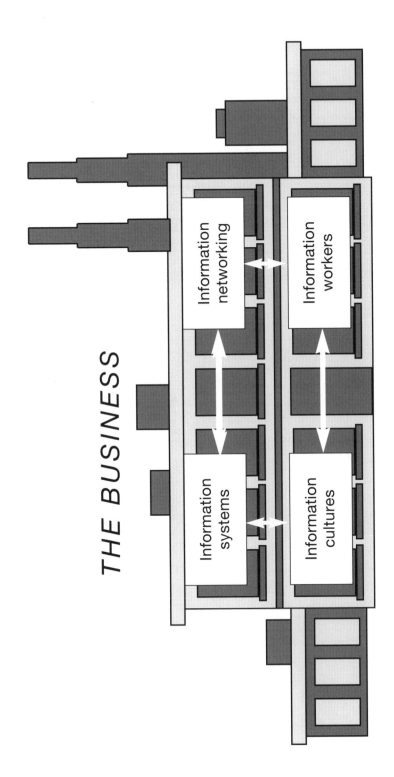

FIGURE 23 The Virtual Organisation

❏ formulating, initiating and bringing about necessary change

❏ generating appropriate viable solutions to problems

❏ developing the necessary collaborative environment in which the sponsorship of capable protégés is more likely to succeed and produce results.

Buchanan and Boddy[11] emphasise the value of strategies that involve using and managing the support offered by the so-called 'invisible team'. Essentially, this consists of those sources of potential collaboration, support and information, which are frequently ignored or not fully exploited. These include:

❏ other stakeholders in the business, such as suppliers and clients or customers

❏ external contractors, subcontractors and support services

❏ internal support functions whose influence, contacts and expertise may not have been effectively elicited and used

❏ mentors, 'fixers' and 'smoothers' who, variously, by education, 'facipulation' or sound 'lubrication' smooth the way, open up possibilities and promote individuals or teams within, across and outside the organisation

❏ gatekeepers who have access to key players and contacts both inside and outside the business.

Such relatively 'invisible' sources of help may open up channels, opportunities and new contacts for those being sponsored that the more obvious relationships may have failed to deliver. Understanding how the organisation *actually* works, knowing who the real influencers and power figures are, and recognising the tribal roots and imperatives of the organisation's culture – as well as being familiar with its information systems – are essential to *effective* sponsorship in today's businesses.

SUMMARY

Mentoring

Coaching is primarily concerned with *finite* learning, development and improvement goals over relatively short periods of time, whereas mentoring is aimed at fulfilling the individual's contributive potential, on a progressive, continuing and *additive* basis. David Megginson[12] distinguishes between the two related processes by describing mentoring as the kind of help that assists people *over* any transition *between* stages, whereas coaching contributes more to a person's development *within* stages. On a comparative basis, mentoring and coaching look like Table 6.

TABLE **6** Coaching v Mentoring

Coaching	Mentoring
• Concentrates on task and role performance	• Focuses on life and the individual as a whole person
• Short-term focus	• Longer-term perspective
• 'Close-up' lens	• 'Wide-angle' and total lens
• Helps people to see and do things differently	• Challenges – and opens up – mindsets and behaviours
• Presents 'models' for learning and development	• Presents a 'mirror' as a basis for learning and development
• Based upon a tutoring relationship, where tutoring tends to be unilateral	• Based upon a learning relationship, where there is often mutual learning
• Results- and outcome-driven	• Values- and vision-driven
• Focus on skills development	• Concern with continuous growth
• Tends to be more active and concerned with specifics	• More conceptual and aimed at general development

In this chapter, the concept of '*plus me*' and the related '*plus role*' are introduced to underline the long-term close relationship between the individual's 'learning journey' and growth as a person and the intrinsic scope for job enrichment and role growth that exist within the vast majority of roles, given imagination, resourcefulness and informed courage on the part of both mentor and mentored. A key concept in the '*plus me*'/'*plus role*' model is that of '*horizons*' in potential. As organisations become 'de-layered' and thus 'flatter', so career patterns are changing from climbing traditional 'promotion ladders' to manoeuvring through the challenges and variety of outlets offered by a '3-D climbing frame' mode of career *progression*. 'Career' now is coming to be seen as the sum total of a working life's experiences in a variety of *lateral*, temporary and transient roles, as well as through vertical moves and promotion opportunities.

Being a mentor is a demanding role, and experience suggests that relatively few directors and managers possess the inclination to operate in what is primarily a helping capacity. A preoccupation with bottom-line results, personal survival and competitive career stakes means that many executives are, perhaps understandably, preoccupied with their own agenda and their own particular lot. Effective mentoring demands a good deal of selflessness at times, as well as long-term perspective and sufficient organisational 'savvy' to create the right climate, opportunities and motivation for learning – and hence development – to become a reality.

The effective mentor, necessarily, helps both to stimulate and give definition to people's aspirational visions – to their hopes, expectations and personal goals. Aligning those aspirations with known corporate pathways helps people to:

- relate to and 'feel' their personal vision

- give realistic definition to their ambitions

- develop a succession of 'horizons' in their visionary thinking to which they can relate their developing talents – and their potential as individuals.

While people's inspiration and vision may, ultimately, be 'internal' and private, the effective mentor acts as stimulus, 'trigger', catalyst and 'enabler' to the envisioning process. That is one of the crucial contributions of mentoring in the sustained progressive management of talent.

In the overall task of 'enabling', mentoring is a key function since it focuses on and is directed towards the developing maturity and self-sufficiency of the individual. In other words, it is in part a long-term process of helping others to learn how to help themselves to grow as people.

Sponsoring

Sponsoring – like coaching and mentoring – is a fundamental talent management process, but one that tends to occur more 'organically', and often in less obviously structured ways than the others. It may often involve a great deal of 'behind the scenes' activity and personal networking.

There are four principal facets to sponsoring:

1 *championing people and their particular talents* – by promoting, publicising and 'pushing' them

2 *protecting them, by acting as an organisational 'umbrella'* – by creating an environment in which they can experiment, take risks and experience failure without punishment

3 *gatekeeping and making available key players to protégés of talent* by creating useful relationships and networks with supportive, helpful 'knowledge' and 'power' figures, both inside and outside the organisation

4 *organisational 'do-how'* – which involves clearing 'road blocks', opening 'doors' and creating opportunities for people to test out, enhance and widen their skills, through legitimate, necessary, frequently challenging activity; essentially this means understanding

- who *knows* about the problem, issue or opportunity

- who *cares* about it

- who *can* do anything about it.

All these functions – and *arts* – of sponsorship are complementary activities to the processes of coaching and mentoring, in pushing forward, developing and using the talents and competencies of identified and untried people of potential and talent within the business.

Championing

Championing – and its kindred talent management activity, protecting – may require a manager to act as 'guardian angel', who cultivates and acts to safeguard people of talent. On the one hand, the manager needs to promote and push contributive competence. On the other hand, he or she may also need to act as patron and ensure some *organisational immunity* until the protégé has acquired sufficient skill in the arts of political self-defence and mature protectionism within his or her particular business domain. Becoming increasingly important in organisational do-how is an understanding of the business in terms of its management information systems and its inevitably growing IT culture, where value is added to information and knowledge through cross-functional activity and collective interaction.

There are thus many facets to sponsoring people of talent. In this chapter, it has been represented as a critical influencing process, which helps to ensure that those who can do will do – as, when and where necessary. Inevitably, much of sponsorship is likely to be based upon *positive* 'gut feel' about others and their capabilities or potential. Intuitive perception may well provide a powerful – and realistic – basis to judgement when it is backed up by other sources of information, such as track record, psychometric data, where available, and verified feedback on behaviour and performance.

ACTION – THEORY INTO PRACTICE

- Please complete the *Talent Mentoring Profile* on page 235.

  - As far as possible, please use it as a 360-degree instrument.

  - Work through the issues – and the actions that you might need to take – with the key players in your team.

  - Discuss the implications of a mentor for *you* with your manager.

- Using the *'plus-me'/'plus role'* model as your basis, identify the development needs, job-enrichment opportunities and mentoring plans for at least two high-performing/high-potential people.

  - In the *'plus me'* part, consider both the *skill* and the *will* elements of strengths and areas for development.

  - Set realistic horizons against which to formulate mentoring plans and actions.

  - In the *'plus role'* part, identify what the individual *does well, what they enjoy doing and what 'stretching' challenges exist in their current role.*

  - Agree how these three motivational elements can be enhanced, or expanded, in a new *'plus role'*.

  - Link personal growth to role enrichment in your mentoring plans.

- 'Brainstorm' with three or four colleagues – especially those with whom you are likely to experience the *creative synergy* that comes from 'peak communication' – ideas for making greater use of mentoring within the areas that you, collectively, manage in the business. Use the strength of collective enthusiasm and mutual support to move things along.

- Please complete the *Talent Sponsoring Profile* on page 239.

  - Work through the *'Action points'* of the profile.

  - Where is the greatest impact that you currently make as a result of sponsorship activities with people of outstanding talent and potential?

  - What more could – and should – you be doing to act as 'patron', 'guardian' or sponsor within the business?

  - Carry out a similar 'brainstorm' exercise to that identified above with talented colleagues to agree how sponsoring could become more of an applied art and help to younger talented people within your organisation. Agree the first actionable steps and start implementing.

Endnotes

1 WILLIAMS M. R. *Enabling – Beyond empowering.* London, Thorogood, 1998.

2 LEWIS G. *The Mentoring Manager.* London, Institute of Personnel and Development/Pitman, 1996.

3 Research conducted internationally, 1996–8, Personal Decisions International.

4 MORRIS S., MEED J. *and* SVERSEN N. *The Knowledge Manager – Adding value in the information age.* London, Pitman, 1996.

5 BENNIS W., PARIKH J. *and* LESSEM R. *Beyond Leadership.* Oxford, Blackwell, 1994.

6 O'CONNOR C. *Proceedings, Hawksmere Adair Leadership Programme.* November 1997.

7 BENNIS W. *and* NANUS B. *Leaders.* New York, Harper & Row, 1985.

8 HIRSCHHORN L. *and* GILMORE T. 'The new boundaries of the boundaryless company'. *Harvard Business Review.* May–June 1992.

9 BUCHANAN D. *and* BODDY D. *The Expertise of the Change Agent.* London, Prentice Hall, 1992.

10 REVANS R. *The ABC of Action Learning.* Bromley, Chartwell-Bratt, 1983.

11 BUCHANAN D. and BODDY D. *The Expertise of the Change Agent.* London, Prentice Hall, 1992.

12 MEGGINSON D. 'Instructor, coach, mentor: three ways of helping for managers'. *MEAD Journal.* Vol. 19, Part 1. Spring 1988.

CHAPTER

Empowering Talent

You know empowerment is working when people down the line start pushing us with their initiatives ... there's a real buzz around the place – you can feel *the excitement.*

Nick Kendal, CEO, Ekco Packaging

Autonomy with Responsibility – 'Freedom within a Framework'

Just as we have seen in previous chapters, managing talent is a process of interweaving coaching, mentoring and sponsoring with intelligent leadership and management. So, too, effective empowerment depends upon the sound interplay of at least four processes (see Table 7).

There are two sides to the empowerment coin:

1 Managers must be willing to let go – and take some risks – so that others can get going (*the 'freedom'*). They must clearly spell out the parameters, imperatives and ground rules within which autonomy

TABLE 7 Effective Empowerment

• clear delegation	⎫ *the manager's*
• appropriate releases of power	⎬ *competency*
• appropriate functional maturity	⎫ *the job-holder's*
• readiness to assume ownership.	⎬ *competency*

and initiative need to be exercised (*the 'framework'*).

2 People, for their part, are committed to taking ownership of both the freedom and the responsibility that it brings. They have the experience and competence necessary to exercise freedom and deliver the goods.

> **66** *Managing talent is a process of interweaving coaching, mentoring and sponsoring with intelligent leadership and management.* **99**

The reality is that in any organised and civilised society the practice of freedom without commensurate responsibility will not be allowed to continue for very long without some form of effective intervention and control. Reason and common sense dictate that autonomy and responsibility must go hand in hand for either to succeed – especially in the management of organised, interdependent human enterprise. Autonomy without appropriate responsibility and responsibility without adequate freedom to act are simply not acceptable.

In discussion, the majority of managers are likely to agree with this as a principle, but as Will Rogers once said: 'Liberty doesn't work as well in practice as it does in speeches.' The practical problems of creating and managing equilibrium inherent in the concept of 'freedom within a framework' lie largely in the following issues:

❑ the *qualitative*, rather than the quantitative, nature of such measures as

- to what extent?
- how far?
- which is the best way?

❑ optimisation v maximisation

- long- v short-term impact
- competing priorities

❑ individual circumstances that are unique or exceptional and, therefore, do not fit existing precedent and 'case law' within the business

❑ the new precedents and 'what-ifs' that are typical of complex business decisions – particularly when moving into new and uncharted territory

❑ change and transformation, as they impact upon the organisation and its business, and the consequent requirement for innovative behaviours, responses and solutions

❏ the need to deal 'politically' and managerially with resistant or revolutionary factions that emerge within the organisation in response to change

❏ the necessary but often contentious process of 'boundary-busting'

❏ the quality of confidence and trust that exists between empowerer and empowered and, therefore, the fundamental 'chemistry' of their working relationship

❏ the 'functional maturity' (personal competence, commitment and confidence) and therefore perceived 'skill and will' of the person being empowered and delegated to.

The behavioural stereotypes in Figure 24 are representative and typical and have been selected to reinforce the need for a *balance* between autonomy and responsibility that is essentially what 'freedom within a framework' seeks to bring about, through effective *talent management.*

High autonomy – low responsibility

'Box 1' in Figure 24 is essentially the area of misadventure, rash decision-making or action, and irresponsible disregard for common sense, objective analysis, valid past experience and even the rule of law. Behaviour may typically be characterised by:

❏ inadequate examination of information and insufficient diagnosis

❏ lack, or abandonment, of sound, evaluative judgement

❏ insufficient identification and explanation of options

❏ inadequate reflection and, hence, hasty, ill-thought-through decision-making

❏ impetuosity, impulsiveness and/or disaffection

❏ 'testosterone' or macho self-presentation

❏ unilateralism and an absence of team-working

❏ pursuit of personal kudos, power or 'glory'

❏ high egocentricity and arrogance.

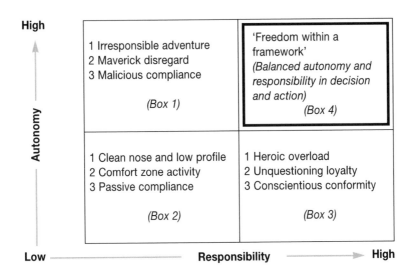

High

Autonomy

1 Irresponsible adventure 2 Maverick disregard 3 Malicious compliance *(Box 1)*	'Freedom within a framework' *(Balanced autonomy and responsibility in decision and action)* *(Box 4)*
1 Clean nose and low profile 2 Comfort zone activity 3 Passive compliance *(Box 2)*	1 Heroic overload 2 Unquestioning loyalty 3 Conscientious conformity *(Box 3)*

Low ————————— **Responsibility** ————→ **High**

FIGURE 24 Freedom within a Framework

This particular 'box', based upon a combination of *high power/personal autonomy but low responsibility*, is not simply the repository for maverick deviation from the norm, or high-handed misadventure and cavalier dismissiveness. Were all the occupants of Box 1 to be brash, ambitious, driving and presumptuous *arrivistes* they would, in fact, present an almost 'ideal' challenge to competent, enabling managers. The bumptious would-be entrepreneur, the indiscipline of the maverick and the lack of restraint of the 'loose cannon' frequently provide the potential 'heart', as well as 'head' *of the talented* for:

☐ differential advantage

☐ boundary-busting

☐ new, creative unorthodoxy and unconventional thinking

☐ readiness to challenge and test established doctrines and dogma

☐ preparedness to reject or overturn the status quo

☐ circumvention of 'orders from above'

☐ the drive to seek answers to the questions 'why?' and 'why not?'

❝ *There is often a wealth of potential competence waiting to be tapped, released and creatively channelled in most organisations.* **❞**

When these attributes are positively managed and led, they can be developed as productive restlessness and channelled into a good deal of added value that more staid, conventional and historically accepted ways of doing things may be incapable of delivering. Such behaviour, too, when intelligently mobilised, can often provide more direct routes to state-of-the-art thinking and practices by short-circuiting obstructive bureaucracy, unnecessary risk-aversion and a dinosaur mentality. On the classic poacher-turned-gamekeeper principle, there is often a wealth of potential competence waiting to be tapped, released and creatively channelled in most organisations.

One likely cause of misadventure, impetuosity and misdirected energy, is that a good many people of potential are:

❐ understretched

❐ underdeveloped

❐ most important of all, underused.

The other, decidedly less attractive and potentially more destructive inhabitants of Box 1 are the *minimalists and maliciously compliant*. Whereas the undisciplined mavericks are usually 'temporary lodgers' and can be moved by intelligent enabling into Box 4, 'freedom within a framework', the organisational malefactors are more likely to be long-term, if not permanent, habitués of Box 1. Frequently intelligent people, whose mental – if not always emotional – potential far exceeds their performance and delivery, these are the individuals whose 'political' and private agenda are more seriously at variance with the official objectives, aims and vision of the business. Such lack of goal congruence and commitment may be compounded by personal antagonism and 'bad chemistry' in their relationships with their manager and/or colleagues. The maliciously compliant emerge in many forms, including:

❐ business-world counterparts of the (fictional) Good Soldier Schweik, who essentially lived by his wits and by carrying out his superiors' orders to the letter – to absolve himself from any blame ('I only did what I was told to do, sir') and prove what incompetent idiots some of his officers were

❏ people who are anti-establishment on principle – or because being 'different' provides them with a perverse form of the kudos, status and recognition that are parodies of those usually offered by formal offices

❏ the 'enemies of opportunity' or 'PPOs' ('project prevention officers'), who typically:

- observe, monitor and criticise
- deny the value of diversity and differentials
- concentrate on risks and risk analysis
- discount or deny the true value of opportunity
- procrastinate, delay and avoid
- overanalyse and so paralyse
- constrain, impede or block, rather than encouraging and empowering

❏ individuals who make greater use than most of 'psychological' or 'power' games in their interactions with others – especially with those who depend upon them or are in hierarchically superior roles; power play, 'politicking' and hence 'power competence' become exceptionally important to some individuals, particularly those whose personal agenda stems from deep-seated resentments or chips – instead of epaulettes – on their shoulders.

Low responsibility – low autonomy

Box 2 is the repository of the unnecessarily careful, essentially risk-averse and 'don't-want-any-hassle' individuals. It is primarily the domain of what White, Hodgson and Crainer[1] term 'difficult learning', which requires overcoming fear of failure, accepting the inherent uncertainty in life and moving out of the 'womb' of comfort zones into the real world. The inhabitants of Box 2 typically demonstrate values, beliefs and behaviours that indicate:

❏ unrealistic reluctance to change, and not bold initiation of transformation and change

❏ complacency and self-protection, and not innovation, creativity and courage

❏ maintaining the status quo, and not breaking the mould

❑ playing things safe, and not pushing out the boundaries

❑ fear of disclosing ignorance, and not readiness to experiment and admit to anxieties about failure and lack of knowledge.

The process of enabling – helping people to see things differently, providing vision and focus – can help create the conditions to bring about the necessary shifts from the former styles of behaviours to the latter.

High responsibility – low autonomy

Box 3 serves to locate the 'willing horses', the hyper-conscientious people who are anxious to please, martyrs to the cause and those whose sense of duty may far exceed their appreciation of professional and managerial reality. Way beyond the demands of the *conscience professionelle*, behaviour and values likely to be encountered amongst the inhabitants of Box 3 often amount to 'perfectionist' standards in dedication, rule adherence, conscientiousness and commitment. In fields where traditional standards of craftsmanship, service or loyalty are essential roots and foundations of success, those whose behaviour and values reflect the 'obedient conformity' and sense of duty of Box 3 are likely to come into their own. Undoubtedly, too, there are times when people temporarily 'leave' other boxes and work for short bursts on a basis of *high responsibility and low autonomy* in order to give maximum compliance and unquestioning support to the dictates of higher authority or the demands of the situation. Where, however, the patterns are largely habitual and out of kilter with the *real* demands of the business, intervention is likely to be essential in order to engender more appropriate and realistic behaviours that depend for effectiveness upon the greater exercise of autonomy, initiative and personal power.

High autonomy – high responsibility

Box 4 is *the 'talent' box* and represents a practical and workable balance between the exercising of personal initiative and freedom and appropriate levels of professional, legal and moral responsibility. One personal aspect of such equilibrium is the *maturity* of the individual, exemplified by the nature and extent of control that he, or she, is able to exercise, legitimately, over his or her own life. This concept is represented diagrammatically by Figure 25, which acknowledges that even the most mature of individuals accepts that some control over his or her activities will – and must – remain in others' hands, in the interest of other people and society in general. The model acknowledges, too, that a good deal of life – especially within a business or working organisation – involves the reciprocation of rights and obligations.

Balance, mutualism and maturity lie at the root of the values and behaviours representative of Box 4; the core theme of 'freedom within a framework' is pursued and continually developed throughout this book.

Understanding What Is 'Mandatory' and 'Discretionary'

Specific and fundamental to the daily working out of the philosophy of 'freedom within a framework' is the need to identify, clarify and crystallise what, within a task, project or role is *mandatory* and what is *discretionary*. This then provides a practical basis for agreeing the degree to which an individual may *give and expect empowerment* – and in which

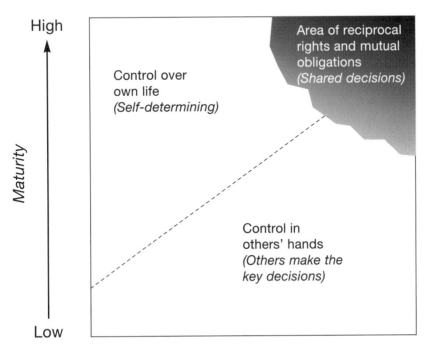

FIGURE 25 Control as an Aspect of Maturity

areas of his or her work. Differentiating between the mandatory and the discretionary allows the job-holder and others to confirm the scope and potential for initiative and enterprise that exists within a project or role – and within the working relationship between the individual, his or her manager and the 'nuclear' contacts of his or her particular role-set. Such differentiation may be based upon a multiplicity of issues, which can vary according to circumstances and occasions, such as:

❑ perceived competence and confidence of the parties involved

❑ competing territorial agendas of the empowerer and empowered

❑ the psychology and politics of pecking order and power differentials

❑ fear, anxiety and a reluctance to 'let go'

❑ genuine pressures of time, but also the 'illusion of urgency' ('it's quicker to do it myself in the circumstances. . .')

❑ individual management and leadership 'styles'.

In Figure 26, the differences between mandatory and discretionary areas of work are presented in terms of role differential in:

❑ *ownership*, and who, therefore, takes charge of which areas of activity

❑ *permission*, and who gives or seeks it

❑ *decision-making*, and who decides what

❑ *action*, and who takes it

❑ *control*, and who exercises it

❑ *referral*, and who, therefore, refers and/or reports to whom.

As a framework for clarifying, confirming and agreeing major parameters for performance outcomes, contributive direction and focus – and for the process of talent management itself – the *mandatory/discretionary* differentiation provides a practical basis for:

❑ the necessarily *interdependent and complementary processes* of empowering and delegating

❑ defining the centrality, relevance and contribution of individual tasks, projects and roles – especially where they are intrinsic to successful group or multifunctional working

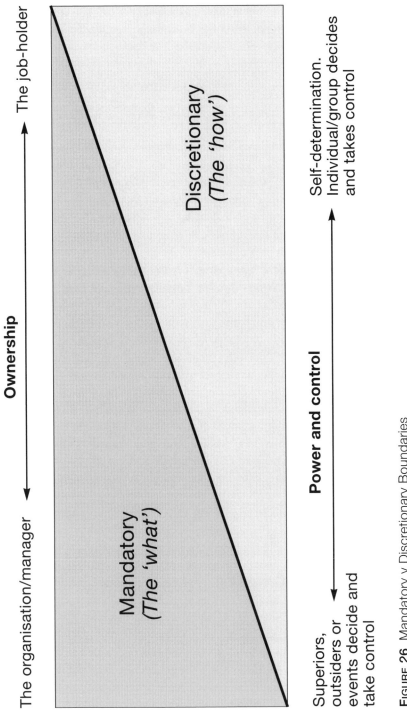

Ownership

The organisation/manager ← → The job-holder

Mandatory
(The 'what')

Discretionary
(The 'how')

Power and control

Superiors, outsiders or events decide and take control ← → Self-determination. Individual/group decides and takes control

FIGURE 26 Mandatory v Discretionary Boundaries

❑ assessing people's performance against expectations within the organisational context of initiative, autonomy, accountability, power and influence

❑ identifying personal – and team – development needs, learning goals and improvement opportunities; this is especially important as people move into increasing uncertainty, organisational transformation and new opportunities, arenas where there is likely to be the need for higher levels of discretionary decision-making and action

❑ establishing individuals' *complementary* needs for longer-term growth and career progression, where with likely decreasing opportunities for 'vertical' promotion, the need for enriched and appropriately varied lateral organisational moves becomes paramount (hence the relevance of the 'plus role' concept defined in Chapter 8).

❝ The process of talent management is frequently a matter of creating and exercising effective 'boundary management'. ❞

The process of talent management – when geared to empowerment, especially – is frequently a matter of creating and exercising effective 'boundary management', between what is believed to be mandatory and what is considered to be legitimate discretionary activity. It is thus about helping people to negotiate, intelligently, the sometimes grey areas of what can amount to a 'no-man's land' between 'can' and 'cannot', or 'must' and 'must not'. Encouraging people to check facts, establish precedent, question, update and give *realistic* definition to custom and practice and test out the myth and ritual that surround some beliefs or practices, may be a key aspect of talent management. This process is fundamental to opening up greater areas of ownership and, hence, initiative, decision-making and control. This is illustrated in Figure 27.

Empowerment with Delegation

The work of Dr John Nicholls[2] of John Nicholls Associates is particularly relevant at this point. Operating out of Northamptonshire, this creative and skilled management consultant has developed several original models of managerial and leadership behaviour. The one illustrated in Figure 28 makes the crucial point that empowerment needs to be given – and managed – in *conjunction with* commensurately effective

'Enabling' and empowering leadership

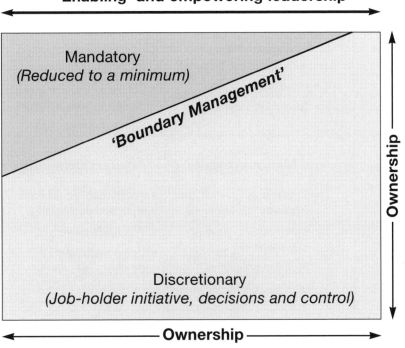

FIGURE 27 The Impact of Talent Management and Empowerment upon Discretionary and Mandatory Boundaries

delegation to establish and clarify parameters, goals and other key outcomes. As a result of coaching directors and managers in empowerment, over many years, the author has adapted and modified Nicholls's original model, primarily in terms of 'labels' and accompanying descriptive detail. His important contribution in this field has been to reinforce and draw attention to the *essential interdependence* of empowering and delegation if they are to be developed and applied as realistic, workable management 'best practices'.

In this adapted version of the model, it is the *genuine coach* who is best able to develop, in conjunction with the job-holder, the most appropriate task and role 'frameworks'. With an *optimal working balance of empowerment* and *delegation*, such frameworks for action are likely to offer the most realistic chances for success of the consequent:

❑ empowering and bestowed freedom to act

❑ ownership and personal sense of accountability

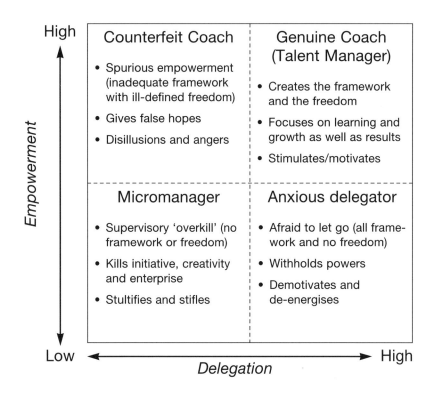

Source: *Dr John Nicholls* (adapted)

FIGURE 28 Empowering with Delegation

❐ commitment to deliver

❐ acceptance of challenge

❐ 'enabling' dialogues between coach and job-holder.

It is also the *genuine coach* who, as a result of professional integrity and personal credibility, is most likely to create – and sustain – the appropriate conditions for the job-holder's learning and continuing growth. The essentially *reflective* environment developed progressively by the genuine coach is that which is likely to be most conducive in helping people to make sense – operationally and strategically – of the organisation and its environment. *In other words, the genuine coach role is central – and critical – to effective talent management.*

Although he or she may clarify parameters and results – and so provide much of the requisite framework – the *anxious delegator* fails to 'let go' sufficiently in order to provide the job-holder with the necessary autonomy and freedom to act. The anxiety of the anxious delegator may have its roots in, for example:

◻ fear of personal failure

◻ reluctance to give power and autonomy to others on the grounds that being in control usually feels the safest position

◻ anxiety about being overtaken by a more capable or confident subordinate in the promotion stakes

◻ fear that, given the requisite autonomy, the job-holder might make a better job of the task than the delegator

◻ a fundamental wish to avoid hassle or vulnerability, by remaining in an established comfort zone and, therefore, position of control over the status quo.

Moving further round the model in a clockwise direction, we come to the *micromanager*, essentially a 'nay-sayer' – sometimes on principle, sometimes out of a general reluctance to rock the boat. Going beyond even the anxious delegator in a desire to avoid hassle or threat in any form, the micromanager maintains obsessively close control over detail and may compulsively 'fine tune' things. Any initiative or creativity that the job-holder *is* able to exercise is largely the result of rebellion on his or her part, through happenstance or by default.

Preoccupation with minutiae and close-quarter 'hands on' supervision usually results in the major, more important issues being neglected. The style, too, is totally inappropriate in the context of today's societal norms and expectations, being essentially:

◻ an anachronism that is alien in current leadership and management 'best practice'

◻ destructive, inhibiting and de-skilling

◻ founded on a form of 'framework' that, because of the total lack of freedom, creates no basis for ownership, accountability or commitment

◻ self-defeating, because of its stultifying and stifling impact on people

❑ 'dead hand' supervision, since it can scarcely claim to be 'management'.

The real joker in the pack is the *counterfeit coach*, since he or she may initially appear quite plausible and well intentioned (and, indeed – somewhat after the manner of the *road to hell* – may be genuinely well intentioned). The spurious empowerment of the counterfeit coach, lacking any real structured framework, usually leads to the raising of unlikely hopes, their subsequent dashing and, as a consequence, disillusion, resentment and anger, on the part of those who were deceived. Typical counterfeit coach behaviour is likely to include some, or all, of the following:

❑ ill-defined areas of freedom and accountability

❑ poor – or no – crystallisation of situations, projects, priorities and work assignments

❑ vague generalisations about opportunities, outcomes, goals and constraints

❑ blandishments, 'blarney' and the raising of unrealistic expectations and false hopes

❑ an absence of 'political' guidance, necessary sponsorship and/or gatekeeping to help the person(s) being empowered to find their way through the organisational 'mazes', pitfalls or barriers that they may need to negotiate in order to 'deliver'

❑ inadequate identification, clarification and exploration of likely options and alternative courses of action

❑ generally too much superficiality and insufficient depth, detail and diagnosis before initiating action

❑ an absence of opportunities for dialogue, analysis and review, during both planning and action stages – hence insufficient reflection

❑ classical communication and transactional problems between managers and subordinates, including 'game playing', hidden agendas and inauthenticity.

'Action learning' projects conducted by the author in a variety of businesses and professional organisations as consultancy assignments indicate that only about 12 per cent of those involved in coaching roles in such projects[3] effectively sustain a 'genuine coach' contribution. Supportive workshops, devoted to empowering, improving coaching skills and creating reflective learning environments appear to raise the percentage, substantially, to typically around 25–30 per cent.

> **❝ The roles of effective mentor, coach or sponsor, are taken willingly and fulfilled effectively by a disturbingly small percentage of managers and directors. ❞**

What is significant, however, is that the roles of effective mentor, coach or sponsor, which have the potential to add enormous value to people's understanding, growth and contribution, are taken willingly and fulfilled effectively by a disturbingly small percentage of managers and directors. The obviously relevant composite skills of *talent management* appear to be developed – and used – regularly by very few executives as part of their *natural* day-to-day leadership and management styles. Even business schools, management colleges and the organisational behaviour faculties of many universities are often far stronger on the *theory* than the best *practices* of empowering, coaching or mentoring.

Yet the evidence of enough real-life examples indicates how the skilful use of such techniques can – and does – pay off. Companies like Quest, the international biotechnology group, Ideal Computer, a UK-based telephone sales, IT hardware and software business of £170 million turnover, and Steelcase, the giant office furniture manufacturer, all show significantly above-average return on investment and/or profit-per-employee growth rates. The managements of all three companies place strong emphasis upon and give active support to the intelligent development and use of empowerment, employee autonomy and the management of talent.

Similarly, an extensive – yet relatively little known – seven-year research project and evaluation of a large sample of European managers, conducted by the Kienbaum Akademie of Düsseldorf, identified the *top two* characteristics of successful organisations as:

❒ effectively developed and used *complementary* contributive competencies of managers and staff

❒ high trust, extensive autonomy and minimal organisational control over people.

Beyond these two strong indicators of effective empowering, the next three characteristics, in order of significance, emerged:

❑ Such organisations possess a high measure of *uniqueness* in the way they conduct their business and manage its resources – especially talent and knowledge.

❑ They possess a strong visionary orientation and sense of direction.

❑ They know and understand their competitors well.

Closer to home, the conclusions of academics like Goffee and Hunt[4] of the London Business School and writers such as Valerie Stewart[5] point convincingly to the value-adding potential of effective empowering, and what are essentially reflective, *enabling* styles of leadership and management, in contributing to organisations' transformation and success.

The Power in Empowerment

Being *empowered* – having the *necessary* power to do what needs to be done – has its roots in many sources (see Table 8).

Authority and power may be bestowed, derived, ascribed, assumed, developed or otherwise acquired. Similarly, influence is normally directly – or indirectly – attributable to personal behaviour, competence and personality – as well as the formal and informal roles, or status, of people within an organisation.

Sources 1 and 3 – *positional authority* and *informational authority* – emerge largely (though not wholly) from the organisational structure, formal role set and *enabling* style of a manager. However, there are also initiatives that can be taken by individuals – and within hierarchical relationships – to enhance their positional and informational power by, for example:

❑ influencing 'upwards' to secure approval and ratification of role enrichment and/or an increased power base

❑ putting into practice the old maxims 'always assume you have the authority of the chief executive, until proved otherwise' or 'it's easier to ask for forgiveness, than for permission'

❑ demonstrably developing both core and specific competencies to the point of undeniable excellence

TABLE 8 Power

1 Positional power	–	job, role, status and the extent of authority conferred by superiors, in terms of budget, resource, headcount and decision parameters
2 The authority of expertise	–	vested in a person's competence, specialist contributive knowledge and skills, or particular – often unique – expertise
3 Informational power	–	the possession of significant facts, data and information that enhance an individual's influence, status and power personally and professionally
4 Influence ('personal power')	–	the quality of alliances, sponsorship and committed support from others, including 'political' backing gained by networking, interpersonal skill and the development of important 'power' relationships
5 Commitment ('ownership')	–	individuals support and own what they create and the commitment that stems from a genuine sense of ownership often gives a person power
6 The power of integrity	–	the individual's trustworthiness, honesty and personal credibility, in the way they conduct themselves and their business, frequently termed 'moral authority'.

❐ building increased centrality into one's role and increasing the relevance, legitimacy and necessity of its contributive outputs

❐ adding value, wherever practicable and appropriate, to others' contributions and/or to outcomes likely to ensure competitive advantage or significant cost reduction.

Clearly, the various sources of executive power and empowerment can interact in many different ways to create *unique* strengths in a manager's – or director's – 'style' and, consequently, *operational effectiveness*. However, what might be identified as the '3 Cs' of empowerment and personal power, are their Credibility, Commitment and Communications:

1 *Credibility* – as an executive, as a professional and as a leader of people. Credibility stems largely from the *power* of a person's

❑ expertise

❑ integrity

❑ influence.

It is backed up by the other three sources of power and authority.

2 *Commitment* – this is backed up by demonstrated personal responsibility and accountability for actions and results. Commitment has many of its roots in the *power* of the individual's

❑ sense of ownership

❑ expertise and conscience professionelle

❑ position and positional obligations.

It is reinforced by the other three sources of power and authority.

3 *Communications* – ie his or her communicative competence and the impact he or she makes on both events and people as a consequence. Communications as a source of authority and influence arise out of the *power* of someone's

❑ position and formal status/roles

❑ information quality and significance

❑ influence and personal 'clout' or 'style'

❑ integrity and trustworthiness

Similarly, it is underpinned by the other sources of personal power.

66 *The synergy of leadership and management, allied to transformed organisational power, can generate intelligent use of power.* 99

In an age of constant change and perpetual transformation, an increasingly relevant source of power is emerging – that of the *transformed organisation*. Not simply an opportunist's charter, the '*power of the transformed organisation*' is essentially the authority to act, or scope for initiative, that arises out of the:

☐ restructuring and reorganisation of the business

☐ disappearance, blurring or weakening of traditional role, territorial and functional boundaries

☐ emergence of new roles, alliances, coalitions and cross-functional working

☐ shifting priorities, imperatives or profit/delivery criteria – for example, added value, intrusive competitor activity or new technology – that require fresh initiatives, behaviours and interactions

☐ appointment of new people and departure of existing people and, hence, the creation of different visions, missions, values and goals.

Ultimately, however, it is the productive synergy of effective leadership and management, allied to transformed organisational power, that can generate the intelligent use of power that is most likely to make empowerment work.

The 'Feel' of Empowerment

So, what does it feel like to be empowered and to work in an empowering organisation? Of the many books that appeared on empowerment throughout the last decade, one of those that most graphically conveys a convincing impression of what being empowered really *feels* like is Valerie Stewart's *The David Solution*.[6] Key themes are 'busting' the bureaucracy and liberating talent. Client comments about empowerment in action – as the result of consultancy assignments – parallel, or confirm, so many of Stewart's conclusions:

☐ 'The two Jims and I [Manufacturing and Finance – together with Sales and Marketing] get together and talk things through regularly, and we come up with our own, joint, solutions' – team leaders, high-tech fasteners.

☐ 'We'll often stay over, at the end of the day, and work out, ourselves, what we will do about a problem we've got to face tomorrow' – supervisor (and operatives), electronics company.

☐ 'It's just so different now, from what it used to be like, even two years ago. We get so much more useful work done and waste a hell of a lot less time than we did' – junior engineer, REC.

❐ 'Today, people are more self-regulating. They control the progress of things, themselves – not us' – plant engineer, engineering company.

Generally, the experience and 'feel' of empowerment in a business indicate the following changes from pre-empowering days:

❐ more egalitarianism and less reliance upon status differentials, with consequent greater accessibility of senior management

❐ values and principles as self-regulatory processes, rather than 'standing orders' or rules

❐ significantly more dialogue than under the previous system of unilateral decision-making, with a greater option generation before decisions are finalised

❐ more direct face-to-face or oral communication, and less formal, protective memo-writing

❐ shift from 'who went wrong – who do we blame?' to 'what went wrong – how do we best prevent it from happening again? What can we learn from this?'

❐ more concentration on seeking and exploiting opportunities than solving problems

❐ less fear of failure and more preparedness to experiment and take less thoroughly calculated risks (although the experience on this is variable).

Talent Management – Continuity of Feedback and Dialogue

Managing talent as a process between individuals relies heavily on continuous discussion and feedback. Proactive and concurrent monitoring, as well as post-event reviews that provide a continuing form of 'finger-on-the-pulse' dialogue, offer a practical and necessary alternative to the polarised extremes of 'micromanaging' and 'laissez faire' leadership.

Talent management is not simply a fortuitous or haphazard affair that arises as the result of serendipity or because a manager happens to feel that it is about time he or she took an interest in a particular member of staff. Rather, it is a well-structured, systematic and continuous process, which provides a *bedrock of organised consistency* between managers and their staff for:

- ❐ agreeing issues, parameters, mutual obligations and requisite outcomes
- ❐ raising and exploring concerns and expectations
- ❐ generating and testing viable options
- ❐ confirming development needs and the means of meeting them
- ❐ initiating and facilitating action – and the support needed
- ❐ providing necessary monitoring, feedback and review
- ❐ stimulating learning, via doing and experiencing.

Its focus, therefore, is upon 'do-how' as well as 'know-how', and it offers the wherewithal for regular structured discussions and interventions about the 'what', 'when', 'where', 'who', 'why' and 'how' of day-to-day and longer-term performance, development and growth. It is, for example, an ideal process for linking personal development to step-by-step job enrichment – and career progression – so that the individual, the role and the business are all growing together, concurrently, in a more logical and productive way. This issue is explored in more detail in Chapter 8.

SUMMARY

To be successful, empowerment depends upon the balanced interplay of at least four factors (see Table 9).

To be satisfying to both parties – and to produce the results of which it can be capable for the organisation – empowerment must obviously be based upon *mutual* respect, trust and confidence. There are reciprocal rights and obligations – as in most relationships – but

TABLE 9 Effective Empowerment

• clear delegation	⎫ *the manager's effectiveness*
• appropriate release of power	⎭
• adequate functional maturity	⎫ *the job-holder's effectiveness*
• preparedness to take ownership.	⎭

in empowerment such mutuality is also bounded by the demands of other organisational and professional imperatives. Customers, suppliers, shareholders, functions up and down the line, various legislative and watchdog bodies, as well as other stakeholders, all influence and limit the mandatory–discretionary boundaries of people at work. Thus empowerment is essentially a matter of *appropriate freedom, within professional, moral and legal frameworks*, where autonomy is necessarily tempered by mature judgement, a sense of responsibility and wisdom on the part of the job-holder.

Just as autonomy and responsibility need to go hand in hand for empowerment to work, *empowerment and delegation need to be in balance* to avoid the traps of the 'counterfeit coach', 'anxious delegator' or 'micromanager' shown in Figure 28. Delegation, however, means much more than handing over well-defined areas of work and specific tasks. It must also be about surrendering spheres of influence, personal kudos and job satisfaction – the giving up, therefore, of sources of recognition, reward and pleasure.

It can involve, too – at a psychological level – giving up part of oneself and not knowing just what it will look like when it eventually comes back. On a more utilitarian plain, delegating work may also strip away excuses for not doing the jobs that really should be done, hence there can be a measure of alibi preservation and protectionism in failing to delegate as thoroughly as reality demands. Another fear may be, 'Will he or she make a better job of it than I did?'

With a progressive shift of power – and power bases – there needs to be a commensurate increase in personal ownership and accountability on the part of those accepting the greater freedom. Enhancing the *will*, as well as the *skill* of those being empowered is where the enabling manager must necessarily adopt the encouraging, supportive roles of *coach*, *mentor* and/or *sponsor*, according to the situation and environment.

The 'power' underlying empowerment springs from many sources – organisational and personal. Those that are *extrinsic* to the person are primarily:

- *positional power*, vested in the role, job, status and formal authority conferred by rank and/or decision parameters

- *informational power*, which stems from the importance of facts, data and information to which an individual has access.

Sources of authority and power *intrinsic* to the individual include:

- *the expertise and competence* that resides in a person's capability and often scarce or unique skills and expertise

- *'personal power', or influence*, deriving from an individual's interpersonal skills, 'style' and development of significant relationships within and without an organisation

- *commitment and 'ownership'*, the power that stems from 'territory' and territorial rights, and hence the possession of a domain, role or job

- *power of integrity*, sometimes referred to as 'moral authority', which arises out of a person's honesty, trustworthiness and the integrity with which he or she conducts business and relates to others.

Empowering people – as a key element of talent management – is not a haphazard process to be largely left to chance. Rather, it depends upon regular 'quality dialogues' and feedback, which ensure that a finger is kept on the pulse of what is happening, day to day, in the transfer and exercise of power. It is regular feedback and dialogue that, ultimately, ensure consistency of both leadership and talent management.

ACTION – THEORY INTO PRACTICE

- Coaching, mentoring and sponsoring may all be viewed as *talent management* processes that can make effective empowerment a reality – given appropriate delegation. Look at your scores, together with any feedback from others, for the *Effective Enabler Profile*, *Talent Coaching Profile*, *Talent Mentoring Profile* and *Talent Sponsoring Profile* in the Appendix. What do the *collective* results tell you about:

  o your management and leadership styles as a manager of talent

  o what, specifically, you need to begin to do *differently* to ensure that empowerment will work in the areas you manage?

- Complete the *Power and Empowerment Profile* on page 242 and respond to the questions about the results of your scores.

- Following exploration and discussion of the outcomes of the questions above, what is your strategy – and action plan – to develop effective, empowered working within your managerial domain?

  o Who will take the lead, and do 'what', 'by when' and in connection with whom, to implement strategies for effective empowerment in the areas that you manage?

  o What are your plans for follow-up and follow-through?

Endnotes

1 WHITE R. P., HODGSON P. and CRAINER S. *The Future of Leadership: A white water revolution*. London, Pitman, 1996.

2 Dr John Nicholls, John Nicholls Associates, the management consultants who developed the original '*Delegation–Empowerment*' Model.

3 Consultancy projects undertaken by Michael Williams & Partners in the USA, Canada, UK, Ireland and seven other countries in Western Europe.

4 GOFFEE R. and HUNT J. *Research Project*. London, London Business School. Internal research, undated.

5 STEWART V. *The David Solution*. Aldershot, Gower, 1993.

6 *Ibid.*

Managing Talent –
New Mindsets, New Actions

The future belongs to the learners – not the knowers.

Anonymous

Towards Strategic Talent Management: Integration with Business Strategy

The information age revolution has led to the most dramatic and far-reaching changes in the business world – and this is just the beginning. The nature and form of talent management, similarly, is changing in order to cope with the learning and development needs of people within rapidly transforming and often networked organisations.

A survey conducted by PDI consultancy, among US and European businesses during the period 1996–8, sought to differentiate between 'state of the practice' and 'state of the art' in talent management. This is illustrated in Table 10.

Though goodwill helps professional competence and know-how immeasurably, effective talent management is not the haphazard by-product of altruism or well-intentioned personal interventions. Neither is it simply the outcome of a close relationship between people who share mutual affection and respect. Rather, it is a conscious, dedicated interplay of processes, inherent in information age leadership, which seek to integrate the recruitment, deployment, development and retention of high performers with the longer-term strategic direction of the

TABLE 10 Practice v State of the Art

STATE OF THE PRACTICE	STATE OF THE ART
• Organisations make decisions about talent management and its outcomes on a decentralised, case-by-case basis.	• *Organisations use talent management systematically and strategically, where the pay-off is greatest.*
• Coaching and mentoring still too often occur once on a 'quick-fix' basis.	• *Talent management is aligned with HR systems to meet business needs.*
• Coaches are selected and managed informally (or not managed at all).	• *Organisations build pools of coaches they can rely on.*
• Organisations do not monitor and evaluate talent management and leave much to chance.	• *Organisations monitor and evaluate talent management against performance results.*
• Talent management is low on the list of management 'musts'.	• *Effective talent management is seen as a major contributor to success – especially competitive advantage.*

business. Without reducing talent management to the mechanistic functioning of a mere 'system' – however good – its success is heavily dependent upon both *sufficient structure* and *formalised consistency*.

The component activities that make up the talent management process need to be effectively implemented, co-ordinated and aligned with the key business strategies of the organisation. Aimed very much at securing competitive advantage, the following activities must form part of a *dedicated, coherent plan* focused on and integrated with the business plan of the company:

❐ a means of sourcing the right sort of talent and high potential for the business – both outside and inside the organisation

❐ clear policies on how appropriate *developmental* positions – as well as key contributory roles – can best be created and exploited expressly to 'grow' and use talent

❐ accessing and releasing high performers where and when they are needed – to misquote a very successful Confederate American General from the Civil War, 'Getting there firstest, with the bestest'

❐ reviewing performance regularly from results and against expectations in order to develop, build and grow competencies

❏ evolving strategies that ensure the retention of high performers and people of potential – by breaking with the worst wasteful and stifling practices of the past – to include

- intelligent but realistic career progression, involving frequent and early appointments to responsible, challenging roles
- flexible and differential reward systems that actively acknowledge high performance and outstanding contributions
- individual 'bespoke' mentoring programmes, supported by shorter-term and role-/project-specific coaching and, where necessary, appropriate sponsorship.

> **❝ The component activities that make up the talent management process need to be effectively implemented, co-ordinated and aligned with the key business strategies of the organisation. ❞**

Stora Enso, a major global timber and paper products company with roots principally in Finland and Sweden, has as its declared vision: *'We will be the leading forest products company in the world.'* It sees the linkage between its mission/vision and dedicated action as the interplay of several key elements of the business, illustrated in Figure 29.

Its description of company culture is that it is a *'glue'* that holds people, strategy and organisation together, in order to achieve requisite business results. One of the declared values of the Stora Enso culture – or 'glue' – is: *'The emphasis is on people – motivated people create success.'* As a consequence, HR systems – and talent management – are expressly linked to the mission and business plan of the company.

According to Professor Lynda Gratton,[1] 'Without the re-engineering of fundamental human resource systems, mission statements are destined to remain rhetorical.' Too often, experience confirms that there is an enormous discrepancy between rhetoric and reality. In many organisations, there is little cohesion or strategic synergy and engagement between business goals and the longer-term aims and objectives of the human resources function – and, hence, those of talent management. Though perhaps not representative, therefore, of the majority of companies, human resource systems – and practices – appear to be integrating effectively with the business strategies and competitive imperatives at Stora Enso. The simplistic model – 'from mission and vision into action' (Figure 29) – and its implementation in operations, technical and commercial functions, appear to be readily recognised

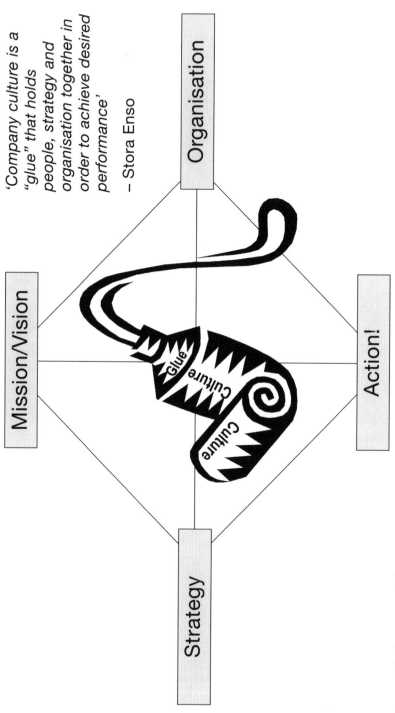

'Company culture is a "glue" that holds people, strategy and organisation together in order to achieve desired performance'

– Stora Enso

Organisation

Mission/Vision

Action!

Culture Glue

Culture

Strategy

FIGURE 29 Company Culture – The Critical 'Glue'

and also *felt* by many employees. Discussions with both senior HR professionals and others would appear to confirm this.

Undoubtedly, talented, high-performing people are pushed through the system into roles where they are able to optimise their potential and contribution at early stages in their careers. *Higher than in many organisations we have worked with is the marked sense of pride, engagement and involvement in the core business of the company.* The commitment encountered, at several levels, seemed to be significantly more than a short-term or tactical response to today's challenges. It was rather a sense of involvement in – and ownership of – the business, with a *strongly shared aspirational element to it.*

The research quoted in the Introduction and Chapter 1 indicates that there are few areas where 'say–do' credibility is as questionable as it frequently is in talent management. The gap between 'the talk' and 'the walk' remains unacceptably high in rather too many organisations. There appear to be several reasons for this lack of alignment and integration between business and human resources strategies. Professor Lynda Gratton of London Business School suggests that one reason is the quality and closeness – or otherwise – of the relationship between those who devise strategy and those (particularly the human resources function) who are charged with implementing it.

In many organisations, HR is not represented at board level and so is rarely party to 'inner cabinet' strategic policy discussions and the formulation of key business strategies. Consequently, HR tends to function at operational levels, with little or no part to play in shaping the strategic direction of the organisation. Lack of involvement in creating the strategic imperatives of a company may:

❏ further reduce, over time, already relatively low levels of business awareness encountered among some HR specialists

❏ result in HR developing and implementing human resource systems that are distanced from and not aligned with the main strategic goals and direction of the business.

Gratton reinforces the point about the dangers of isolation for the HR function and its failure to influence the strategic management of talent when she states: 'Without a grounded frame of reference they can become overly influenced by the "flavour of the month", participating in initiatives which quickly lose momentum.' There are certainly also plenty of consultants and business schools who will eagerly peddle yet more enticing and plausible 'flavours' for those anxious to establish credibility and centrality with their boards. The rush for panaceas may, in such circumstances, lead to a search for 'solutions' to problems that are:

❑ effects, or symptoms, but not causes

❑ inadequately defined

❑ not the real issues that need to be confronted.

Another source of pressure on the HR function is the short-term demands for 'quick fixes' and other 'urgent priorities', imposed by the board or senior colleagues from operations, sales and marketing or customer services. In such an environment, leveraging talent to meet the demands of strategic intent and the longer-term growth of the business largely becomes sacrificed to the 'priorities' of the moment and what is often *illusory* urgency. Building integration between HR – especially the intelligent management of talent – and the strategic 'engine' of the business is likely to involve at least the following:

❑ focusing on the consequences of, for example, a failure to manage and leverage talent effectively, in pursuing the strategic goals of the business

❑ directly involving senior/specialist HR executives in cross-functional discussions leading to decisions about strategic intent and strategy formulation

❑ reinforcing alignment and integration by increasing line management's (and others') understanding of what talent management is and what their roles – and accountability – are in making talent management a corporate priority and, hence, a critical strategic imperative.

Figure 30 illustrates the progressive integration and alignment of HR strategies, especially talent management, with the strategies and imperatives defined as necessary to move a business from its current position or set of conditions ('x') to an articulated new state of affairs ('y').

❝ The shift from 'human resource' management to 'talent management' is one of the big leadership challenges of the new millennium. ❞

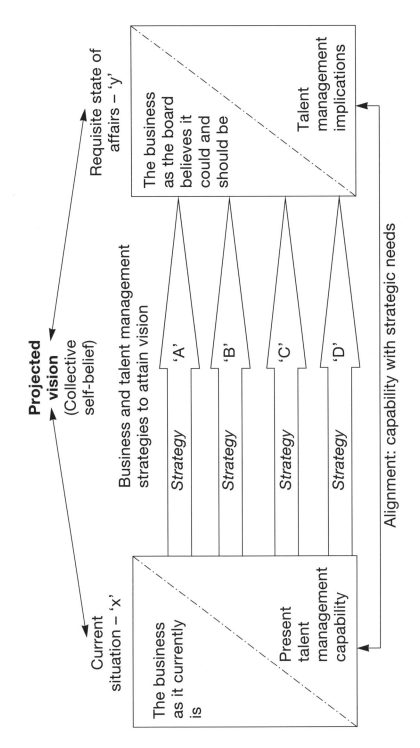

FIGURE 30 Alignment of Talent Management with Business Strategy

The shift from 'human resource' management to 'talent management' is one of the big leadership challenges of the new millennium. As Professor Pierre Casse[2] of the Business Innovation Network asks:

☐ What does the challenge mean for managers?

☐ How can leaders make the necessary change?

☐ Can the new leadership skills – and mindsets – be learned?

And, one might add:

☐ What are the crucial implications for HR professionals and how can they best meet such a challenge?

As Casse says, people are not resources – they *have* resources, which is significantly different. The task facing both leaders and HR professionals is to create the right environments, so that high intelligence, outstanding competencies and energy can be channelled and used to the full. The role of the leader, in business, is changing fundamentally to that of 'a nurturer of talents, a catalyst, in search of synergy'.

Much of Casse's work was undertaken in large multinationals like Nestlé, Nokia, Olivetti and Philips, where he found that there appear to be three key success factors that are identified with tomorrow's leaders:

☐ behavioural flexibility and the ability to adjust rapidly

☐ mental innovation and inventiveness in finding and exploiting new opportunities

☐ people orientation and a concern to release talent.

Our own conclusions from working in such global organisations as ABN AMRO, AstraZeneca, Generali, ING Group, Baxter Healthcare, Stora Enso – and many others – are generally similar, namely that we now need:

☐ a necessary movement away from traditional 'human resource' thinking, to finding ways to maximise the sourcing, release and use of creative brainpower and ability, at *individual, team and organisational* levels.

- ❐ a 'nose' for real opportunity and the ability to open up, develop and exploit such possibilities quickly

- ❐ a high capacity to mobilise people from different disciplines, functions and locations to generate the productive collaboration necessary to make the right things happen for the business.

In-Depth Approach to the Development of Strategic Management

The members of an executive board are primarily responsible for the strategic management of their business. The scope of this strategic role is much wider than the operational role through which many executives reach the boardroom. Strategic management is often a matter of personal *style and power*; much less often it is a matter of teamwork. The development of truly strategic team management requires an in-depth and conscious approach to how the strategic perspective is generated.

In adopting a real strategic perspective, executives are working with a curious double standard. On the one hand, they have to challenge the reality and relevance of taken-for-granted assumptions. On the other, they have to support and even create the myths that feed the organisational identity. A large corporation like IBM can carry its myths into society with great power, but even so has to subject them to revision as forces of change outside its control and influence impact upon the organisation.

The way executives can work at this, aided by HR professionals, is in terms of perceptions and images. The executives' perceptions essentially determine the nature of the questions they are able to ask. By stimulating the range and radical nature of questioning, their perceptual field can be opened up considerably. This is an important means of testing the reality and preparing the ground for strategy formulation. The images in the mind of the executive, particularly those bound up with his or her aspirations and drives, provide the form and direction of thrust that will be transmitted to the organisation. These images are usually latent rather than conscious. With the help of the right HR professional, the executive can give these appropriate form and develop the visionary basis for the strategy of the business – including talent management.

The vertical line AC in Figure 31, represents the basic *raison d'être* of the organisation. The interplay between activity and myth creates the

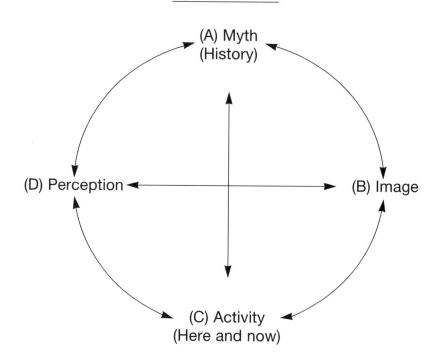

Source: *Tony Hodgson and Michael Williams*

FIGURE 31 Strategic Management

rituals, products, ethos and style of the enterprise, both as a community
and as a culture. The horizontal line DB in Figure 32 represents the
power of strategic management, which must extend the perceptions
beyond activity and myth, but also visualise selected futures *that do not
yet exist.* In the long term, this 'stretching' changes the dominant myth
(by lines DA and BA) and the shape of the activity (by lines DC and BA).
Thus we can represent the in-depth work of strategic management as
the interplay of forces shown in Figure 32.

The realities of the total world in which the organisation functions
may be far greater and richer than presumed. To identify this richness,
we need to distinguish between the positive and negative aspects of
executives' perceptions and visions, as well as the positive and negative
aspects of the organisation's mythology and activity.

The negative aspects are those that decrease the organisation's hold
on reality. They are the blindness and fantasy that run away with the
organisation's resources, talent and energy. The positive aspects are
those that increase the organisation's hold on reality and, indeed, help

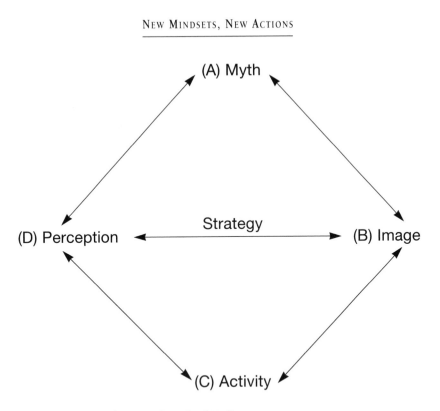

Source: *Tony Hodgson and Michael Williams*

FIGURE 32 The Power of Strategic Management

to create – and add value to – that reality. For example, the negative side of myth can be related to the sacred cows, totems and taboos held too dearly and unquestioningly. Yet these beliefs may be leading the organisation, lemming-like, to rush over some unseen cliff. The positive side of myth can be related to *the values for which the company stands* – such as service, quality, competitiveness or excellence. The negative side of activity can be related to the irrelevance, waste, self-vested interests, 'sleep' and inertia in the organisation. The positive side of activity emerges in the effectiveness, creativity and capacity for delivery that the organisation demonstrates.

Executives operating at the strategic levels are themselves subject to the same unconscious forces of myth-belief and activity-blindness as anyone else in the corporate community. Thus their questioning and envisioning of the strategic future cannot be properly developed unless they are willing to subject their own internal processes of thought, feeling and action to reflective scrutiny. Generally, they have achieved high positions through success. One possible danger is that they have a natural tendency to follow the same pattern. The pattern may no longer fit the present or the future.

The crucial involvement of the HR/organisational development specialist is now apparent. To develop strategic management he or she must provide a stimulus to the executive and the top team to question the basis of their understanding by:

☐ eliciting questions and visions about the present and the future

☐ challenging the current myths to help distil the positive from the negative

☐ reminding the executives that their style and behaviour has to be consistent with the strategic approach that they are advocating.

This is a delicate, tough and intellectually demanding role to play, but one that can release tremendous creative energy for the enterprise. It is also one in which talent management, at the highest levels, truly adds value to the business and to the effectiveness of the organisation's management.

The 'Heroic Journey' – Getting Talent Management Right

At a time when it has become partly an issue of fashionable political correctness to play down heroes and to talk about 'post-heroic' leadership, it was refreshing to see a recent powerful attack on such doctrinaire thinking by George MacDonald Fraser,[3] who wrote: 'Of one thing I'm sure: my country needs heroes now . . . and I don't see any coming up.'

More than ever before, it would seem, now *is* the time for heroes and people of talent and self-belief, in business and in our professions and great institutions. If the world we are living and working in is going to become progressively tougher, more ambiguous and less certain, then not only do we need people with well-developed intellects, high strategic awareness and visionary competence as our leaders – we need them to have courage and resolve, too. As organisations function less and less as 'corporations' and more and more as *enterprises* and embark upon 'heroic journeys', then it seems only fitting that they should be led by people who possess the courage and spirit of adventurers, explorers and pathfinders.

66 *Vision – with its connotations of aspiration, opportunity and thus risk-taking – without any requirement for courage and heroism is little more than a contradiction in terms.* **99**

Vision – with its connotations of aspiration, opportunity and thus risk-taking – without any requirement for courage and heroism is little more than a contradiction in terms. Taking two dictionary definitions of the words 'hero' and 'heroine', it would seem that there is little to quarrel about over the value and relevance of such people:

☐ 'man/woman of superhuman qualities'

☐ 'man/woman admired for achievements and noble qualities'.

Managing today, in order to shape the organisation's tomorrow, involves:

☐ ensuring the *continuous transformation* of the business in the most appropriate directions

☐ constant informed scenario-building, evaluation and adaptive rebuilding

☐ making sense of and imposing some coherence and order upon the sometimes capricious link between speculative opportunism and uncertainty, in trying to read the future intelligently

☐ taking major decisions about the shape, direction, positioning and profitability of the organisation on the basis of frequently imperfect information and knowledge

☐ continually relating the organisation to the changing, sometimes contradictory, imperatives and paradoxes of its wider environment

☐ doing all of the above while maintaining competitive advantage and profit, securing people's willing commitment, and running the business, day to day, in the meantime.

Hardly stuff for the fainthearted!

With the changing shape and nature of organisations and new patterns of working, the 'heroic journey' involves, too, the core challenges of *managing the business while managing people's potential* – the very essence of talent management and organisational learning. Chapters 7 and 8 cover the coaching and mentoring responsibilities and competencies of the manager as a developer of talent in the short and longer term. More importantly, they offer ideas for harnessing and *using* people's talents within the context of the enhanced personal contribution of the individual and the fulfilment of his or her potential.

The tools and techniques identified in these two chapters, especially, are aimed at opening up necessary dialogues between people to create freer-flowing exchanges of ideas, expectations and feedback. They are offered, too, as a means of not only developing people, but of demonstrating that value is put on their knowledge – and the learning that is involved in enhancing their knowledge, skill and personal contribution.

Being a hero or heroine is thus not simply a matter of always leading from the front, grabbing personal kudos or playing the pied piper. In today's world of empowerment, taking ownership and assuming greater degrees of autonomy, it is also about *leading from behind* – catalysing, facilitating and enabling so that *others* may learn, succeed and take credit for success.

To increase *influence* and credibility, some formal authority has to be abandoned. No longer does the size of epaulettes – or the number of 'stars' on them – necessarily equate with contributive knowledge and competence. Moreover, as Tom Cannon[4] points out, 'Collaboration is more important than control', and 'Performance is more important than deference.'

Authoritarianism is being replaced by *authoritative* expertise, knowledge and competence and, at a time when the radical is coming to be accepted as the norm, innovative, creative and well-informed knowledge workers are coming into their own. What is more, they *expect* to be led by people who value, respect and know how to release and use their knowledge. Never before, probably, has the leadership competence of so many managers been so critically put to the test, as it is in the information age, where talent management is coming to be one of *the* hallmarks of the effective executive. As Patrick Dixon's research[5] would seem to indicate, the leadership of capable, creative, high performers is going to be even more important in tomorrow's world.

In strongly interdependent organisations, talent management is no longer the prerogative of the individual leader or manager – although personal *enabling* will continue to be an essential set of competencies for leaders as individuals. Now, *talent management strategies* are essential to catalyse and facilitate *organisational* learning, the development and use of *collective* knowledge and the effective interaction of multifunctional networks.

People in organisations give of their best, and collaborate, when they have confidence in leadership that *values* their contribution – by actions, not merely the 'right' words. In times of change, especially, winning hearts and minds is a matter of trust, credibility and mutual respect. None of these are gained by 'quick fixes', nor necessarily 'on the cheap'. Commitment is a process based upon *reciprocal* rights and obligations, and while styles of leadership need to adapt to the changing norms of society as well as of business, the credibility of leaders remains rooted in the examples *they* set, and the values by which they live, work and lead, day by day.

That is – and will remain – the essence of the leader's heroic journey. Good luck – enjoy the journey!

ACTION – THEORY INTO PRACTICE

Please complete the following 'Personal Board of Directors'.

'Personal board of directors': *the 'heroic journey'*

The purpose of this exercise is for you to think about your own development as a person and, especially, to identify the principal people in your life who have made a significant impact upon your thinking, behaviour and development as a manager and leader. Consider, for example, those people who have changed your life in some way and from whom you have learned to 'grow' as a person – especially in a leadership or professional role. Include positive and negative contacts from whom you have learned critical messages about life.

Objectives

- to crystallise the impact people have had upon you, *so that you can continue to draw lessons from – and capitalise upon – the experience*
- to let those who sit on your 'Personal Board of Directors' know that they are there – and why
- to develop the quality of relationships with the people that *you* manage and/or with whom you work – including superiors – *so that they would 'appoint' you to their Personal Board of Directors.*

The task

- Identify those who have made important differences to your life (state their relationship to you).

- *Highlight the key management and leadership lessons you learned from them.*

- Summarise on the 'table top', as succinctly as possible, the *collective impact* that those relationships have had upon your life, your thinking and your development as a person – and as a manager/leader or professional.

On page 206 is an example of an individual's *Personal Board of Directors*, with the key messages received from each 'director', together with a summary of key learning 'on the table'.

- What does the exercise tell you about the talent management in your life? How could you have made more of the critical messages you were given?

- What ideas emerge from the *Personal Board of Directors* exercise for you to use in managing the talent of your own people – especially the high performers and people of potential?

- Use the model – or your own derivative of it – as a basis for developing more powerful coaching and mentoring strategies within the areas that you manage

- Think of the concept of a 'heroic journey'. What would be the key milestones or staging posts in that journey for you and your team? How will you stimulate, focus and perpetuate learning in your team? Organise a half-day meeting/workshop to define, 'shape' and plan the journey for an appropriate period of time – focusing on the journey itself, not just the destination, on the principle that 'It's better to travel than to arrive...'

My Personal Board of Directors:

Key people who have shaped/are shaping my life as a manager/leader

ME

SUMMARY

- It's really up to me.
- *Live* life.

- Don't waste talent and effort.

- Focus on the 'crime', not the criminal.

- It's people, not 'things', that really matter.

- I'll find a way – or make one.

- You're only as good as your *next* job.

- Adaptability and innovation are crucial to success.

- Quality and professionalism are musts.

- Hard and tough are okay. Harsh and unjust are unacceptable.

- Be courteous and considerate, *but* if you're forced to fight – go for it!

Wife BRENDA
Don't judge – there's always another side to the story. Be loyal, be loving, be consistent.

Son JONATHAN
Egalitarianism. Balance and perspective. You could also see it *this* way!

Mother DOROTHY
It's okay to have fun and to laugh at life – and at yourself. Live each day at a time.

Troop Commander DON
Don't give in – go that extra one step. It's okay to take tough decisions, when necessary.

Col. Yevgenny Galko
Russian teacher. Don't talk about it – go there!

Boss DENNIS
Sensitivity, awareness of others, listening. Ask 'Why?' and not 'Why not?'

Friend ROY
Try new things. Experiment. Innovate. Be resourceful and adaptable.

Colleague RAY
Be real, but let vision, hopes and rainbows shape your efforts and those who work with you.

Daughter SUSIE
Life is for real – live it. Don't compromise standards, but don't waste time on 'perfection'. Being boring is a real crime.

Grandfather RUTHERFORD
Caring and gentleness. Never be cruel.

Father SIDNEY
If a job's worth doing it's worth doing well. Love of things Celtic and Gaelic.

School bully GEOFF
Fight back and fight to win. Never tolerate injustice.

Personnel Manager REG
Life is largely what *you* make of it. Nobody owes you a living.

Boss GRAHAM
Identify, build and *use talent well*.

Colleague MAVIS
Cut the crap – have the courage to be yourself.

Neighbour TREVOR
You're never too old. Life's too short to drink cheap wine.

Endnotes

1   GRATTON L. 'Implementing strategic intent: human resource processes as a
    force for change', *Business Strategy Review*. Vol. 5, No.1. Spring 1994.

2   CASSE P. 'People are not resources'. *Journal of European Industrial Training*.
    Vol. 18, No.5, 1994.

3   MACDONALD FRASER G. 'Where have all the heroes gone?' *Telegraph
    Weekend*. 3 January 1998.

4   CANNON T., in Watts, S., 'Career directors have a charter to learn how to do
    their job'. *Sunday Telegraph*. 18 July 1999.

5   DIXON P. *Futurewise: Six faces of global change*. London, HarperCollins,
    1998.

Appendix

Talent Management Profile

Think about what happens in your organisation.

How much time, energy and thought consciously goes into *developing and managing talent*?

How are leaders, at all levels, encouraged and trained to coach and develop their people – especially those in leadership roles?

Please circle the score that most realistically reflects what actually happens.

In our organisation . . .

	Never	Sometimes	Always
1 Recruitment We deliberately recruit people with high leadership talent, as well as technical/specialist skills.	1	2 3 4	5
We especially look for leaders who will coach and develop talent around them.	1	2 3 4	5
2 Placement and promotion We promote people on their ability to develop others, as well as for their technical/specialist competence.	1	2 3 4	5
We have a clear idea about what skills are needed by people to develop and manage others' talents.	1	2 3 4	5

	Never	Sometimes	Always

3 Performance reviews
People agree, with their managers, talent management objectives for coaching and developing their people.
1   2 3 4   5

People are assessed for their ability to coach, develop and manage others' talents and contribution.
1   2 3 4   5

Talent management is given as much significance, in appraisal, as the achievement of performance targets.
1   2 3 4   5

4 Bonuses and rewards
Salary increases and merit awards are based upon talent management, as well as other aspects of job performance.
1   2 3 4   5

5 Personal and career development
We have a clear idea about what we mean by 'potential'. People's potential is regularly reviewed and plans are implemented to fulfil that potential.
1   2 3 4   5

Development and coaching are consciously aimed at enhancing people's talent management skills, as well as technical/job competence.
1   2 3 4   5

Managers and specialists are encouraged to develop as role models in the coaching and mentoring of other people.
1   2 3 4   5

6 Organisational change
When people are moved to new roles they are developed and trained to lead, coach and manage in changed situations or different circumstances.
1   2 3 4   5

7 Retention of talent
We have well-developed policies – supported by sound talent management practices – that enable us to retain our best people.
1   2 3 4   5

Your Scores

Scores of 4 and 5 reflect talent management of the quality now needed to recruit, progress and use people of potential in global organisations. If you scored 3 or less for any questions, it might be helpful to consider:

1 **Questions 1–2**

   ❏ How structured and focused are your recruitment advertisements and role descriptions for new recruits? Do they need tightening up or redefining?

   ❏ What are your selection criteria for 'leaders'?

   ● Are they sufficiently well defined and clear?

   ● Are you considering wide enough ranges of likely candidates, on grounds of gender, age, experience and culture?

   ❏ How effective are your selection processes?

   ● Are your biographical interviews as focused as they should be?

   ● Do you ask the right questions of new candidates?

   ● Do you make sufficient use of tools and techniques, other than the interview eg psychometric profiles, assessment centres, discussion groups and other 'screening' procedures?

2 **Questions 3–4**

   ❏ Do you build in enough clear objectives into people's appraisals/performance reviews to ensure that they give sufficient time and focused energy to the development of *their* staff?

   ❏ Do you expressly reward people for the way they manage and develop the talent and abilities of their staff?

3 **Questions 5–7**

   ❏ How well do you identify and seek to fulfil your people's potential through 'quality dialogues', formal reviews and other forms of feedback and discussion? Do you do this sufficiently often and in enough practical detail?

   ❏ How well do you consciously develop your people as 'leaders of others', ie as coaches and mentors?

   ❏ How do you identify *role model* coaches and mentors – and what part do *you* play in developing the 'leader-manager' coach and mentor role model within your spheres of influence?

   ❏ Are you developing yourself – and your key players – sufficiently as *transformational leaders*, capable of identifying, leading and capitalising upon necessary change?

   ❏ Is enough conscious thought and action currently being given to strategic talent management aimed – especially – at retaining your best people?
   If not, what do you need to do to change attitudes, thinking – and action – to

ensure that more effective and appropriate management of talent takes place within your areas of influence and control?

Action

Looking at your scores, what are:

❏ the three major priorities in talent management that your organisation needs to address urgently

❏ the three major priorities that you, personally, need to deal with and take action on

❏ the first *actionable steps* that you need to take?

Emotional Intelligence Profile*

Emotional literacy

Factor 1: Self-awareness

Consider what has been happening to you recently and how typically you have reacted to events. Please circle, for each question, the score that most *realistically* describes you.

		Very often	Quite often	Occasionally	Very rarely
1	I am very aware of what will bring out both the best and the worst in me.	3	2	1	0
2	I am not afraid to show my feelings – including tears – in the right situation.	3	2	1	0
3	I recognise and can describe the physical sensations brought on by my different emotions.	3	2	1	0
4	When I read a story, or see a play, or film, I really become involved with the characters.	3	2	1	0
5	I am an open person that most people can 'read' quite easily and recognise how I feel.	3	2	1	0
6	I understand why my energy level fluctuates and what drains or revitalises me.	3	2	1	0
7	My attention wanders at times and I often don't know why.	0	1	2	3
8	I know how to wind down and can let go of things whenever I need to.	3	2	1	0
9	I don't know why I trigger negative reactions in some people.	0	1	2	3
10	I hate to fail and be seen to have failed.	0	1	2	3
11	I know how to maintain my concentration on a task and sustain focus when I need to.	3	2	1	0

		Very often	Quite often	Occasionally	Very rarely
12	I am clear about what I need to do in order to become a more aware and sensitive person.	3	2	1	0
13	I enjoy being me and I don't want to be anybody else.	3	2	1	0
14	Other people's opinions of me are a good measure for me to judge myself by.	0	1	2	3
15	I usually know how to recharge my emotional – and physical – 'batteries', when they run low.	3	2	1	0

Factor 1 – *Self-awareness*

Total Score: _____

Emotional literacy

Factor 2: Awareness of others

Consider what has been happening to you recently and how typically you have reacted to events. Please circle, for each question, the score that most *realistically* describes you.

		Very often	Quite often	Occasionally	Very rarely
1	I quickly develop a good 'feel' for a group or team when I first meet them.	3	2	1	0
2	I'm good at 'reading between the lines' with people and picking up their unspoken agenda.	3	2	1	0
3	I can normally sense when it is the right time to raise difficult issues with people.	3	2	1	0
4	I usually hide my feelings and emotions in front of others.	0	1	2	3
5	I quickly sense when others are upset or unhappy.	3	2	1	0
6	I don't find it easy to go out to others and ask for their help.	0	1	2	3
7	I generally consider other people's feelings before I give them my opinions or ideas.	3	2	1	0
8	People who know me well quickly recognise how I feel, or what mood I am in.	3	2	1	0
9	I quickly recognise how I antagonise or frustrate other people.	3	2	1	0
10	I have no difficulty in adapting my behaviour and 'style' to suit different people and occasions.	3	2	1	0
11	People who know me would say I am someone who values them.	3	2	1	0
12	I express my appreciation and recognition when somebody has done something well.	3	2	1	0

	Very often	Quite often	Occasionally	Very rarely
13 When I am in difficulties there are not many people I can really count on.	0	1	2	3
14 I quickly sense how other people feel about me when I am with them.	3	2	1	0
15 I feel uncomfortable when people try to get close to me.	0	1	2	3

Factor 2 – *Awareness of others*
                        Total Score:

Emotional integrity

Factor 3: Trust

Consider what has been happening to you recently and how typically you have reacted to events. Please circle, for each question, the score that most *realistically* describes you.

		Very often	*Quite often*	*Occasionally*	*Very rarely*
1	People who know me would say I had high credibility as a person and as a professional, ie they believe me and believe *in* me.	3	2	1	0
2	People who know me would consider me to be completely trustworthy.	3	2	1	0
3	I would be described as consistent by the people I work with.	3	2	1	0
4	The people I know both give to me and accept from me feedback about our working relationship and our respective work performance.	3	2	1	0
5	People know they can speak their minds and open their hearts to me, and that what they tell me will remain with me.	3	2	1	0
6	People who know me recognise that I do have their interests at heart.	3	2	1	0
7	I know that if I left confidential papers lying around on my desk some people would read them and start prying.	0	1	2	3
8	People generally would consider me to be reliable and dependable.	3	2	1	0
9	I don't feel that I can act upon what some members of my team/ workgroup tell me.	0	1	2	3
10	I feel quite comfortable in asking people in my team for support and back-up when I need it.	3	2	1	0

	Very often	Quite often	Occasionally	Very rarely
11 There are people here who would be only too happy to see me fall flat on my face.	0	1	2	3
12 There are people in my team/ colleagues whom I just don't trust.	0	1	2	3

Factor 3 – *Trust*

Total Score: _____

Emotional competence

Factor 4: Leadership

Consider what has been happening to you recently and how typically you have reacted to events. Please circle, for each question, the score that most *realistically* describes you.

	Very often	*Quite often*	*Occasionally*	*Very rarely*
1 People know that I take their roles and contributions seriously.	3	2	1	0
2 I make a point of giving sufficient autonomy and power to my staff to enable them to use their talents to maximum effect.	3	2	1	0
3 I work at helping people to derive a high level of 'buzz' and challenge from their jobs.	3	2	1	0
4 I consciously create opportunities for people's personal growth and development.	3	2	1	0
5 I believe I am not really a good listener and I don't give my people enough time when they need it.	0	1	2	3
6 I take an active interest in people's career progression and discuss this with them.	3	2	1	0
7 I really could do considerably more for my team members, by acting as a sponsor, or 'door-opener', to enable them to grow within the organisation.	0	1	2	3
8 Those who know me would describe me as an effective visionary leader, who is capable of describing and working towards requisite future conditions.	3	2	1	0
9 I don't really give sufficient time, as an effective coach and mentor, to my staff.	0	1	2	3

		Very often	Quite often	Occasionally	Very rarely
10	I need to involve people in decision-making and ownership of results more than I currently do.	0	1	2	3
11	I give very full and explicit, constructive feedback to people about their performance and contribution.	3	2	1	0
12	I make sure that people are clear about the responsibilities, scope and outputs of their jobs.	3	2	1	0
13	I put a high level of energy into developing effective work relationships with each of my people.	3	2	1	0
14	I need to put considerably more effort into issues from other people's perspectives.	0	1	2	3
15	I am always conscious of the impact of what I say – and how I say it – on the person to whom I am talking.	3	2	1	0

Factor 4 – *Leadership*

Total Score: _____

Emotional competence

Factor 5: Intuition

Consider what has been happening to you recently and how typically you have reacted to events. Please circle, for each question, the score that most *realistically* describes you.

		Very often	Quite often	Occasionally	Very rarely
1	The real basis of success, in many of my decisions, is a final intuitive 'leap'.	3	2	1	0
2	When it comes to spotting opportunities, or possibilities, in situations, I rely on sensing and 'feel'.	3	2	1	0
3	I come to important conclusions through systematic investigation, rather than as the result of some nagging 'inner voice'.	0	1	2	3
4	When exercising judgement, there are occasions when I just *know* that I'm right.	3	2	1	0
5	I rely strongly on my ability to visualise outcomes and consequences in exercising significant choice.	3	2	1	0
6	I just don't have confidence in hunches; it's hard facts that count in the real world.	0	1	2	3
7	There are times, in making decisions, when my heart rules my head.	3	2	1	0
8	When something does not *feel* right, I start to concentrate on it and look at it more closely.	3	2	1	0
9	I have an excellent and natural sense of timing in taking action.	3	2	1	0
10	I believe that reality is largely an illusion that can be overcome by relying on instinct.	3	2	1	0
11	Real breakthroughs come about as a result of detailed analysis, logic and hard work.	0	1	2	3

		Very often	Quite often	Occasionally	Very rarely
12	I have a well-developed instinct for knowing when to 'go for the jugular', or when to duck.	3	2	1	0
13	The more complex the problem, or issue, the more I rely on 'gut feel'.	3	2	1	0
14	In management, there are few short cuts to worthwhile results.	0	1	2	3
15	One of the most important strengths as a professional is being able to see the potential in situations.	3	2	1	0

Factor 5 – _Intuition_

Total Score: _____

Emotional competence

Factor 6: Transformational competence

Consider what has been happening to you recently and how typically you have reacted to events. Please circle, for each question, the score that most *realistically* describes you.

		Very often	*Quite often*	*Occasionally*	*Very rarely*
1	I *know* in which direction we should be moving, as a business, in order to become more successful.	3	2	1	0
2	I have faith and confidence in my ideas for introducing necessary major changes.	3	2	1	0
3	I *sense* when it is the right time to change direction, or do something different, in order to take the organisation forward.	3	2	1	0
4	People who know me well would say that I am somewhat conservative and not inclined to rush into change.	0	1	2	3
5	My staff would say that I am always ready to champion their feasible recommendations for change, even where there is a risk of failure.	3	2	1	0
6	I am much more an implementer, monitor or manager, than I am an innovator or inventor.	0	1	2	3
7	I am someone who is unlikely to remain in a 'comfort zone' for more than a very short time.	3	2	1	0
8	I quickly become bored and find myself anxious to get involved in new ideas and new projects.	3	2	1	0
9	Those who know me would say that my ability to transform situations and move things forward is one of my greatest strengths.	3	2	1	0

	Very often	Quite often	Occasionally	Very rarely
10 Generally, I am happier preserving traditions and stability, and getting on with what I'm paid to do, rather than looking for ways to change things.	0	1	2	3
11 Common sense and experience usually tell me that there is really little that is new under the sun.	0	1	2	3
12 Uncertainty is the only certainty today, and adaptability is a much more important strength than reliability or dependability.	3	2	1	0
13 I feel confident about going into situations where I know it is impossible to predict the outcomes with any guaranteed accuracy.	3	2	1	0
14 Fear of failure, or looking foolish, if things go wrong is just not an issue for me.	3	2	1	0
15 People who know me well would say that I am more inclined to protect my reputation, or keep a low profile, than take major risks.	0	1	2	3

Factor 6 – *Transformational competence*
Total Score:

Emotional synergy

Factor 7: Interaction and 'flow'

Consider what has been happening to you recently and how typically you have reacted to events. Please circle, for each question, the score that most *realistically* describes you.

		Very often	Quite often	Occasionally	Very rarely
1	I come away from meetings feeling I would never have progressed things so far working by myself.	3	2	1	0
2	In working on a problem with some people, I find we just keep building on and enhancing one another's ideas and escalating creativity.	3	2	1	0
3	I find that tapping into others' intuition, or hunches, is not particularly profitable.	0	1	2	3
4	I practise 'management by walking around', in order to bounce ideas off other people and act as a sounding board to them.	3	2	1	0
5	My colleagues and I regularly exchange feedback on our respective contributions and results.	3	2	1	0
6	At least 40 per cent of my time is spent 'networking' with others, ie engaging in direct, profitable *oral* communication.	3	2	1	0
7	I find it productive to make controversial or challenging statements in problem-solving discussions with my colleagues.	3	2	1	0
8	As a rule, I produce better solutions to problems or generate more effective ideas when working alone.	0	1	2	3
9	Adrenalin flows whenever we get together as a team and new ideas start to pour out.	3	2	1	0

	Very often	Quite often	Occasionally	Very rarely
10 Some days I feel really 'at one' with the task at hand and completely on top of things.	3	2	1	0
11 I can become so absorbed in my work that I just lose all track of time.	3	2	1	0
12 On occasions, it would be accurate and not immodest to describe my performance as 'effortless excellence'.	3	2	1	0
13 The people I work with use common sense and work quite hard, but we really don't experience 'synergy' as such.	0	1	2	3
14 Some days I instinctively *know* I'm on a winning streak and just can't lose.	3	2	1	0
15 When I work with some people, the 'chemistry' between us is just right and the 'buzz' is unbelievable.	3	2	1	0

Factor 7 – *Interaction and 'flow'*
Total Score: _____

Emotional synergy

Factor 8: Positive collaboration

Consider what has been happening to you recently and how typically you have reacted to events. Please circle, for each question, the score that most *realistically* describes you.

	Very often	*Quite often*	*Occasionally*	*Very rarely*
1 I believe in the old adage 'If you want a job done properly, do it yourself.'	0	1	2	3
2 I know who to go to in order to find the answers I need for my work.	3	2	1	0
3 I normally find a way round most problems, especially when I take time out to discuss likely solutions with others.	3	2	1	0
4 I believe one of the most important things in success is to share learning and continually update knowledge as a team.	3	2	1	0
5 I don't find it easy to ask other people for help.	0	1	2	3
6 I can readily change my own behaviour in order to adapt to others' moods and feelings.	3	2	1	0
7 I quickly recognise other people's reactions to what I say or do.	3	2	1	0
8 Generally I can get positive responses and good co-operation from colleagues and staff.	3	2	1	0
9 People go out of their way to help me. Collaboration here is very good.	3	2	1	0
10 I have reputation for being supportive and co-operative when people need help.	3	2	1	0

Factor 8 – *Positive collaboration*
                                    Total Score: _____

Interpreting your scores

In any self-scoring instrument, there is always the risk of some motivational distortion, and hence modification, exaggeration and/or playing down of certain characteristics. The tendency to identify with the 'norm' and the 'socially desirable' can be very strong at times. As with any mirror, we sometimes see – or hope to see – what we want to see and reject what we don't want to see. While this is, to some extent, natural, a distorted and therefore, inaccurate picture does not give us the feedback that is most relevant, useful and personally profitable.

With this in mind, quickly calculate your scores and see if they do reflect you as accurately and realistically as possible.

1 Scores of 3 obviously indicate very high levels of *potentially effective emotional intelligence*. A great many 3s, however, might beg the question 'Do you walk on water as well?'

   A score of 3 implies a need to continue to build on – and further develop – existing successful interpersonal skills, 'social radar' and intuitive competence.

2 A score of 2 suggests behaviours that, for the most part, represent potentially effective and 'above average' EQ.

   The major implication of scores of 2 is to identify *specifically* what you still need to do differently, in order to be consistently effective, by enhancing existing skills and developing new competences.

3 Scores of 1 indicate areas of significant, or major, development.

   What exactly needs to be improved, or introduced, to strengthen your repertoire of competences, should be identified and worked upon.

4 A score of 0 indicates not simply a lack of skill, but also one of absence of application, or use.

   With 0 scores, possibly personal values, 'mindsets' and attitudes may well need to be explored to find great 'fit' and compatibility between behaviours, results, roles and relationships.

There are also implications for *taking responsibility for personal learning*, as well as the processes of acquiring or building necessary competences and developing more effective 'style', as a leader, manager and professional.

Profile Summary: Your *EQ* profile

	Emotional literacy		Emotional integrity	Emotional competence			Emotional synergy	
	Self-awareness	Awareness of others	Trust	Leadership	Intuition	Transformational competence	Interaction and 'flow'	Positive collaboration
FACTOR	1	2	3	4	5	6	7	8
Your scores								
Effective behaviour	35–45	35–45	28–36	35–45	35–45	35–45	35–45	25–30
Development needed	29–34	29–34	23–27	29–34	29–34	29–34	29–34	21–24
Ineffective behaviours	0–28	0–28	0–22	0–28	0–28	0–28	0–28	0–20

How to score the profile summary:

1 Put your total scores, for each factor, under the appropriate heading, 1–8.
2 Put a cross as appropriate against each factor, which represents your score, ie 'Effective behaviour', 'Development Needed' or 'Ineffective Behaviours'.

What do you need to develop?

Consider your scores in response to the questions. What, exactly, are the specific issues behind, especially, the lower scores? What are the *real* development needs, against each of the following factors.

1 Self-awareness

   How strong, clear and consistent is your self-image? Where does it need greater certainty and coherence?

2 Awareness of others

   Do you pay enough attention and give enough time to others – particularly those closest to you?

3 Trust

   To what extent do your actions and attitudes contribute to distrust amongst those close to you at work (and at home)?

4 Leadership

   How consistent is the example you set and, therefore, your 'say–do' credibility?

5 Intuition

   Is your sensing of situations as developed as it should be, and do you have sufficient confidence to rely on 'gut feel' as well as logic?

6 Transformational competence

   Do you regularly put sufficient energy and commitment into changing things that should be changed? How often do you stay in a comfort zone instead of moving out of it and taking necessary risks?

7 Interaction and 'flow'

   Is there enough 'peak communication', 'buzz' and adrenalin in your work relationships? How will you increase this so that there is more contributive interaction?

8 Positive collaboration

   How effective are you in collaborating with others whilst maintaining your personal integrity?

Talent Coaching Profile

Background

A critical factor in the *impact* of coaching is the quality, relevance and consistency of the learning that takes place as a consequence of the coach's competence, style and techniques. For all coaches and developers, there remains, however, the question of what is the most appropriate and effective form of learning for a particular individual. The *Talent Coaching Profile*, developed by Michael Williams & Partners, should indicate where your style of coaching is likely to be successful – or less so – in the key areas of generating learning, development and improved performance for people of talent.

Please answer the questions as objectively, accurately and realistically as you can. 'Fudging' the results doesn't help anyone – least of all you or those you coach.

Scoring

Under each statement, circle the score that most accurately reflects how you typically behave in enabling others to learn and develop.

1 When agreeing expected performance levels with someone, I deliberately start from where they are *now* – not from where I want them to be, even with high performers.
Rarely   0   1   2   3   4   5   6   7   Frequently

2 When selecting or planning assignments for people to undertake, I try to see the project and its various aspects from *their* point of view and level of experience and competence.
Rarely   0   1   2   3   4   5   6   7   Frequently

3 When I look for, or create, development opportunities for others, I consciously build in challenge, responsibility and some form of leadership role for them.
Rarely   0   1   2   3   4   5   6   7   Frequently

4 As an essential part of their learning and development, I am prepared to allow people to take risks by trying out new ways of doing things, although it could result in poor performance or even failure.
Rarely   0   1   2   3   4   5   6   7   Frequently

5 I am prepared to devote time helping people to understand projects, problems or tasks, and work through possible solutions, plans and actions with them in discussion.
Rarely   0   1   2   3   4   5   6   7   Frequently

6 I give people maximum freedom to develop their own solutions to problems or challenges, and so come up with their own ideas wherever possible.
Rarely   0   1   2   3   4   5   6   7   Frequently

7   To ensure ownership of their own development and improvement, I actively encourage people to monitor, evaluate and review their own progress, and put forward their own ideas to improve performance and develop themselves.
Rarely   0   1   2   3   4   5   6   7   Frequently

8   When considering how best to meet people's development needs, I would, jointly with the person(s) being coached, develop personal improvement plans that consisted of at least three major learning activities, including new, developmental roles where possible.
Rarely   0   1   2   3   4   5   6   7   Frequently

9   Improvement action plans for my staff involve a rich variety of development sources, including external tutors from, typically, customers, business schools, professional bodies, management consultancies and other organisations.
Rarely   0   1   2   3   4   5   6   7   Frequently

10   My manager (or other appropriate authority figure) and I meet in order for my coaching to take place and to develop my performance and contributive competence.
Rarely   0   1   2   3   4   5   6   7   Frequently

Your Scores

If you score 5 or less on any question, it might be helpful to consider the following:

1   **Questions 1–3**

   ❐ Are you making the most effective use of questions such as those spelled out in the COACH model in Figure 17?

   ❐ Are you effectively using the coaching sequence (or something similar) illustrated on page 131?

   ❐ Specifically, are you asking enough questions and listening carefully to the other person's responses?

   ❐ Are you building in sufficient challenges, and 'adrenaline' elements into the other person's role (see Chapter 1)?

2   **Questions 4–7**

   ❐ Are you spelling out, in sufficient detail and depth, the parameters to the 'framework' within which the other person can exercise his/her discretion and take initiatives?

   ❐ Do you need to give others more encouragement to experiment, try out new ideas and take some risks?

   ❐ Look again at the EAR coaching model in Figure 18. Are you using sufficient reflective 'open' questions to guide and steer without unnecessarily constraining the other person's ideas and proposals?

3 Questions 8–9

❏ Have you identified, in sufficient detail, with the other person, his/her real development needs?

❏ Do you make sufficiently sure that they understand the exact nature/extent of their need to improve, or develop?

❏ Are the training plans that you jointly evolve relevant to the development needs of the individual, and do they adequately cover all that needs to be undertaken to improve performance/develop within their current role?

4 Question 10

❏ Are you creating the right opportunities for your superior(s) to be able to give you the feedback and coaching that you need?

❏ Do you pursue those opportunities, yourself, with sufficient energy, consistency and determination?

❏ Do you build sufficiently upon your boss's ideas and suggestions and work at them, with enough commitment and follow-through?

Some actions you might now take

❏ Talk through your scores with your manager and ask for *specific* feedback from him or her about your abilities as a coach, identifying 'plusses' and 'minuses' about your coaching ability, especially in relation to 'high-flyers'.

❏ Discuss the results of this profile with your own staff – especially the 'high-flyers' – and ask them for reactions and specific feedback. How do they look upon you as a coach? What are their views of your *strengths* and *areas for development*?

❏ Where you manage managers – give them the profile and use the results as a basis for a review of coaching practices within your function, project or team.

❏ Develop coaching improvement action plans for yourself and any others in your team for whom the profile suggests development needs and action.

❏ Give your manager a copy of the profile and give him or her specific feedback on the scores. Suggest how he or she might develop and improve as a coach.

Developing Coaching Skills – a 'Coaching Challenge' Workshop

Set up a workshop of up to 12 people to explore coaching. During this session you will have an opportunity to discuss your 'coaching challenge'. This may be a direct report, a colleague or a boss. With a tutor or facilitator, you can decide on the precise allocation of time during this session. As a suggestion, you might consider the following procedure:

❒ Select a member of your team who can role play your 'challenge' person, or who could role play you, while you play the role of your 'coaching challenge'.

❒ Divide into groups of three and find a suitable location in which to conduct your group work (your tutor will move from group to group).

❒ Use up to 35 minutes per participant; the following schedule may help:

1 Briefing (**10 minutes**)
Person 'A' briefs person 'B'. Person 'C' listens carefully, making notes as necessary.
During this period try to identify whether the issues are 'job- or system-based' or 'interpersonal'.

2 Role-play (**10 minutes**)
Role-play a past or future conversation or dialogue. The observer should observe behaviour, attitude, body language, voice, techniques and any other indicators of the coaching 'style' of person 'B'.

3 Review (**10–15 minutes**)
Person 'C' and person 'B' feed back their observations on the discussion, including approaches, verbal style and body language. They 'coach' person 'A' as needed.

At the end of your session, quickly check that you are clear about what happened. You will then have 15 minutes, approximately, in which to summarise your key learning points on overhead transparencies or flipcharts, and prepare to present this to the rest of the participants.

Talent Mentoring Profile

Introduction

A major factor in the *impact* of mentoring is the quality and relevance of the learning and development that is taking place, as a consequence of the mentor's competence, style and techniques. For all mentors and developers, however, there remains the question of, 'What is the most appropriate and effective form of learning for a particular individual?'

The *Talent Mentoring Profile*, developed by Michael Williams & Partners, should indicate where your style of mentoring is likely to be successful in the key areas of generating learning, development and longer-term growth for others – particularly for those of outstanding talent and high potential.

Please answer the questions as objectively, accurately and realistically as you can. 'Fudging' the results doesn't help anyone – least of all you and those you mentor.

Scoring

Under each statement, circle the score that most accurately reflects how you typically behave in actively helping others to learn, develop and realise their potential as individuals.

1   I devote 3–4 hours within the working week to helping others – especially people of high talent – with their longer-term development and growth *(excluding coaching on specific assignments)*.
Rarely   0   1   2   3   4   5   6   7   Frequently

2   When considering the people in my team, I consciously think of their potential and how it might be more appropriately developed and used, and I discuss this with them.
Rarely   0   1   2   3   4   5   6   7   Frequently

3   I explore ways of consciously aligning talented people's medium- and longer-term development and growth with the foreseeable changing direction and transformation of the business.
Rarely   0   1   2   3   4   5   6   7   Frequently

4   I actively encourage my staff to think about their longer-term development, and to come up with challenges, ideas and initiatives to help them grow as individuals.
Rarely   0   1   2   3   4   5   6   7   Frequently

5   I keep myself up to date with what is considered to be *current best practice* in mentoring, by reading and discussions with leading business school tutors or consultants.
Rarely   0   1   2   3   4   5   6   7   Frequently

6   I equally keep myself au fait with organisational changes and, therefore, the changing patterns – and opportunities – for career progression and personal development within the business.
    Rarely   0   1   2   3   4   5   6   7   Frequently

7   In mentoring people, I help them to work on issues such as development of their 'style', confidence and mindset, as well as working on their longer-term skill and competence development.
    Rarely   0   1   2   3   4   5   6   7   Frequently

8   As a manager, I actively involve other mentors in the longer-term development of my staff – especially talented individuals. Such external sources of help include both people inside and outside the organisation.
    Rarely   0   1   2   3   4   5   6   7   Frequently

9   I develop and review, together with my staff, medium-term individual personal development *plans* for them – with actions and activities programmed against broad but realistic timescales.
    Rarely   0   1   2   3   4   5   6   7   Frequently

10 I take active steps with my manager/team leader to ensure that my medium-term development is a 'live', ongoing process, and meet with him or her to discuss my personal growth and contribution within the business.
    Rarely   0   1   2   3   4   5   6   7   Frequently

Your Scores

If you scored 5 or less on any question, it might be helpful to consider the following:

1   **Questions 1–4**

    ❐ How creatively do you use time to have 'quality dialogues' with your people about their aspirations, career progression and development? Do you make sufficient use of lunch hours, journeys together, short 'retreats' or simply 'quiet' half-hours together?

    ❐ How actively do you seek to create, with others, learning opportunities within their jobs, on special assignments or with the help of internal/external tutors and mentors other than yourself?

    ❐ Have you agreed, in sufficient detail, what the individual's potential really is? Can you give clear definition to their potential and how it should best be realised?

    ❐ Using the 'Plus Me' and 'Plus Role' models in Figures 21 and 22, identify the personal development needs and potential fulfilment plans for your people. Then relate that personal growth to progressive job enrichment via the 'Plus Role' concept, finding ways to increase and enhance for people

    what they *enjoy* doing in their role
    what they *do well*
    what *challenges* or 'strategies' they need.

Ensure that you build in enough 'pull' and *retention* factors into the individual's development and work experiences (see Chapter 1).

2 **Questions 5–6**

❒ Do you ensure that you really keep up to date with what is considered to be current best practice in mentoring by reading and discussions with leading specialists?

❒ Think about how you currently keep abreast of organisational changes – and the emerging scope for career progression in your company. Do you really know what is going on and how the business is transforming, and what it should look like in, say, 12–18 months' time?

❒ Talk with those in the know – both colleagues and superiors – and consciously keep up to date with organisational changes in your company.

3 **Questions 7–9**

❒ Are you always the best person to mentor those who report to you, or should you 'stage manage' the mentoring of your people by identifying and organising mentoring by a group of internal/external mentors and tutors?

❒ If you are the principal mentor, go through the list of mentoring activities on pages 144–7.
Which of these do you need to put more thought, time and energy into? Which need to be done in different ways – and how – in order to ensure that effective mentoring is taking place for your people.

4 **Question 10**

❒ Over the last 4/5 years have you had at least one mentoring session per month and up to six days' formal training/development in managerial and leadership issues?
If not, you might want to think about ensuring that this starts to happen with effect from this month.

❒ Do you spend sufficient time with mentors – inside or outside the organisation – on such issues as your longer-term career progression and development?

❒ Have you a current personal development plan which is 'live' and regularly reviewed against changes in the business, and your likely future with the company?
If not, this is something you might need to talk through with your boss and initiate.

Some actions you might now take

❒ Talk through your scores with your manager and ask for *specific* feedback from him or her about your abilities as a mentor, identifying 'plusses' and 'minuses' about your ability and commitment.

❏ Discuss the results of this profile with your own staff – especially those of high-fliers – and ask them for reactions and specific feedback. How do they look upon you as a mentor? What are their views of your *strengths* and *areas for development*?

❏ Where you manage managers – give them the profile and use the results as a basis for a review of mentoring practices within your function, project or team.

❏ Develop mentoring improvement action plans for yourself and any others in your team for whom the profile suggests development needs and action.

❏ Give your manager a copy of the profile and give him or her specific feedback on the scores. Suggest how he or she might develop and improve as a mentor.

❏ Bring in a specialist (internal or external) to develop and run a mentoring techniques and skills programme for you, your manager, colleagues and staff.

Talent Sponsoring Profile

Introduction

Fundamental to effective sponsorship is the ability to recognise – and promote and progress – people of real talent, who can make more of an impact on the business than they are at present, given the openings and opportunities. For managers operating in the role of sponsor, however, there remains the question: what are likely to be the most effective strategies and tactics in sponsoring a particular individual – or group of people – within the environment and domains where they are being promoted as persons of talent and potential?

The *Talent Sponsoring Profile*, developed by Michael Williams & Partners, should give you personal feedback, indicating your potential strengths, weaknesses and preferences in the different but complementary processes that make up sponsoring.

Please answer the questions as objectively, accurately and realistically as you can. 'Fudging' the results helps no one – least of all you and those you sponsor.

Scoring

Under each statement, circle the score that most accurately reflects how you typically behave in sponsoring talented people within your organisation.

1   I actively sponsor people of talent and potential by publicising and promoting them to top people or key players in the organisation.
   Rarely   0   1   2   3   4   5   6   7   Frequently

2   I keep up to date in my knowledge of current career-role opportunities, throughout the business, so that I can recommend likely individuals when such job changes occur in the organisation.
   Rarely   0   1   2   3   4   5   6   7   Frequently

3   Generally, I am able to enthuse others about protégés. I become aware of and manage to facilitate placement within the organisation of people of potential and talent.
   Rarely   0   1   2   3   4   5   6   7   Frequently

4   I am prepared to 'go out on a limb' in order to support young up-and-coming talented people and help them into roles and work for which they appear eminently suitable.
   Rarely   0   1   2   3   4   5   6   7   Frequently

5   I possess – and exercise – sufficient power and influence within the organisation to be able to sponsor, 'push' and place people of talent in roles where their competence will be appreciated, developed and used to effect.
   Rarely   0   1   2   3   4   5   6   7   Frequently

6   People would consider me to be someone who has established professional patronage and sponsorship as necessary alternatives to the 'old boy network' and the 'halo effect', in my area of the organisation.
Rarely   0   1   2   3   4   5   6   7   Frequently

7   I am thought of as a person who possesses a high level of 'political' realism and acumen, and who is able to get things done within the business – including successfully sponsoring people of talent – as a result of effective 'backstage' activity and/or 'facipulation'.
Rarely   0   1   2   3   4   5   6   7   Frequently

8   In my understanding of the business I would claim that I have a well-developed and sophisticated understanding of our management information systems and the influence of IT generally upon our organisation and its working.
Rarely   0   1   2   3   4   5   6   7   Frequently

9   I can act as an organisational 'umbrella' in order to give a realistic degree of protection to new or 'untried' people of talent when they start to take action within new appointments.
Rarely   0   1   2   3   4   5   6   7   Frequently

10   I am effective as a 'gatekeeper' because of my range of contacts inside – and outside – the organisation that I can call upon as sources of help and support, especially in the sponsorship and placement of people of talent and potential.
Rarely   0   1   2   3   4   5   6   7   Frequently

Your Scores

If you scored 5 or less on any question, it might be helpful to consider the following:

1   **Questions 1–4**

   ❏ Do you do all that you should to draw top management's attention to people of high capability who might be employed elsewhere, to greater effect, within the company?

   ❏ Do you keep sufficiently abreast of organisation and job changes, so that you know when a likely opening will become available for a person of talent whose presence would add critical value to the role?

2   **Questions 5–8**

   ❏ Do you believe that you need to exercise more strategic patronage and power of sponsorship to stimulate a talent management mindset, so that people begin to look more actively at the intelligent movement of talent around the business?

   ❏ Do you need to develop more skill in 'back stage' activity and political acumen in order to ensure that you sponsor talent with the best sense of timing and chance of success?

3 **Questions 9–10**

❑ Do you make enough of the potential learning experience that your suppliers, customers, customers' customers and other external stakeholders could offer as development opportunities for your best people?

❑ Should you be developing a wider range of professional – and personal – contacts both within and outside the organisation, in order to build up a greater variety of developmental experiences for people of oustanding ability?

Some actions you might now take

❑ Talk through your scores with your manager and ask for *specific* feedback from him or her about your ability as a sponsor, identifying 'plusses' and 'minuses' about your sponsoring ability and commitment.

❑ Discuss the results of this profile with your own staff, and ask them for reactions and specific feedback. How do they look upon you as a sponsor? What are their views of your *strengths* and *areas for development as a champion of others' talents*?

❑ Where you manage managers – give them the profile and use the results as a basis for a review of sponsoring practices within your function, domain or team as a whole.

❑ Develop sponsoring improvement action plans for yourself and any others in your team for whom the profile suggests development needs and action.

❑ Give your manager a copy of the profile and then specific feedback on his or her scores. Suggest how he or she might develop and improve as a champion and sponsor of people's talents and potential within the business.

Power and Empowerment Profile

This instrument, the *Power and Empowerment Profile*, has been developed by Michael Williams & Partners to complement their existing range of management and leadership psychometric profiles. It can, however, be used as a profile in its own right, to identify the extent of *power and empowerment* exercised by individuals and teams in companies and other organisations.

Authority, Influence and Power – the Bases of Empowerment

Using the rating scale, please identify what you believe to be the extent of *power and empowerment* that you have in your current job. Be as objective as you can in your scoring.

Extent of Power

None ◄———————► Total

	0	1	2	3	4	5

A Positional Authority

1   Authority over budget and control of 'spend', ie make appropriate financial decisions.

2   Selection, promotion and appointment of staff.

3   Removal of staff from role.

4   Appraisal and development of staff.

5   Reward of staff.

6   Quality and extent of empowerment from superiors, generally.

B Authority of Expertise

7   Possess specialist/unique skills necessary to success in the job.

8   Have extensive job knowledge and breadth/depth of experience.

9   Possess important competences that my superiors may not have.

10   Am highly qualified vocationally and/or professionally.

Extent of Power

None ◄————► Total

	0	1	2	3	4	5

11 Regarded as someone who is good in a crisis and who handles the unexpected well.

12 Seen as possessing high potential, especially creativity and conceptual competence.

C Information Authority

13 Have access to information generally unavailable to others.

14 Have access to information that may be denied to my superiors.

15 Possess important organisational and 'political' information and knowledge.

16 Am in a privileged position for informing/ communicating to others.

17 Have access to key decision-makers and/or am a focal point in decision-making.

18 Possess clear vision and the ability to conceptualise the bridge between the current and the requisite state of the business.

D Influence ('Personal Power')

19 Networking extensively to gain support, informally, through alliances at all levels.

20 Socialising with superiors and others.

21 Degree to which people do what you want because they like and/or respect you.

22 Practise MBWA ('management-by-walkabout') regularly and give recognition to people, personally, face-to-face.

23 Am a member/official of relevant influential steering groups, task forces and/or committees, or 'in groups'.

24 Possess perceived 'political' awareness and competence and handle organisational 'politics' effectively.

Extent of Power

None ◄──────► Total

	0	1	2	3	4	5

E Ownership and Commitment

25 Extent to which I participate in defining the vision and goals of the department/business.

26 Degree to which I say 'what' will be done.

27 Extent to which I say 'how' it will be done.

28 Degree to which I propose, initiate and implement change.

29 Extent to which I take initiatives of real significance in my job.

30 Degree to which I feel personal 'ownership' of my job and its success, or failure, in results.

F Authority of Integrity

31 Extent to which people believe in me, as well as believe me.

32 Degree to which subordinates trust me and feel 'safe' about what I do.

33 The trust peers and colleagues put in me and what I do.

34 The extent of trust placed in me and my actions by superiors.

35 My self-rating for integrity and 'straight dealing'.

36 How others at work who really know me would rate me for trustworthiness and consistent dependability.

Your Power and Empowerment Profile

1 Add up your scores, under each of the six principal sources of power and empowerment and write these, against each heading, in the spaces below.

2 Put your overall rating in the Total Score box.

A. Positional Authority   Your score . . .   (Max 30)

B. Authority of Expertise   Your score . . .   (Max 30)

C. Informational Authority   Your score . . .   (Max 30)

D. Influence ('Personal Power')   Your score . . .   (Max 30)

E. 'Ownership' and Commitment   Your score . . .   (Max 30)

F. Authority of Integrity   Your score . . .   (Max 30)

Your total power and empowerment score   [＿＿＿＿＿]   (Max 180)

Implications of Your Scores

From your scores, please consider the following factors about your own use of power and empowerment.

1 Which are your strongest power bases at work?

2 Which are your weakest?

3 What should you now do to develop and capitalise upon your strongest power base(s) by enhancing your own empowerment?

4 What action will you take to improve things in your weakest areas of power in order to increase your own empowerment?

5 What should you do, specifically, to improve the extent to which your superiors empower you:

❑ in yourself?

❑ with them?

6 What are the implications of your scores about how *you* empower those who report to you?

7 What specific actions should you now begin to take to increase the extent of your empowerment of your staff?

8 Any other thoughts, concerns or intentions?

Index

added value considerations 6, 7, 9, 10,
    18, 23, 24, 26, 37, 57, 62, 90, 97,
    98, 120, 126, 146, 170, 182, 183,
    202
assessment centres 70, 78
attracting talent 29–31
autonomy, as an attraction for talent 23
    as a need for talented people 29–30,
        102, 124, 149
    'freedom within a framework' 29, 102,
        128, 135, 166–173
    levels of responsibility and 166–173
    see also empowerment

best-practice considerations 2, 6, 12, 26,
    67, 88, 149
brand image (of an organisation) 24, 28,
    29
business management, strategic see
    strategic management of a business
business strategy and HR management
    195–202
business strategy and talent management
    see management of talent,
    integration of business strategy

challenge, as a need for talented people
    29–30, 32, 57

change
    challenge of 5, 7–8, 24
    coping with new technology 5, 7, 9,
        71
    coping with new values 5, 168
    initiation of 6, 77
    mechanics of (illustrated) 56
    need/pressure for 55
    requiring flexibility 7
    response to 7–8
    vision of the desired result of 55–7
choosing an organisation to work for
    21–5
coaching and mentoring of talent 17, 18,
    19, 31, 32, 37, 60, 65, 72, 73, 78,
    87, 102, 106, 109, 114, 117,
    119–120, 138, 147–8, 161–2, 181,
    188
    as an attraction for talented people 23,
        24, 31
coaching as differentiated from
        mentoring 120–134, 135–6, 138,
        140–141, 144, 161–2, 181, 193
    leadership and management aspects
        (COACH) of 124–6
    stages in the process 130–134, 135–6
    style and techniques 129–130
    the coaching leader 119–134, 135–6

common sense as an attribute of talent 36

competenc(i)es, building/developing the requisite 18, 65, 119–120, 144, 183
diverse/complementary 7, 22, 29, 40–44, 48, 86
hierarchy of 88–90, 119
in relation to emotional/intuitive intelligence 46–7

competitive advantage, definition of 81–2
guaranteed by talent 2, 6, 18, 57, 65, 77, 146

competitive disadvantage in lack of talent 10

corporate-speak v entrepreneur-speak 8

creativity as an attribute of talent 38–9

cross-cultural effectiveness as an attribute of talent 36

cultural differences, sensitivity to 7

culture of an organisation see organisational culture

development of talent 1, 2, 3, 6, 11, 12, 14, 17, 18–19, 26, 29–32, 39, 73–6, 78, 106, 146, 187
action plan for 146, 192
as an attraction for talented people 23, 24
by means of coaching see coaching as differentiated from mentoring
continuous 17, 39
major factors contributing to 30–32
personal development plans 74

development of talent management skills 57–64

dialogue, styles and levels of 57–64, 186–7, 189
see also EAR technique; listening; management of talent, relationships/dialogue; peak communication level

discretionary and mandatory elements of a job 173–6

EAR technique of questioning and listening 58–64, 69
diagram of 59, 132

in relation to coaching dialogue 132

ecological considerations see environmental ('green') imperatives

emotional intelligence (EQ), as an attribute of talent 43–8, 49–50, 92
the five key aspects of 47, 49

empowerment 18, 23, 24, 26, 30, 104, 106, 109, 110, 117, 128, 134, 149, 166–189
four key factors in 187
power (and the 'three Cs') in 182–5, 188–9
the 'feel' of 185–6
with delegation 176–182, 188

enabling leadership 101–116, 117, 152, 162, 172, 182, 183, 204
as a four-function process 104–108, 117
as a mindset 108–114
as the responsibility of a team 153
leader as 'hub' not 'head' 104–105, 117

entrepreneurs 8, 9
entrepreneur-speak 8

environmental ('green') imperatives 8, 9

exciting job, as an attraction for talent 23, 24, 30–31, 32, 102

'family feeling' within an organisation 7

feedback to aid development 29, 63–4, 72, 73, 78, 87, 93, 134, 146, 148, 186–7, 189

First Quench case study 114–116

'five-fold grading' see selection interview framework

'flow' as a state of effortless excellence at work 47–8, 61, 86, 144

four imperatives of talent management see management of talent

globalisation, effects of 7, 9, 17, 108
the 'global village' 7, 108

'helicopter' quality of perceptual overview 36, 110

'high-flyers' 29, 31, 37, 87–8

horizons in potential see identifying potential/talent, horizons

human resource strategies 10, 66–7
  in relation to business strategy
      195–202

'ideas factories' 104–106
identifying potential/talent 1, 3, 18, 78,
      106, 140–144, 154
  creating the means for 67–73
  horizons in potential 142–7, 161–2
information networks 9
intellectual satisfaction 21
intelligence, as an attribute of talent
      37–9
  mobilisation of 86, 97
integrative thinking 112
intuition and intuitive expertise 43–8
  in synergy with IQ and cognitive
      reasoning 44
investing in the best 3
IT see change, coping with new
      technology

knowledge
  as a primary factor of competitive
      advantage 81–5
  checking up on/validating/monitoring
      94–6
  five traditional levels of 91–2, 99
  hierarchy of 88–90
  managing the transfer of 86–7, 97–8,
      99, 103
  new perspective processes 85–6
  seven critical factors for the
      management of 97–8
  ten imperatives for the management of
      86–98
  two forms: explicit and tacit 82–6, 88,
      90, 99, 103, 115

leadership in managing talent see
      management of talent, leadership
leadership qualities and skills 7, 9, 12,
      13, 26, 37, 42–3, 50, 54, 58, 60,
      66, 75–6, 198, 204–205
  coaching see coaching as differentiated
      from mentoring, the coaching
      leader
  enabling see enabling leadership

learning cycle (Kolb's/adapted) 40–43,
      123
listening, as an important element of
      dialogue 58, 60, 63, 135, 140–141

mandatory and discretionary elements of
      a job 173–6
management of knowledge see
      knowledge, ten imperatives for the
      management of
management of talent 1–3, 5–6, 8,
      10–17, 18, 22, 24, 28–32, 37,
      40–48, 53, 54–67, 75, 77–8,
      101–116, 119–134, 138–160, 181,
      191–205, 207
  as a corporate priority 12, 15–16, 18,
      54–67, 77
  as a crucial executive skill 6, 10–11,
      15, 18, 57–67, 77
  as an attraction for talented people 23,
      24, 31
  enabling leadership for see enabling
      leadership
  facilitators and 12, 63–4, 112
  four imperatives of 2, 11–17, 18, 32,
      53, 75, 76, 77, 107–108
  gatekeeping 156, 160, 163
  getting it right 202–205
  in teams 42
  integration with business strategy
      191–202
  integration with HR management/
      strategy 195–202
  leadership within/for 2, 7, 12, 13, 22,
      29, 31, 55, 64–7, 72, 76, 98,
      101–116, 119–134, 155, 185
  organisational strategies for 5, 6, 12,
      16, 18, 29, 54–7, 64–7,
      199–202, 204
  relationships/dialogue within 2, 8, 9,
      46, 58–64, 104
management of time 30
management styles 22, 26, 28–9, 59,
      64–7, 101, 104–105, 183
  versatility in 58
mentoring as differentiated from
      coaching 120–121, 138–153,
      161–2, 193

definition/characteristics of (good)
148–153, 162
micromanaging and the micromanager
178–180, 186, 188
mistakes/failures as means of learning 29,
30, 72, 87, 186

'need to know' basis for information
distribution 93–4

organisational culture and ethic 22, 26–7
definition of 27
disparate levels of 27
tribal 27–9
organisational performance ethic 24, 30
organisational strategy re talent see
management of talent,
organisational strategy
organisational visions and values 10, 12,
18, 19, 22, 26, 28–9, 32, 71–2, 96
organisation's reputation 24, 28
organisation's role in the market place
22, 24, 28

peak communication level 61–3, 86, 90,
150
power (and authority) 182–5, 204
of the transformed organisation 184–5
the three Cs and 183–4
professionalism, development of 90,
92–3
promotion of talented people see
rewarding talent

recognition of talent see identifying poten-
tial/talent; talent, recognition of
recruitment practices 6, 10, 29
outsourced 70
resourcefulness as an attribute of talent
36
rewarding talent 16–17, 19, 23, 24, 29,
31–2, 53, 73, 78, 193
total package for 32
with rapid and frequent promotion
16–17, 23, 24, 31, 78

selecting talent see talent, selection of
selection interview framework 69–70

self-reliance as an attribute of talent 35
social responsibilities 8, 9
sponsoring, as an enablement factor 106,
109, 117, 138, 153–160, 162–3,
188, 193
championing, as a means of 154–5,
158, 163
the four aspects of 153–160, 162–3
status, as an attraction for talent 21, 25
Stora Enso case study 193–5
strategic management of a business
199–202
stress 89–92
synergy, as an attraction for talent 23,
24, 40–43
promoting improved productivity/
effectiveness 1, 7, 9, 29, 43–4,
48, 75, 86, 90, 92, 97, 99, 106,
119, 126, 147, 198
see also teams and team-working

talent
and authority figures 2
and budgets 3; see also rewarding
talent
definition and examination of 34–50,
57, 140
development of see development of
talent
key factors that contribute to 37
management of see management of
talent
recognition within an organisation of
2, 32, 67, 72
selection of 2, 12, 14, 16, 18, 67–76,
78
using, making full use of 2, 12, 18,
40–43
see also war for talent
teaching as part of talent management 12
the teaching organisation 12
teams and team-working 7, 9, 24, 26,
27–9, 42–3, 47, 71, 95, 98, 99,
120, 134, 152
and hierarchies 119
as a combination of complementarities
40–43
see also synergy

technological change(s) *see* change, coping with new technology

time management *see* management of time

tolerance as an attribute of talent 36

tribes and tribalism within/around an organisation 27–9

triple bottom line 9, 104

'virtual' organisation(s) 7, 8, 9, 27, 113, 119
  diagram of 159

visions and values *see* organisational visions and values

war for talent, the nature of the 1–2, 5–20, 109

winning company/organisation, the 23–7

winning environment (to attract/retain talent) 2, 12, 13–15, 17, 18, 21–33, 48, 53, 77